Cavendish
Publishing
Limited

EQUITY & TRUSTS

L B Curzon
Barrister

First published in Great Britain 1993 by Cavendish Publishing
Limited, 23A Countess Road, London NW5 2XH.
Telephone: 071-485 0303   Facsimile: 071-485 0304

British Library Cataloguing in Publication Data

Curzon L B
Equity & Trusts - (Lecture Notes Series)
I Title II Series
344.20604

ISBN 1-874241-62-7

Cover photograph by Jerome Yeats
Printed and bound in Great Britain

Preface

This text comprises a series of lecture notes designed specifically for students who are preparing for first examinations in Equity and Trusts. At the end of each chapter will be found a summary intended for those who wish to make a swift revision of the essential features of the subject-matter of the chapter. The text is intended to be read in conjunction with Questions and Answers in Equity and Trusts (Cavendish Publishing Limited 1993).

A large number of case references will be found in each chapter, testimony to the very important role of judicial decision in the development of the law of trusts from its early days as 'a creature of Equity'. It is hoped that these references may lead students to an exploration of the extensive literature which has grown around the doctrines of Equity.

L B Curzon
1993

Outline of Table of Contents

Detailed Table of Contents

Table of Cases

Table of Statutes

Chapter 1

The Essence of Equity

In this text we examine the trust in detail. The significance of the trust is stated by Maitland, in his *Selected Essays*, thus:

> 'If we were asked what is the greatest and most distinctive achievement performed by Englishmen in the field of jurisprudence, I cannot think that we should have any better answer to give than this, namely, the development from century to century of the trust idea.'

The trust, based essentially on the concept of a 'settlor' entrusting property to a 'trustee' on the understanding that he shall take care of it for the benefit of a third person (the 'beneficiary'), is a creature of equity: its principles are derived from equitable doctrines; its development mirrors the very growth and refinement of equity. It is essential, therefore, that a survey be made, initially, of the nature of equity, its doctrines and remedies.

1.1 The trust – a creature of equity

The popular definition of equity refers to 'the quality of being equal or fair; impartiality; even-handed dealing' and notes its derivation from *aequus* (= even, fair). Popular usage has in mind ideas of that which is just or right, associated with 'conscience' or so-called 'natural justice'. A highly-specialised meaning of the term has evolved and may be traced through the writings of jurists and others.

1.2 The meaning of equity

Aristotle (384-322 BC), in his *Ethics*, writes:

> 'That which is equitable is just, not legally just, simply a correction of legal justice. This is so because law is universal, but it is not possible to make universal statements about some things. When the law makes a universal statement and a case arises out of it which is not embraced in that statement, it becomes right, when the law-maker falls into error by over-simplifying, to correct the omission ... this is the nature of the equitable, to correct the law where, because of its universality, it is defective.'

1.2.1 Aristotle

In his *Rhetoric* he notes:

> 'It is equity to pardon the human failing, to look to the law giver and not to the law, to the spirit and not to the letter; to the intention and not to the action ...'

1.2.2	Cicero	Cicero (106–43 BC) argued:

'What law ... what treaty cannot be invalidated and torn to pieces if we choose to bend facts to words and leave out of the question the intention, design and authority of those who wrote them?'

1.2.3	Aquinas	Aquinas (1226-74) wrote:

'Laws that are rightly enacted prove deficient where to observe them would be to offend against natural right. In such cases judgment should be delivered, not according to the letter of the law, but by recourse to equity, this being what the law-giver aimed at.'

1.2.4	Christopher St Germain	Christopher St Germain (1460-1540) argued:

'In some cases it is necessary to leave the words of the law and to follow that which reason and justice requireth, and to that intent equity ordained; that is to say, to temper and mitigate the rigour of the law ... And such an equity must always be observed in every law of man ... And the wise man saith: Be not overmuch legal, for extreme legality does extreme wrong.'

1.2.5	Lord Cowper	Lord Cowper spoke of equity, in *Dudley v Dudley* (1705), thus:

'Now equity is no part of the law, but a moral virtue, which qualifies, moderates and reforms the rigour, harshness and edge of the law, and it is a universal truth; it does also assist the law where it is defective and weak in the constitution (which is the life of the law) and defends the law from crafty evasions, delusions, invented and contrived to evade and delude the common law whereby such as have undoubted right are made remediless; and this is the office of equity to support and protect the common law from shifts and crafty contrivances against the justice of the law. Equity therefore does not destroy the law, nor create it, but assists it.'

1.3	**Equity and the common law**	Maine (1822-88) speaks of equity as:

'Any body of rules existing by the side of the original civil law, founded on distinct principles and claiming incidentally to supersede the civil law in virtue of a superior sanctity inherent in those principles.'

Equitable doctrines tend to appear in legal systems when the general rules of those systems fail to correspond to the needs of a changing society and when the continued application of those rules, far from assisting the growth of the law, acts as a fetter upon its further development. In circumstances such as these, supplementary rules tend to emerge, designed to fill in gaps within the legal system and to modify the harshness produced by a over-rigid application of the system's general rules.

We shall consider equity as, in essence, a system of doctrines and procedures which developed side by side with the common law and statute law, having originated in the doctrines and procedures evolved by the old Court of Chancery in its attempts to remedy some of the defects of the common law.

In its beginnings equity grew from the common law; it has never existed independently of it.

Equity is a modification of, and hence a supplement to, the common law. 'Equity came to fulfil the law, and not to destroy it.' Its origins and growth can be comprehended only within the context of the common law. In some historical circumstances it has appeared to rival the common law. Today, however, as a result of its development, and the Judicature Acts 1873-5 in particular, law and equity stand not in rivalry, but as integral parts of one system.

Equity arose and developed in its early days as a reaction to the rigours and inadequacies of the common law. The unavailability of writs for some who needed them, their high costs, their inapplicability to many types of complaint, procedural difficulties and the dominance of technicalities meant that the common law was losing touch with the requirements of the community. *Denom v Scot* (1343) exemplifies the problems. X sued Y on a debt and Y pleaded truthfully that X had received payment following a previous judgment. The deed recording the obligation had not been cancelled. Y was ordered to pay again.

1.4   The general development of equity

From the 13th to the 16th centuries, developments stemmed from the Chancellor's office - the Chancery - from which writs were issued. New writs were invented to cover new complaints; the Statute of Westminster 1285 empowered the Chancery to issue writs based on variations of existing formulae to meet cases which were novel but of 'a similar nature' (*in consimili casu*) to decided cases. The Court of Chancery grew from the practices of the Chancellor and his staff in hearing petitions addressed to the King and in issuing appropriate decrees. Defendants were obliged to give evidence on oath and the Chancellor could, at his discretion, issue declarations of right commanding defendants to perform, or abstain from performing, some act.

1.4.1   13th-16th centuries

The 17th and 18th centuries witnessed a decisive struggle between Chancery and the common law courts, provoked in part by the jealousy of Coke, the Lord Chief Justice, in the face of the growing popularity of Chancery. In the *Earl of Oxford's Case* (1615), Lord Ellesmere, the Chancellor, granted relief in

1.4.2   17th & 18th centuries

equity against certain claims of Merton College which had been upheld by the common law judges. Coke declared that he would no longer hear any counsel who had participated in the bringing of bills in equity directed against the judgments of the common law. Ellesmere appealed to the King (James I) to resolve the dispute. James referred the matter to his Attorney-General, Bacon (a bitter enemy of Coke). The decision favoured Chancery; the Chancellor was instructed that he had no need to refrain from giving relief in equity. Ellesmere's exposition of the role of Chancery was upheld: 'The cause why there is Chancery is for that men's actions are so diverse and infinite that it is impossible to make any general law which may aptly meet with every particular act and not fail in some circumstances'. Coke was humbled (and later dismissed). Chancery flourished, with a burgeoning of doctrines and precedents. By the end of the 18th century, the great equitable doctrines of the trust, the injunction, specific performance had been formulated.

| 1.4.3 | 19th century |

The 19th century saw common law courts permitted to utilise certain procedures hitherto allowed only in Chancery. The Judicature Acts 1873-5 established one Supreme Court of Judicature and effectively fused the administration of equity and law. Under s 25(1), the rules of equity were to prevail in the event of a conflict between equitable and common law rules.

| 1.4.4 | The situation today |

The situation today is summed up in the Supreme Court Act 1981, s 49:

(1) Every court exercising jurisdiction in England or Wales in any civil cause or matter shall continue to administer law and equity on the basis that, wherever there is any conflict or variance between the rules of equity and the rules of the common law with reference to the same matter, the rules of equity shall prevail.

(2) Every such court shall give the same effect as hitherto (a) to all equitable estates, titles, rights, reliefs, defences and counterclaims, and to all equitable duties and liabilities ...

'The two systems of substantive and adjectival law formerly administered by courts of law and equity have surely mingled now': *per* Lord Diplock in *United Scientific Holdings v Burnley BC* (1978).

1.5   Maxims of equity

Some of the maxims enumerated here enshrine old common law brocards; others date from the early practices of the Court of Chancery.

The ecclesiastical background of the early Chancellors was responsible for the formative equitable doctrine that equity proceeded, not necessarily against a person's goods, but against his *conscience* and his person. Any law, according to the early Chancellors, ought to be according to God's law, and equity would not hesitate to act on the conscience. *Per* Browne-Wilkinson VC in *Grant v Edwards* (1986): 'Equity acts on the conscience of the legal owner to prevent him from acting in an unconscionable manner by defeating the common intention'. See also *Gibbon v Mitchell* (1990), in which a voluntary transaction to confer a bounty on another would be set aside if it had an effect which had not been intended by the maker of the deed.

1.5.1 Equity acts on the conscience

The Chancery Court tended to issue its orders upon *a person* so that he was commanded (eg, by injunction or decree of specific performance) to do, or refrain from doing, an act. The order was supported by attachment, writ of sequestration, committal for contempt, etc. See *Penn v Lord Baltimore* (1750); *Ewing v Orr-Ewing* (1833) - 'The courts of equity in England are, and always have been, courts of conscience, operating *in personam* '... and not *in rem*'. And in the exercise of this personal jurisdiction they have always been accustomed to compel the performance of contracts and trusts as to subjects which were not either locally or *ratione domicilii* within their jurisdiction': *per* Lord Selbourne LC. Note, too, the early case of *Rochefoucauld v Boustead* (1897) in which a trust involving land in Ceylon was enforced.

1.5.2 Equity acts *in personam*

The maxim 'equity follows the law' has been construed: in the literal sense, so that an equitable right may not generally override a legal right; in the sense that equity has adopted some of the rules of the common law; in the sense that, unless there is a good reason for deviating from the law, equity will follow it.

Note *Hopkins v Hopkins* (1739), *per* Lord Hardwicke: 'Trust estates, which are the creatures of equity, shall be governed by the same rules as legal estates so as to preserve the uniform rule of property.'

The deviation of equity from the rules of law may be illustrated by the case in which equity allowed the redemption of mortgaged property to take place after the contractual date for repayment. See, eg, *Kreglinger v New Patagonia Meat Co* (1914). Note *Stickland v Aldridge* (1804). Equity gave, in general, no relief to younger brothers and sisters excluded in the event of an intestacy. Where, however, an eldest son had prevailed upon his father not to make a will,

1.5.3 Equity follows the law

on the understanding that he would share the estate with his brothers and sisters, equity (mindful of the need to act upon the conscience) recognised the essential validity of the rule at law but made the eldest son a trustee of the land for himself and the other children.

| 1.5.4 | Where there are equal equities the law prevails | Where, for example, a person purchases a legal estate for valuable consideration and, at the time, is without any notice of the existence of an equitable interest in the land, the legal estate will generally pass to him free from that interest. |

Thus, A, owner of Blackacre, forges, with intent to defraud, a duplicate set of title documents to that property. In pursuance of his plan to defraud he deposits the genuine title deeds with B in return for a loan. Later, he purports to convey Blackacre to C for value and gives the forged documents to C. C has no notice of an equitable mortgage; his rights will be superior to B's. The equities are equal in that neither B nor C is at fault. The law prevails, so that priority goes to the legal owner: *Pilcher v Rawlins* (1872). 'Such a purchaser's plea of a purchase for valuable consideration without notice is an absolute, unqualified, unanswerable defence, and an unanswerable plea to the jurisdiction of this court': *per* James LJ.

| 1.5.5 | Where there are equal equities the first in time prevails | *Qui prior est tempore potior est jure.* (He who is first in time has the strongest claim in law.) In general, interests and estates will rank in priority according to the order of their creation; in the case of equities being equal, the first in time will prevail. See *Cave v Cave* (1880), in which a sole trustee used trust money, in breach of the terms of the trust, so as to purchase land. He took the conveyance in his brother's name. The brother mortgaged the land by legal mortgage to X, and then to Y by way of an equitable mortgage. Neither X nor Y had any notice whatsoever of the existence of the trust. It was held that X's legal mortgage had priority over the beneficiaries' equitable interests. Y's mortgage, since it was created later in time, was *postponed* to the beneficiaries' interests. |

| 1.5.6 | Equitable remedies are discretionary | See Chapter 3. Common law remedies could be claimed as of right. The early Court of Chancery dispensed its remedies solely at the Chancellor's discretion. Today, equitable remedies are granted at the discretion of the court, subject to settled rules, where it is equitable and just in all the circumstances of the case to do so. See *Flight v Bolland* (1828), in which the court refused a decree of specific performance to an infant who had requested performance of a contract. The court exercised its discretion so as to take account of the fact that, because of plaintiff's infancy, the contract could not be enforced against him. Lack of the element of 'mutuality' in the contract means that the court will not grant, in its discretion, specific performance. |

Per Lord Camden in *Smith v Clay* (1767):

'A court of equity has always refused its aid to stale demands where a party has slept upon his rights and acquiesced for a great length of time. Nothing can call forth this court into activity but conscience, good faith and reasonable diligence.'

The equitable doctrine of *laches* asserts that negligence or unreasonable delay in the assertion or enforcing of a right will defeat equities. In cases turning upon laches (see, eg, *Lindsay Petroleum v Hurd* (1874)), consideration will be given to the length of the delay and the nature of acts done during the interval. *Per* Lord Selborne: 'The doctrine of *laches* in courts of equity is not an arbitrary or a technical doctrine. Where it would be practically unjust to give a remedy, either because the party has by his conduct done that which might fairly be regarded as an equivalent to a waiver of it, or where by his conduct and neglect he has, though perhaps not waiving that remedy, put the other party in a situation in which it would not be reasonable to place him if the remedy were afterwards to be asserted, in either of these cases lapse of time and delay are most material'.

Note also *Pollard v Clayton* (1855), in which X agreed to mine and sell Y all the coal in a particular mine. For some time X carried out the agreement but then refused any further deliveries, and sold the coal to other persons. Y was referred to X's solicitors but waited for almost a year before bringing an action. The court held that his delay had barred his equitable claim for specific performance.

The Limitation Act 1980 regulates the periods of time within which certain claims in equity may be brought, eg, claims against a trustee for a breach of trust (see s 21).

The maxim 'Equality is equity' is exemplified by equity's dislike of the joint tenancy and its tendency to favour the tenancy in common. See, eg, *Lake v Craddock* (1732). Note, also, equity's leaning against double portions (as where a testator gives his son a legacy and, later in his lifetime, makes a gift to him, it is presumed that the gift is a substitute for the legacy: see *Ex p Pye* (1811)). See 2.3.7.

In *Jones v Maynard* (1951), a husband and wife had paid into and withdrawn from time to time from a joint banking account; after their divorce, the balance in the account was held to belong to them jointly, being considered by the court as 'a joint purse'. *Per* Vaisey J: 'I think that the principle which applies here is Plato's definition of equality as a "sort of justice". If you cannot find any other, equality is the proper basis'.

1.5.7   Delay defeats equity

1.5.8   Equality is equity

See also *Bower's Trusts* (1942), in which a settlement included a clause directing that a fund be held for persons in unequal shares. An accruer clause concerning shares failing to vest did not state the proportions. It was held that the accruer was to be in equal shares. In *Burrough v Philcox* (1840), a trust in favour of a testator's nephews and nieces was created, subject to a power to appoint in the testator's child. On the child's failure to appoint, it was held that the property was to be divided equally among the objects of the trust.

| 1.5.9 | He who seeks equity must do equity |

A plaintiff who seeks equitable relief must, before obtaining that relief, do that which is right and fair by the defendant. In *Chappell v Times Newspapers* (1975), the Court of Appeal emphasised that plaintiffs, by their refusal to undertake to refrain from disruptive action during an industrial dispute, had not shown themselves willing to perform their side of contracts of employment and could not seek equitable relief when they were not prepared to act equitably. *Per* Lord Cranworth in *Jorden v Money* (1854).

> 'If a person makes a false representation to another, and that other acts on it as a *prima facie* proposition, the person who made the false representation shall not afterwards be allowed for his own benefit to set up that which he said was false.'

Since a decree of specific performance may not be awarded against a minor, it will not be awarded to him - mutuality is lacking and in circumstances such as these an equitable remedy cannot be granted. See *Lumley v Ravenscroft* (1895). See 1.5.6 above.

| 1.5.10 | He who comes to equity must come with clean hands |

The plaintiff must have a clear conscience as regards the past. See *Overton v Banister* (1844) in which a minor fraudulently misrepresented her age and persuaded trustees to pay money to her; later, when she came of age, she sued them for payment of the sum again, but her claim was not allowed. Note Lord Eyre, in *Dering v Earl of Winchelsea* (1787): 'A man must come into a court of equity with clean hands; but when this is said it does not mean a general depravity; it must have an immediate and necessary relation to the equity sued for; it must be a depravity in a legal as well as in a moral sense'.

In *Tinsley v Milligan* (1983), the House of Lords considered whether a party, founding himself on a legal or equitable title acquired in the course of carrying through an illegal transaction, could recover so long as he was not forced to plead or rely on the illegality.

(i) *The facts.* X and Y had lived together for some years in a house which they ran as a lodging house. The purchase price was provided jointly and they agreed that the title was to be taken solely in X's name so as to facilitate Y's false claims on the Department of Social Security. X and Y fell out; X claimed possession of the property and Y counterclaimed for a declaration that X held the property on trust for X and Y in equal shares. X appealed from the judge's dismissal of her claim for possession. The judge held that X held the property on trust for X and Y in equal shares. The Court of Appeal dismissed X's subsequent appeal.

(ii) *House of Lords.* Per Lord Browne-Wilkinson: the time had come to decide clearly that the rule was the same whether a plaintiff founded himself upon a legal or equitable title. He was entitled to recover if he was not forced to plead or rely on the illegality, even if it emerged that the title on which he relied was acquired in the course of carrying through an illegal transaction. Y had established a resulting trust (see 8.1.1) by showing that she had contributed to the price of the house and that there was a common understanding between X and Y that they owned the house equally. Y had no need to prove why the house was conveyed into X's name alone, since that fact was irrelevant to her claim. It sufficed to show that the house was in fact vested in X alone. The illegality emerged only because X sought to raise it. Having established those facts, Y had raised the presumption of a resulting trust and there was no evidence to rebut the presumption. Therefore Y ought to succeed.

In *Bannister v Bannister* (1948), P gave D an oral promise that D could stay for as long as she desired in a rent-free cottage. In return, D sold P the cottage at a relatively low price, and also an adjoining property. The conveyance did not refer to P's promise. P claimed possession of the cottage, arguing that the trust was invalid because of an absence of writing (see Law of Property Act 1925, s 53(1)). It was held that fraud on P's part had been shown; the plea relating to absence of writing failed. Note, however, *Midland Bank Trust Co v Green* (1981) in which equity did *not* intervene in circumstances which appeared to suggest use of the Land Charges Act 1972 as a cloak for fraud.

1.5.11   Equity will not permit a statute to be used as a cloak for fraud

(i) *The facts.* W owned land in fee simple and granted his son, G, an option to buy the land at a specified price of £22,500. G failed to register the option as required under the Land Charges Act 1972. W later discovered G's failure to register and swiftly conveyed the land to his wife, E, for a nominal price of £500 (although the land had by then doubled in price). G's attempt to exercise his option was met by E's refusal to sell. The judge at first instance ruled that the unregistered option did not bind E's estate. His decision had been reached 'with regret'; he was unable to allow his 'subjective moral judgment to stand in the way of the clear meaning of a statutory provision'.

(ii) *Court of Appeal.* Lord Denning, enunciating the reversal of the lower court's ruling, held that E had not given money or money's worth and that her payment was 'grotesquely small'. Payment at an undervalue was unacceptable. Fraud unravels everything. 'No court in the land would allow unwary innocents to be deprived of their rightful dues.' The conduct of W and E towards G constituted 'a plot'.

(iii) *House of Lords.* The lower court's ruling was reinstated. The omission of any requirement of good faith from the Land Charges Act 1925 was deliberate. 'The case is plain: the Act is clear and definite. Intended as it was to provide a simple and understandable system for the protection of title to land, it should not be read down or glossed: to do so would destroy the usefulness of the Act.'

1.5.12   Equity does not suffer a wrong to be without a remedy

Per Lord Holt in *Ashby v White* (1704): 'If plaintiff has a right, he must of necessity have a means to vindicate it, and a remedy if he is injured in the exercise or enjoyment of it.'

The maxim has in mind only those wrongs capable of judicial redress.

1.5.13   Equity looks to the substance and intent rather than to the form

Per Romilly MR in *Parkin v Thorold* (1852): 'If [a court of equity] finds that, by insisting on the form the substance will be defeated, it holds it inequitable to allow a person to insist on such form and thereby defeat the substance.'

This is exemplified in equity's attitude to the mortgage: 'Once a mortgage, always a mortgage' (so that the equitable right to redeem may be exercised in any transaction which is substantially a mortgage: *Re Lovegrove* (1935)).

Note *Metropolitan Electric v Ginder* (1901). X had agreed to take from Y all the electrical energy he needed for his premises. Later, Y asked for an injunction (see 3.8) which would prevent X's taking any electrical energy from Z. The court held that, in substance, the agreement did not oblige X to take any electricity; but it meant, in essence, that X could not obtain such energy from anyone other than Y.

1.5.14   Equity looks on that as done which ought to be done

A contract to perform an act is treated in equity as if the act had been performed, and equity will consider the parties to the contract as possessing the rights, duties and remedies they would have had if the act had been performed. See *Walsh v Lonsdale* (1882).

Where a person is under an obligation to perform an act and he later performs another act closely resembling a performance of that obligation, equity will assume that he had an intention to fulfil the obligation. 'Where a man covenants to do an act, and he does an act which may be converted to a completion of this covenant, it shall be supposed that he meant to complete it': *per* Kenyon MR. Note the doctrines of performance and satisfaction (see Chapter 2) and *Lechmere v Lady Lechmere* (1735).

Under early common law there was no remedy for a breach of trust. Assume that X, who owned Blackacre in fee simple, made a conveyance of Blackacre to Y, instructing him to hold it upon trust for Z. Common law gave no remedy against Y if he used the property for his own, and not for Z's, benefit. But the Court of Chancery would enforce the trust against Y for the benefit of Z. Z was regarded as the beneficial, or equitable, owner, ie, the person entitled to the benefit in equity, possessing an *equitable interest* in Blackacre.

The Court of Chancery would 'act upon the conscience' of Y and enforce his holding of the property for the beneficial owner, Z. Z's interest manifested itself in a right *in personam* available against Y. During the 15th century, Z's interest became enforceable not only against Y, but against Y's heirs, or against a purchaser of Blackacre who took with notice of Z's interest.

In time an equitable interest became capable of enforcement against everyone *except* a purchaser of the legal estate without notice. Today, an equitable interest gives way, in general, only to a *bona fide* purchaser for value of the legal estate who takes without actual, constructive or imputed notice.

Examples of equitable interests other than the trust include: the equitable lien; the equitable charge; the restrictive covenant; the estate contract; the equitable easement and profits.

Note Law of Property Act 1925, s 1(3), by which all estates, interests and charges in or over land save those mentioned in ss 1(1) and 1(2), take effect as equitable interests. See also *Tinsley v Milligan* (1993).

It is doubtful whether new rights in equity are capable of creation now. In *Re Diplock* (1948), the Court of Appeal stated that if a claim in equity were to be made:

'... it must be shown to have an ancestry founded in history and in the practice and precedents of the courts administering equity jurisdiction. It is not sufficient that because we think that the "justice" of the present case requires it, we should invent such a jurisdiction for the first time.'

1.6 The nature of equitable interests

Note also Law of Property Act 1925, s 4(1):

'... After the commencement of this Act ... an equitable interest in land shall only be capable of being validly created in any case in which an equivalent equitable interest in property real or personal could have been validly created before such commencement.'

The Essence of Equity

The principles and development of the trust (based on X entrusting property to Y for the benefit of Z) reflect concepts of equity.

    The trust must be seen within the wider framework of equitable principles.

The trust - a creature of equity

'Equity' reflects, in popular usage, even-handed impartiality.

    In legal theory, it is a system of doctrines and procedures which developed side by side with the common law and statute law, having originated in the doctrines and procedures evolved by the old Court of Chancery in its attempts to remedy some of the defects of the common law and temper the harshness produced by a too-rigid application of its rules.

    Essentially equity was created as a modification of, and a supplement to, the common law.

    As a result of its development, courts exercising jurisdiction in England or Wales now administer law and equity on the basis that, in the event of a conflict between their rules, equity shall prevail: Supreme Court Act 1981, s 49.

The meaning of equity

Maxims of equity date from the early practices of the Court of Chancery.

Maxims of equity

1   Equity acts on the conscience.
2   Equity acts *in personam*.
3   Equity follows the law.
4   Where there are equal equities the law prevails.
5   Where there are equal equities the first in time prevails.
6   Equitable remedies are discretionary.
7   Delay defeats equity.
8   Equality is equity.
9   He who seeks equity must do equity.
10   He who comes to equity must come with clean hands.
11   Equity will not permit a statute to be used as a cloak for fraud.
12   Equity does not suffer a wrong to be without a remedy.
13   Equity looks to the substance and intent rather than to the form.
14   Equity looks on that as done which ought to be done.
15   Equity imputes an intention to fulfil an obligation.

The nature of equitable interests

The equitable interest is fundamental to the law of trusts. It arose, in this context, when the Court of Chancery enforced the holding of property for the beneficial owner.

In time the equitable interest became enforceable against everyone *except* the *bona fide* purchaser of the legal estate without notice.

Examples of equitable interests: equitable lien, restrictive covenant, estate contract, equitable easement.

The creation of new rights in equity is now very unlikely.

A claim in equity must be established on the basis of precedent: see *Re Diplock* (1948). Note Law of Property Act 1925, s 4(1): the creation of an equitable interest after 1925 is possible *only* when an equivalent interest (in property) might have been created before that date.

Chapter 2

Equitable Doctrines

Conversion, in equity, is a notional change, under certain circumstances, of real into personal property (land into money), or personal to real property (money into land), which arises as soon as the duty to convert arises. Thus, P gives personalty on trust to Q and R to purchase land and to hold it for S. A devises land to B and C to sell and hold the proceeds of that sale for D. In these cases the equitable doctrine of conversion operates so that there is a notional conversion by which, in the first example, the personalty is considered as realty,and, in the second example, the land is considered as money. *Per* Sewell MR in *Fletcher v Ashburner* (1779):

> 'Nothing is better established than this principle that money directed to be employed in the purchase of land, directed to be sold and turned into money, are to be considered as that species of property into which they are directed to be converted; and this in whatever manner the direction is given, whether by will, by way of contract, marriage articles, settlement, or otherwise; and whether the money is actually deposited, or only covenanted to be paid, whether the land is actually conveyed, or only agreed to be conveyed, the owner of the fund, or the contracting parties, may make land money, or money land.'

The equitable principle at the basis of the doctrine is 'Equity looks on that as done which ought to be done'. Where, therefore, a person is under an obligation to sell realty and convert it into money, or to employ money in the purchase of realty, equity will look on the property as being, for all purposes, in its converted state from the particular time when that obligation arose. The doctrine operates in the case of wills, deeds and contracts.

Note the comments of Pollock MR in *Re Twopeny's Settlement* (1924): 'Where the quality of real estate is "imperatively and definitely" fixed upon personalty (or vice versa) equity will treat the personalty (or realty as the case may be) as having acquired the quality indicated, even though it is not found to have been actually turned into realty or personalty; because equity treats what ought to be done as done, and will not allow the rights of beneficiaries to be altered by a failure on the part of the trustees to carry out their trust'.

2.1.1   **Circumstances in which the doctrine of conversion operates**

The circumstances in which the doctrine of conversion operates are as follows.

- By order of the court

  The court may direct the purchase or sale of realty and in such a case conversion is considered to have taken place at the date of the order. Where the court directs a sale under statute, the doctrine may come into play: thus, under the Mental Health Act 1983, s 101, where the court directs the sale of a patient's real property, the property which represents it is treated as real property while it remains in his estate.

- By valid contract for the sale or purchase of land

  Vaisey J set out the general rule in *Hillingdon Estates v Stonefield Estates* (1952): 'When there is a contract by A to sell land to B at a certain price, B becomes the owner in equity of the land, subject, of course, to his obligation to perform his part of the contract by paying the purchase money; but subject to that, the land is the land of B, the purchaser. What is the position of A, the vendor? He has, it is true, the legal estate in the land, but, for many purposes, from the moment the contract is entered into he holds it as trustee for B, the purchaser. True, he has certain rights in the land remaining, but all those rights are conditioned and limited by the circumstances that they are all referable to his right to recover and receive the purchase money. His interest in the land when he has entered into a contract for sale is not an interest in land; it is an interest in personal estate, in a sum of money'.

  The contract must be one which is specifically enforceable. In such a case the purchaser is considered as having an interest in realty; the seller is considered as having an interest in personalty.

  (i) Should a purchaser die before completion, his interest is regarded as real property and will pass to the person entitled to his real property.

  (ii) Should a vendor die before completion, his right to receive the purchase money passes to the person entitled to his personal property.

  (iii) In the case of an option to purchase, the rules are as follows. Where the option to purchase freehold land is given in a lease and exercised during the lessor's life, it operates as a conversion of his interest to personalty. Where an option is exercised after the lessor's death, it operates as a conversion of the property to personalty: *Lawes v Bennett* (1785).

- Under a trust

  The general rule is that where a settlor or testator directs trustees to sell or purchase realty, the property is considered as having been converted from the time of the direction, provided that the direction is imperative.

  (i)   Direction under a deed: conversion takes place at the time of the deed's execution. Direction under will: conversion takes place at the time of the testator's death. See *Re Grimthorpe* (1908).

  (ii) Direction to convert not imperative, and conversion optional: the property is considered as having been converted unless there is an actual conversion. See *Re Dyson* (1910).

  (iii) Direction offends perpetuities rule: no conversion in equity even if an actual conversion has been made.

  (iv) Trustees given discretion as to time of purchase or sale: property is considered as having been converted from the time when the instrument containing the direction has come into operation.

  (v)   Trust to either sell or retain land: construed as trust to sell with power to postpone sale, hence a conversion: see Law of Property Act 1925, s 25(4).

- Note Settled Land Act 1925, s 75(5) (uninvested or unapplied capital money arising under the Act may be treated as land), and Partnership Act 1890, s 22 (land which has become partnership property). 'Capital money arising under this Act while remaining uninvested or unapplied, and securities on which an investment of any such capital money is made shall for all purposes of disposition, transmission and devolution be treated as land, and shall be held for and go to the same persons successively, in the same manner and for and in the same estates, interests, and trusts, as the land wherefrom the money arises would, if not disposed of, have been held and have gone under the settlement': Settled Land Act 1925, s 75(5). 'Where land or any heritable interest therein has become partnership property, it shall, unless the contrary intention appears, be treated as between the parties (including the representatives of a deceased partner), and also as between the heirs of a deceased partner, and his executors and administrators as personal or movable and not as real or heritable estate': Partnership Act 1890, s 22.

In the case of a *total failure of conversion* (as where A devises land to B and C as trustees to sell and hold the proceeds of sale for D, and D pre-deceases A, so that there is a total failure of

2.1.2   Failure of conversion

the objects of conversion) no conversion is possible whether the direction is in a will or deed. But in the case of a *partial failure* (as where A devises land to B and C as trustees to sell and hold the proceeds of sale for D and E, and E pre-deceases A, so that there is a partial failure of the objects of conversion), if the conversion was directed *by deed* the property reverts to the settlor in its converted form (*Griffith v Ricketts* (1849)); if directed by *will*, the property passes to the person entitled to it in its unconverted form, but that person takes it in its converted form (*Re Walpole* (1933)).

2.1.3   Reconversion

Reconversion is the notional process whereby property which has been subject to notional conversion is treated as having been restored to its original state. It must be distinguished from 'failure of conversion' in which it is assumed that, since the objects of the conversion failed, the conversion never took place. Reconversion assumes a prior, effective conversion. Thus, A devises land to B and C on trust to sell and pay proceeds of sale to D. As a result of the doctrine of conversion, D is entitled to the property in its converted form (realty) at the time of D's death. He can elect to take the property in its actual or converted form. Should he elect to take the land, then reconversion has taken place.

Reconversion may come about by operation of law, eg, where a trust has failed or come to an end, and the property was in the possession of a person who was absolutely entitled and who has died without making a declaration concerning that property. See *Re Cook* (1948). *Per* Byrne J in *Re Douglas* and *Powell's Contract* (1902):

'It is necessary to have sufficient evidence of the election to be derived from declarations or acts and conduct of the parties, and where it is sought to establish such an election by a person or persons only entitled so to elect subject to the rights of third persons to insist upon a sale, it must be shown in like manner that such persons have assented.'

2.2   **Election**

A person who takes a benefit under an instrument must accept or reject that instrument *as a whole*; he must elect between approbation and reprobation. The doctrine derives fundamentally from the concept expressed in the maxim: *Qui sentit commodum sentire debet et onus, et e contra.* (He who enjoys the benefit ought also to bear the burden, and vice versa). *Per* Lord Cairns in *Codrington v Codrington* (1875):

'Where a deed or will professes to make a general disposition of property for the benefit of a person named in it, such person cannot accept a benefit under the instrument without at the same time conforming to all its provisions, and renouncing every right inconsistent with them.'

See also *Re Edwards* (1958).

For example, assume that A makes a gift of his property, Pl, by deed or will, to B, and, in the same instrument he purports to make a gift of B's property, P2, to C. Equity puts B 'to his election', so that he may either elect to take under the instrument, in which case B will take Pl and C will take P2, *or* elect to take against the instrument, in which case B retains P2 and claims Pl. B is then compelled to compensate C out of Pl. *Per* Buckley J in *Re Mengel's WT* (1962):

> 'The doctrine of election does not depend upon the intention of the testator and, indeed, the case in which the testator frames his will with the conscious intention of bringing the doctrine into play must be very rare. In the great majority of cases to which the doctrine is applicable it applies because the testator has made a mistake.'

Certain conditions for election are essential. (The names used here, A, B, C, refer to the example above.) All these conditions must exist when the instrument comes into operation.

2.2.1   Conditions for election

- There must be a clear intention (which must appear from the will itself, for example) by the donor to dispose of property which he does not own. Whether he mistakenly thought the property was his own is of no relevance: *Welby v Welby* (1813). 'But what is the intention that the court must apprehend upon clear evidence? ... The intention that must be clearly demonstrated in evidence to the court is an intention to do the particular thing - to give the property which the party has not a right to give, and to give a benefit to a person who has an interest in the property. These two intentions being ascertained upon clear evidence, the law draws the conclusion. It is a conclusion of equity ...': *per* Lord O'Hagan in *Cooper v Cooper* (1874).

- There must be a gift of A's property to B by deed or will: *Birmingham v Kirwan* (1805).

- There must be a purported gift of B's property to C: *Cooper v Cooper* (1874).

- The property given by A to B must be available for C's compensation: *Re Tongue* (1915).

- B's property, which A has purported to give to C, must be freely alienable by B: *Re Lord Chesham* (1886). Note also *Re Dicey* (1957), in which X left by will her house to her son, Y, and 'two freehold houses' in a named road to her grandson, Z. X did not possess the freehold of the houses, having only a life interest under the provisions of a settlement by which, at her death, the houses were to be sold and one-half of the proceeds were to go to Y. It was held that Y had a beneficial interest which he could transfer. He should elect whether to take under the terms of X's will and transfer his interest to Z, or take against the will, offering compensation to Z for not receiving the houses.

2.2.2   Problems in relation to election

The following types of problem may arise in relation to election.

- Death of elector

  An election made by the elector before his death binds his personal representatives and those claiming through him: *Cavan v Pulteney* (1795). Where no election has been made and the elector's entire property passes to one person, that person must elect: *Cooper v Cooper* (1874).

- Testator's limited interest in property

  Where a testator purports to dispose of property which is not entirely his own, but in which he has merely a limited interest, 'the court will lean as far as possible to a construction which would make him deal only with that to which he was entitled': *per* Page Wood VC in *Howells v Jenkins* (1863).

- Delay in election

  Election is not inferred merely from lapse of time. But where there is a limited time for election, failure to elect within that time may be regarded as tantamount to an election against the instrument.

- Express or implied election

  Election may be express, in which case it must be communicated to those likely to be affected (see *Re Shepherd* (1943)) or implied from the elector's conduct.

- Knowledge of rights

  'There must be, in the first place, [to constitute a settled and concluded election] clear proof that the person put to his election was aware of the nature and extent of his rights': *per* Romilly MR in *Worthington v Wiginton* (1855).

2.3   **Satisfaction**

Where X is under an obligation to provide for Y, or to give him something, and X gives Y something else, there may be a presumption that X's gift was made with the intention of satisfying his obligation to Y. Lord Romilly referred, in *Lord Chichester v Coventry* (1867), to satisfaction as 'the donation of a thing with the intention that it is to be taken either wholly or in part in extinguishment of some prior claim of the donee'.

'Equity imputes an intent to fulfil an obligation.' Where, eg, a father covenants to provide his child with a portion and he later provides a portion for that child in his will, there will be a presumption, in certain circumstances, that the portion given by will was in satisfaction of the covenant. The child may not take the portion under the will and also claim under the covenant. In *Herne v Herne* (1706), H covenanted that at his death, his wife, W, should have a legacy of £800 and that this would not exclude W taking the benefit of any other gifts he might confer on her 'by will or writing'. H bequeathed W a legacy of £1000. It was held that the legacy was to be taken in satisfaction of the covenant of £800.

2.3.1 Essence of the doctrine of satisfaction

The general rule is that equity imputes to the donor an intention to give the legacy in satisfaction of the debt. *Per* Trevor MR in *Talbott v Duke of Shrewsbury* (1714):

2.3.3 Satisfaction of debts by legacies

> 'If one, being indebted to another in a sum of money, does by his will give him a sum of money as great as, or greater than, the debt, without taking any notice at all of the debt, this shall, nevertheless, be in satisfaction of the debt, so that he shall not have both the debt and the legacy.'

For example, assume that D owes C £1,000. D does not pay C during his lifetime and, by a will made later, bequeaths to C a legacy of £1000. There is then a presumption that the legacy was intended to satisfy the debt, so that C would not be able to claim both legacy and debt.

The doctrine has no application in the following circumstances.

2.3.4 Circumstances in which election has no application

- Where the debt was contracted after the will was made or contemporaneously with it. In such a case no intention to fulfil the obligation may be presumed: *Horlock v Wiggins* (1888).

- Where the legacy is less than the debt. In such a case no intention to satisfy is presumed, and the creditor can claim legacy and debt: *Atkinson v Webb* (1704).

- Where the legacy is not as beneficial to the creditor as the debt, eg, where the legacy is contingent or uncertain: *Re Rattenbury* (1906).

- Where the legacy and debt are of a different nature: *Eastwood v Vinke* (1731).

- Where the testator indicates a contrary intention: *Re Manners* (1949). *Per* Evershed MR: 'It seems tolerably clear that direction for payment either of debts and legacies, or of debts *simpliciter* is treated as being, whether or not artifically - and I do not think it is particularly artificial - something which *prima facie* takes the case altogether out of the rule.'

| 2.3.5 | Satisfaction of a portion-debt by a legacy |

In general, equity 'leans against double portions'. A *portion* is a gift of money or other property made to a child by a father or by one standing *in loco parentis* in order to establish the child in life or make permanent provision for him. A *portion-debt* arises from a covenant to give a portion. *Per* Cotton LJ in *Montagu v Earl of Sandwich* (1886):

> 'As between father and son the presumption arises that a father does not intend to give double portions to his children; that is to say if a father has made a provision by way of covenant in favour of his child before the date of his will, then unless it appears upon the will or by parol testimony that he intends to give the benefit conferred by the will in addition to that which is already secured to the child by covenant, then the child will not take both.'

Note the explanation given by Lord Cottenham in *Pym v Lockyer* (1841): 'All the decisions upon questions of double portions depend upon the declared or presumed intentions of the donor. The presumption of equity is against double portions because it is not thought probable, when the object appears to be to make a provision, and that object has been effected by one instrument, that a repetition of it in a second should be intended as an addition to the first. The second provision, therefore, is presumed to be intended as a substitution for, and not as an addition to, that first given'.

For example, assume that X is Y's father and covenants, in Y's marriage settlement, to pay the trustees £100,000. In a will made at a later date, he leaves Y a legacy of £100,000, but dies without paying any money to the trustees. The legacy may be presumed to be in satisfaction of the portion-debt.

Where the legacy is equal to the promised portion, or exceeds it, satisfaction of the portion-debt is presumed. Where the legacy is less than the promised portion, satisfaction *pro tanto* is presumed: *Warren v Warren* (1783).

| 2.3.6 | Satisfaction of a portion-debt by a portion |

Where X, father of Y, or who stands *in loco parentis* to Y, has undertaken to give Y a portion and, later in X's lifetime, X makes provision for Y, there is a presumption that the provision was made in satisfaction of the portion-debt.

| 2.3.7 | Satisfaction or ademption of a legacy by a portion |

Where X, Y's father, or standing *in loco parentis* to Y, gives Y a legacy and later makes a gift in Y's favour, there is a presumption 'that the gift *inter vivos* was either wholly or in part a substitute for, or an ademption of, the legacy':

per Lord Selborne in *Re Pollock* (1885). There is no such presumption where X pays a sum of money to Y before the will is made. Note that ademption or satisfaction is only *pro tanto*.

'Where a father gives a legacy to a child, the legacy coming from a father to his child must be understood as a portion, though it is not so described in the will; and afterwards advancing a portion for that child, though there may be slight circumstances of difference between that advance and the portion, and a difference in amount, yet the father will be intended to have the same purpose in each instance; and the advance is, therefore, an ademption of the legacy': *per* Lord Eldon in *Ex p Pye* (1811).

It should be noted that a stranger, that is, a person who is not the donor's child, or to whom the donor does not stand *in loco parentis*, may not benefit from ademption or satisfaction; further, there is no ademption or satisfaction in the case of a gift to a stranger. Suppose that A leaves property in equal shares to B and C, who are A's children, and to D, who is not. During A's lifetime he advances money to B and D. B must account for the advance, whereas D need not. D will receive one-third of A's property. The advance made to B will be added to the remaining two-thirds of the property so as to produce equality between B and C: *Re Heather* (1906.)

Where two legacies are given to one person, the legacies may be considered, in the absence of evidence as to the testator's intentions, as substitutional.

2.3.8   Satisfaction of legacies by legacies

- Legacies in same instruments

  If the legacies are of the same amount there is a presumption that they are substitutional; if of different amounts, there is a presumption that they are cumulative, and both are payable. See *Masters v Masters* (1718); *Garth v Meyrick* (1779).

- Legacies in different instruments

  If the legacies are of the same amounts and the same reasons for the gifts are given, there is a presumption of satisfaction. If the legacies are of different amounts, both are payable. If different reasons for the gifts are given, both are payable: *Re Bagnall* (1949).

Where a person covenants to perform a particular act and later performs an act 'which may be converted to a completion of this covenant, it shall be supposed that he meant to complete it': *per* Kenyon MR in *Sowden v Sowden* (1785). 'Equity imputes an intention to fulfil an obligation'; hence, what is done may be regarded as a step to fulfilment of the obligation.

2.4   **Performance**

2.4.1	Performance differs from satisfaction	In the case of satisfaction the thing done may not be the same as the thing agreed to be done. In the case of performance the same act which was the basis of the covenant is assumed to have been done.
2.4.2	Covenant to purchase and settle land	Assume that A, prior to his marriage, and in consideration of it, covenants to purchase certain land and to settle it on B (his wife) and their children. Following the marriage, A purchases land of a similar nature and value, but does not make the settlement. Equity assumes that the purchase was for the purpose of performing the covenant. On A's death, the rights of B and the children will be considered in equity as the rights they would have possessed had the land been settled upon them: *Lechmere v Lady Lechmere* (1735).
2.4.3	Covenant to purchase land of a given value	A covenant to purchase land of a given value may be performed *pro tanto* by the purchase of land of a smaller value. A covenant for the purchase of freehold land is not performed by the purchase of leasehold land. A covenant to purchase land at some future time is not considered as performed by purchases prior to that covenant.
2.4.4	Covenant to leave money by will	In the absence of a contrary intention, or a breach of the covenant, a covenant to leave money by will will be considered as having been performed fully or *pro tanto* where the covenantor dies intestate and the covenantee takes under the intestacy. Thus, in *Oliver v Brickland* (1732), a husband (H) had covenanted to pay his wife (W) a sum of money within two years of their marriage. H died intestate more than two years later, having failed to make the payment. W was held to be entitled not only to her share on intestacy, but also (because there had been a breach of covenant) to the sum H had covenanted to pay.

In *Blandy v Wildmore* (1716), a husband covenanted to leave his wife £620 under the terms of his will. Later he died intestate; following the rules then in force concerning intestacy, his wife became entitled to a sum in excess of £620. It was held that since the covenant had not been broken, it was to be treated as having been performed, so that the wife was not able to recover £620 as a debt over and above her share under the intestacy rules.

Equitable Doctrines

Conversion is a notional change of real into personal and personal to real property which arises as soon as the duty to convert arises.

It is based on the equitable principle: 'Equity looks on that as done which ought to be done'.

The doctrine operates: by order of the court; by valid contract for the sale or purchase of land; under a trust; and under statute, eg, Settled Land Act 1925, s 75(5), Partnership Act 1980, s 22.

Failure of conversion: where there is *total failure*, no conversion possible; where there is *partial failure*, if conversion was directed by deed, property reverts to the settlor in converted form, if directed by will, property passes to the person entitled to it in unconverted form, although he takes it in the converted form.

Reconversion: property which has been subject to notional conversion is treated as having been restored to original state. It may come about through operation of law. See *Re Cook* (1948).

The essence of election: he who enjoys the benefit ought also to bear the burden, and vice versa.

For example, A makes gift of his property, Pl, by deed or will to B. In the same instrument he purports to make a gift of B's property, P2, to C. Equity puts B 'to his election', so that B may elect to take under the instrument, or against it. In the former case, B takes Pl; C takes P2. In the latter case, B retains P2 and claims Pl, and B compensates C out of Pl.

The conditions for election: clear intention by A to dispose of property he does not own; gift to B by deed or will; gift of B's property to C; property given by A to B must be available for C's compensation; B's property, which A has purported to give to C, must be freely alienable by B.

Election may be express or implied from the conduct of the elector.

The essence of satisfaction: where X is under an obligation to provide for Y, or to give him something, and X gives something else, there may be a presumption that X's gift was made with the intention of satisfying his obligation to Y. See *Lord Chichester v Coventry* (1867).

Conversion

Election

Satisfaction

Satisfaction of debts by legacies. Equity imputes an intention to the donor to give the legacy in satisfaction of the debt. This has no application where the legacy is less than the debt or where the debt was contracted after the will was made or contemporaneously with it.

Satisfaction of a portion-debt by a legacy. Equity 'leans against double portions'.

Satisfaction of a portion-debt by a portion. Assume that X, Y's father, undertakes to give Y a portion and, later, makes provision, in Y's lifetime, for Y. The presumption is that the provision was made in satisfaction of the portion-debt.

Satisfaction or ademption of legacy by portion. There is a presumption that the gift *inter vivos* was either wholly or in part a substitute for, or an ademption of, the legacy.

Satisfaction of legacies by legacies may be considered substitutional, if of the same amount in the same instrument.

Performance

Where a person covenants to perform a particular act and later performs an act which may be converted to a completion of this covenant, 'it shall be supposed that he meant to complete it'.

Equity imputes an intention to fulfil an obligation.

Performance differs from satisfaction: in the case of satisfaction, the thing done may not be the same as the thing agreed to be done; in the case of performance, the same act which was the basis of the covenant is assumed to have been done.

A covenant to purchase land of a given value may be performed *pro tanto* by the purchase of land of a smaller value.

Chapter 3

Equitable Remedies

Equitable remedies, at one time available only in the Court of Chancery, are now available in all courts exercising jurisdiction in civil causes: Supreme Court Act 1981, s 49.

    In their essence, equitable remedies are *discretionary*; hence they would not be available to a plaintiff whose conduct indicated that he was 'unwilling to do equity'. The discretion of the court is now exercised in accordance with settled principles.

    Equitable remedies are available, in general, only in the absence of an appropriate and adequate common law remedy. See, eg, *Beswick v Beswick* (1968).

3.1 Nature of equitable remedies

A decree of specific performance is an order of the court instructing a party to an agreement to perform his obligations according to the terms of that agreement. The remedy is discretionary and is granted only where the appropriate remedy at law is inadequate, and where 'under all the circumstances it is just and equitable to do so': *per* Lord Parker in *Stickney v Keeble* (1915). Breach of contract is not always essential to an action for specific performance: *Marks v Lilley* (1959). The decree issues against an individual defendant: refusal to comply is treated as a contempt of court.

3.2 Specific performance

Under the Chancery Amendment Act 1858, the Court of Chancery was empowered to award damages in addition to or *in lieu* of specific performance or an injunction. See now the Supreme Court Act 1981, s 50: 'Where the Court of Appeal or the High Court has jurisdiction to entertain an application for an injunction or specific performance, it may award damages in addition to, or in substitution for, an injunction or specific performance'.

3.2.1 Discretion to award damages

The following are examples of contracts which are specifically enforceable:

3.2.2 Contracts specifically enforceable

- Contracts for the sale or purchase of land or the grant of a lease. In such cases damages are rarely considered as adequate compensation.

- Contracts concerning personal property. Under this heading may be found contracts for chattels of unusual rarity (*Thorn v Commissioners of Public Works* (1863) - stones from Westminster Bridge). Where shares cannot ordinarily be bought on the open market, specific performance may be ordered (see *Duncuft v Albrecht* (1841)).

- See Sale of Goods Act 1979, s 52, giving the buyer (but not the seller) the right to invoke the discretion of the court and request a decree that the contract be specifically performed.

  (1) In any action for breach of contract to deliver specific or ascertained goods, the court may, if it thinks fit, on the plaintiff's application, by its judgment or decree direct that the contract shall be performed specifically, without giving the defendant the option of retaining the goods on payment of damages.

  (2) The plaintiff's application may be made at any time before judgment or decree.

  (3) The judgment or decree may be unconditional, or on such terms and conditions as to damages, payment of the price, and otherwise, as seems just to the court. Note that where a buyer gives a seller some reason to believe that he will claim damages only, and not call for specific performance, that buyer may be estopped from altering his decision should the seller have changed his position because of acting to his detriment by relying upon his belief: *Meng Leong v Jip Hong Traders* (1985).

The following are examples of contracts which are not specifically enforceable:

3.2.3   Contracts not specifically enforceable

- Contracts made for no consideration ('Equity will not aid a volunteer': see *Jefferys v Jefferys* (1841); contracts tainted with immorality or illegality (see *Cartwright v Cartwright* (1853); contracts for arbitration (see *Bremer Vulkan v S India Shipping Corp* (1981)); contracts determinable at will (since 'Equity like nature does nothing in vain' so that, eg, contracts likely to be dissolved within a short period of time will not be specifically enforced' see *Lavery v Pursell* (1888) - refusal in the case of a tenancy for a year).

- Contracts involving the loan and payment of money; contracts for personal services (see *Page One Records Ltd v Britton* (1968)); Trade Union and Labour Relations (Consolidation) Act 1992, s 236 (forbidding a court to order by specific performance an employee to do any work or attend at any place for the doing of any work); contracts lacking mutuality. ('One party to a bargain shall not be held bound to that bargain when he cannot enforce it against the other': *per* Kekewich J in *Wylson v Dunn* (1887).)

- Contracts involving constant supervision. See *Ryan v Mutual Tontine* (1893). In that case, X, lessor of a flat in a block of flats, agreed to appoint a resident porter. Y was appointed; it was found that he was often absent from his duties so as to perform other duties in a nearby club. During Y's frequent absences his duties as porter were carried out by persons who were not resident on the premises. It was held that a breach of contract had been committed, but a decree of specific performance was refused; the only remedy was an action for damages. A continuing contract which had to be performed from one day to another by a series of acts would not be specifically enforced. Note *Posner v Scott-Lewis* (1987), in which the court stated that relevant considerations were: is there a sufficient definition of what has to be done in order to comply with the court order; will enforcing compliance involve an unacceptable degree of court superintendence; what are the hardships likely to be suffered by the parties if the order is made or refused?

Some defences to an action for specific performance are derived from equity's insistence that its discretion shall be exercised only where the parties have behaved fairly. There will be no order where the contract is shown to be incomplete, or uncertain (see *Taylor v Portington* (1855)), or illegal, or where plaintiff has failed to come to equity 'with clean hands' (see *Smith v Harrison* (1857)). Where a decree might cause the defendant unnecessary hardship, it will be refused, or where there has been unnecessary delay by the plaintiff in performing his part of the contract. See now Law of Property Act 1925, s 41. A misrepresentation by the plaintiff, or a mistake of a fundamental character may ground a defence. See also the Misrepresentation Act 1967.

3.2.4   Defences

Where a written document, as the result of a common mistake of the parties, does not accurately express an agreement between those parties, equity has the power to rectify the writing: *Craddock Bros v Hunt* (1923). *Per* Cozens-Hardy MR in *Lovell & Christmas Ltd v Wall* (1911):

3.3   Rectification

> 'The essence of rectification is to bring the document which was expressed and intended to be in pursuance of a prior agreement into harmony with that prior agreement. It presupposes a prior contract and it requires proof that by common mistake the final completed instrument as extended fails to give proper effect to the prior contract. For this purpose evidence of what took place prior to the execution of the completed document is obviously admissible and indeed essential.'

Rectification is not of the agreement itself, merely of the instrument recording the agreement: *Mackenzie v Coulson* (1869). 'Courts of Equity do not rectify contracts; they may and do rectify instruments purporting to have been made in pursuance of the terms of contracts': *per* James VC. It is intended to correct, and not improve, a document: *Whiteside v Whiteside* (1950). The effect of rectification is that the document is read as if drawn originally in its rectified form.

Under the Administration of Justice Act 1982, s 20, a court may order rectification of a will if satisfied that it fails to carry out the testator's intentions because of a clerical error or a failure to understand his instructions. Save with permission of the court, application for an order of rectification may not be made after the end of six months from the date on which a grant of probate or of letters of administration is first taken out.

3.3.1	Essentials for the grant of rectification

The essentials for the grant of rectification are as follows: a prior completed agreement must exist; parties' intentions should have continued unchanged up to the execution of the instrument (*Fowler v Fowler* (1859)); there must be very clear evidence that the mistakes are common to both parties (*Tucker v Bennett* (1887)); the fault to be cured must be literal ('Rectification is concerned with contracts and documents, not with intentions': *per* Lord Denning in *FE Rose Ltd v Pim & Co* (1953)); rectification must represent the exact agreement of the parties as it was when the instrument was executed (*Fowler v Fowler* (1859)); there must be no appropriate alternative remedy (*Walker Property Investments v Walker* (1947)).

3.3.2	Grounds for the refusal of rectification

Grounds for the refusal of rectification include the following: where the mistake is merely unilateral (but not where one party is mistaken and the other is guilty of actual or constructive fraud); where there is an alternative suitable remedy; where a *bona fide* purchaser for value without notice who has acquired the instrument may be prejudiced by rectification; where the contract can no longer be performed (see *Borrowman v Rossell* (1864); where excessive delay prevents a claim (see *Beale v Kyte* (1907)); where acquiescence can be proved (see *Fredensen v Rothschild* (1941)).

3.4   Rescission

The right to rescind a contract is a right which a party has, in particular circumstances, to set aside the contract because of some fundamental flaw and to be restored to his former position. It differs from discharge of contract by breach: in the latter case damages may be recovered, but they are not available to a party who has rescinded. Its availability depends on the general possibility of *restitutio integrum*. In the event of rescission all property must be returned and accounts taken of profit and losses; he who rescinds is to be placed in the position he would have occupied had the agreement not been made.

Grounds upon which rescission may be available include: fraudulent misrepresentation; innocent misrepresentation (see now the Misrepresentation Act 1967, s 2(1)); non-disclosure in contracts *uberrimae fidei*; constructive fraud; fundamental mistake; term in a contract under which parties may rescind on the occurrence of certain events.

3.4.1   Grounds for rescission

Limitations on the right to rescind include the following: impossibility of *restitutio in integrum*, as where the parties cannot be restored to their original position (see *Clarke v Dickson* (1959); *O'Sullivan v Management Agency* (1985)); where an innocent third party has acquired rights for value under the contract and has given consideration; where the contract has been affirmed expressly or by implication. It was held by the Court of Appeal in *Cornish v Midland Bank* (1985) that a bank which chooses to give advice to a customer concerning the effect of a mortgage document that the customer is on the point of signing in the bank's favour has a duty of care not to misstate the effects of that document, but the remedy available will be limited only to damages against the bank and will not be extended so as to set aside the mortgage unless undue influence on the part of the bank can be shown.

3.4.2   Limitations on the right to rescind

Rescission may be available under the Misrepresentation Act 1967, ss 1, 2(1). Under s 2(2) damages may be awarded *in lieu* of rescission if the court is of the opinion 'that it would be equitable to do so, having regard to the nature of the misrepresentation and the loss that would be caused by it if the contract were upheld, as well as to the loss that rescission would cause to the other party'.

3.4.3   Misrepresentation Act 1967

Under certain circumstances, where the existence of a seemingly valid document which is, in fact, void, may cause embarrassment to the plaintiff, eg, because an action may be brought on it, the court can order the document to be delivered up for cancellation. See *Cooper v Joel* (1859) - guarantee obtained as the result of misrepresentation; *Peake v Highfield* (1826) - forged document.

3.5   Delivery up and cancellation

The remedy applies to all kinds of document, eg, insurance policies, negotiable instruments. See *Kemp v Prior* (1802). The document must be entirely void. See *Ideal Bedding Co v Holland* (1907).

Because the remedy is discretionary it will be granted only where the plaintiff is prepared to do equity. In *Lodge v National Union Investment Co* (1907), securities which had been given under an illegal moneylending contract were ordered to be delivered up only on the condition that the borrower repaid the outstanding part of the loan.

3.6   Receivers

Where the preservation of property is endangered, a receiver may be appointed in order to preserve the property for the benefit of persons entitled to it. He may be appointed out of court, in which case he is an agent for those who have made the appointment: see *Ford v Rackham* (1853).

A receiver appointed by the court is considered to be an officer of the court. He is personally liable for his acts and is entitled to remuneration. Nominations for appointment may be made by a party to an action. For appointment of the official receiver, see the Insolvency Act 1986, s 32. Note the comments of Lord Hardwicke in *Skip v Harwood* (1747): The power to appoint a receiver is 'a discretionary power exercised by the court with as great utility to the subject as any sort of authority that belongs to them, and is provisional only for the more speedy getting in of a party's estate, and securing it for the benefit of such person who shall appear to be entitled, and does not at all affect the right'.

In particular, the court will make an appointment: where an executor or trustee is mismanaging or misapplying the assets (*Swale v Swale* (1856)); where a partnership is at an end, and the business must be sold and the assets realised (*Pini v Roncoroni* (1892)); where the security of a company is in jeopardy.

3.7   Account

The court may order an account so that sums due from one party to another might be investigated, eg, as incidental to an injunction (*Neilson v Betts* (1871)); where there are mutual accounts (*Phillips v Phillips* (1852)); where accounts are unusually complicated (*O'Connor v Spaight* (1804)). Accounts may be reopened where there has been fraud or mistake, or under the Consumer Credit Act 1974, s 137(1) (in the case of an extortionate credit bargain, the credit agreement may be reopened so as to do justice between the parties). Note the Limitation Act 1980, s 23.

Note the concept of 'settled accounts': the general principle at the basis of such a plea is that the account has been agreed for valuable consideration and ought not to be re-opened. 'Where A owes, or may owe, B money, and B owes, or may owe, A money, and in their accounts they strike a balance and agree that balance, that truly represents the financial result of their transactions. There is mutuality in it, and whereas A may be giving up something or B may be giving up something, for the purpose of settling the matter between them, they expressly or by implication agree to a conventional position which is established by striking a balance, and that results in what is called a settled account': *per* Romer J in *Anglo-American Asphalt Co v Crowley Russell & Co* (1945).

An injunction is an order of the court directing a party to refrain from doing or continuing to do some act complained of, or restraining that party from continuing some omission.

General principles concerning the award of the injunction include the following:

- The remedy, although discretionary, must be awarded 'according to sufficient legal reasoning or on settled legal principles': *per* Jessel MR in *Day v Brownrigg* (1878). It will not be granted where damages are considered to be an adequate remedy: *Wood v Sutcliffe* (1851).

- The right must be in the plaintiff: *Thorne v BBC* (1967). The remedy is *in personam*. See *Castanho v Brown & Root Ltd* (1981).

- Issue of an injunction requires that the plaintiff shall come to the court 'with clean hands'. Thus an injunction may be refused where plaintiff is in breach of the agreement in issue: *Jackson v Hamlyn* (1953). 'Many cases have occurred in which judgments are applied for and are granted or refused, not upon the ground of the right possessed by the parties, but upon the ground of their conduct and dealings before they applied to the court for the injunction to preserve and protect that right': *per* Lord Eldon in *Blakemore v Glamorganshire Canal Navigation* (1832).

- Breach of an injunction is a contempt of court which may result in imprisonment by committal, or a fine. See *Isaacs v Robertson* (1985); *Times Newspapers v A-G* (1991).

- See Supreme Court Act 1981, s 37, empowering the High Court to grant injunctions 'in all cases in which it appears to the court just and convenient to do so'.

An injunction may be classified under the following headings:

- *Prohibitory*, forbidding the commission, continuation or repetition of a wrongful act; *mandatory*, restraining the continuation of some omission by directing the doing of a positive act.

- *Interlocutory*, an injunction of a temporary nature granted on interlocutory application, intended to maintain the *status quo* until the trial; *perpetual*, granted after an action has been heard.

- *Quia timet*, intended to restrain a threatened activity where, as yet, plaintiff's rights are not infringed; *ex parte*, granted in a very urgent case before the court has the opportunity of hearing the other side: see *Bates v Lord Hailsham* (1972).

3.8.3	The interlocutory injunction	The interlocutory injunction is intended to keep the parties' position in *status quo*, as far as that is possible, until the trial: *Jones v Pacaya Rubber* (1911). The grant is discretionary and the court must be satisfied that it is probable that the plaintiff will be entitled to relief at a subsequent trial: see *Khashoggi v Smith* (1980); *Leisure Data v Bell* (1988).

In *American Cyanamid Co v Ethicon Ltd* (1975), the House of Lords held that there was no rule requiring plaintiff to establish a *prima facie* case for the grant of an interlocutory injunction: the court had to be satisfied that an important question was in issue; the balance of convenience should be the governing consideration, so that the adequacy of damages must be considered first; should the balance of convenience not favour either party clearly, the parties' relative strength must be considered; the court must not, however, try the action. See *Cayne v Global Resources* (1984): these principles are guidelines rather than rules.

Unreasonable delay by the plaintiff in bringing an action, construed reasonably as acquiescence, may result in the refusal of an interlocutory injunction, as may the plaintiff's being in breach of an agreement in issue. See *Russell v Watts* (1883); *Jackson v Hamlyn* (1953). 'If a party, having a right, stands by and sees another dealing with the property in a manner inconsistent with that right, and makes no objection while the act is in progress, he cannot afterwards complain': *per* Lord Cottenham in *Duke of Leeds v Earl of Amherst* (1846).

3.8.4	The perpetual injunction	The perpetual injunction will not be granted where an award of damages might be appropriate. It is available where the injury is of a continuing nature. The court will consider not only the rights of the parties to the action, but also the surrounding circumstances, and the rights of others who may be involved: *Wood v Sutcliffe* (1851). Damages may be awarded *in lieu* of an injunction: Supreme Court Act 1981, s 50.

Principles of such an award were discussed in *Shelfer v City of London Electric Lighting Co* (1895): damages may be awarded in the discretion of the court where the injury complained of is slight, where it can be estimated in, and compensated by, money, and where the grant of an injunction would be oppressive to defendant. See *Allen v Gulf Refining Ltd* (1980) in which Lord Denning suggested that damages should be awarded *in lieu* where an injunction would act so as 'to stop a great enterprise and render it useless'. The following points should be noted carefully:

- In *Armstrong v Sheppard Ltd* (1959), an injunction was refused where the court had been misled by plaintiff, who, in fact, had not suffered any real damage. 'A proprietor who establishes a proprietary right is *ex debito justitiae* entitled to an injunction, unless it can be said against him that he has raised such an equity that it is no longer open to him to assert his legal or proprietary right': *per* Lord Evershed.

• Laches will not generally act as a bar to the exercise of plaintiff's right to the grant of a perpetual injunction unless plaintiff, in full knowledge of the facts, has delayed unreasonably. 'To justify the court in refusing to interfere at the hearing of a cause there must be a much stronger case of acquiescence than is required upon an interlocutory application, for at the hearing of a cause it is the duty of the court to decide upon the rights of the parties, and the dismissal of a bill on the grounds of acquiescence amounts to a decision that a right which has once existed is absolutely and forever lost': *per* Lord Turner in *Johnson v Wyatt* (1863). See also *Bulmer v Bollinger* (1975).

• Plaintiff must show that he has some appreciable right or interest in the subject matter of the complaint for which a perpetual injunction is sought: *Day v Brownrigg* (1878), in which an injunction was refused where defendant had used the name of plaintiff's adjoining house, since there is no right to the exclusive use of the name of a house. 'You must have in our law injury as well as damage ... If a man erects a wall on his own property and thereby destroys the view from the house of the plaintiff he may damage him to an enormous extent. He may destroy three-fourths of the value of the house, but still, if he has the right to erect a wall the mere fact of thereby causing damage to the plaintiff does not give the plaintiff a right of action': *per* Jessel MR.

Where an act is threatened which, if performed, would cause a party considerable damage for which monetary damages would be an inadequate remedy, that party can apply for a *quia timet* injunction. The principles to be applied in a grant of a mandatory *quia timet* injunction were stated in *Redland Bricks Ltd v Morris* (1970), thus: the plaintiff must demonstrate a strong probability of grave damage occurring to him in the future; he must show that damages would be an inadequate remedy and that the cost to the defendant of preventing the continuance or recurrence of the wrongful act must be taken into account; the court must ensure that the defendant is aware of precisely what he has to do. See *Trawnick v Gordon Lennox* (1985).

3.8.5   The *quia timet* injunction

Examples of the use of injunctions include: contract for personal services (*Warner Bros v Nelson* (1937)); improper use of confidential information (*X v Y* (1988)); breach of trust (*Rigall v Foster* (1853)); restraint of one party to a marriage

3.8.6   Examples of the use of injunctions

from using violence against the other party (see Domestic Violence and Matrimonial Proceedings Act 1976, s 2(1)); infringement of copyright (see Copyright, Designs and Patents Act 1988, s 96); prevention of publication of a libel (see *Herbage v The Times* (1981)); breach of negative statutory duty (see *Portsmouth CC v Richards* (1988)); right of purchaser under right-to-buy legislation where necessary conditions are established (see *Taylor v Newham LBC* (1993)).

3.9 *Mareva* injunctions

See *Mareva Compania Naviera SA v International Bulk Carriers SA* (1980). The fundamental purpose of the injunction is 'to prevent foreign parties from causing assets to be removed from the jurisdiction in order to avoid the risk of having to satisfy any judgment which may be entered against them in pending proceedings in this country': *Iraqui Ministry of Defence v Arcepey Shipping* (1980).

Essentially, the *Mareva* injunction comprises an order made against the defendant *in personam* and intended to ensure that assets will be available to satisfy whatever judgment is obtained against the defendant by the plaintiff: see *Derby & Co v Weldon* (1989).

3.9.1 General principles

The following principles apply to the issue of the *Mareva* injunction.

- The plaintiff must have a 'good, arguable case' and must make full and frank disclosure of all material matters within his knowledge: see *Commercial Bank of the Near East v A* (1989). He must demonstrate the existence of a legal or equitable right requiring protection: *Allen v Jambo Holdings* (1980). The injunction will be granted only in support of a cause of action arising out of an actual or threatened invasion of a legal or equitable right of the plaintiff: *Zucker v Tyndall Holdings* (1992).

- The plaintiff must give grounds for believing that the defendant has assets in this country. 'Assets', which must be identified as precisely as possible, include cash and other property, goodwill, choses in action. He must show, also, that there are grounds for believing that there is a real risk of the removal of assets from the jurisdiction so as to defeat the ends of justice.

- The plaintiff must give an undertaking in damages, in the event of his claim failing.

- An interlocutory injunction will be granted on an *ex parte* application preventing defendant from removing his assets until the pending action has been heard.

- The defendant is obliged to obey the order; contempt proceedings will follow a failure to obey.

See *Third Chandris Shipping Corp v Unimarine SA* (1979); *Polly Peck International plc v Nadir* (1992) (grant of injunction against a bank).

See *Anton Piller KG v Manufacturing Processes Ltd* (1976). An *Anton Piller* order is an interlocutory, mandatory injunction, obtained *ex parte*, designed to prevent a defendant from concealing, removing or destroying vital evidence in the form of documents or movable property. The order requires the defendant to permit the plaintiff to enter the defendant's premises so as to inspect and make copies of relevant documents and other appropriate material. Failure to comply with the order is a contempt of court. Note the Supreme Court Act 1981, s 37.

3.10   *Anton Piller* orders

For the pre-conditions to the making of an *Anton Piller* order, note the observations of Ormrod LJ:

3.10.1   Pre-conditions

'First, there must be an extremely strong *prima facie* case. Secondly, the damage, potential or actual, must be very serious for the plaintiff. Thirdly, there must be clear evidence that the defendants have in their possession incriminating documents or things, and that there is a real possibility that they may destroy such material before an application *inter partes* may be made.'

'The inspection should do no harm to defendant's case': *per* Lord Denning.

Dillon J, in *Booker McConnell v Plascow* (1985) suggested the following safeguards: the defendant be supplied by the plaintiff's solicitor with copies of relevant documents; liberty to the defendant to apply to the court (by short notice) to vary or discharge the order; cross-undertaking in damages.

3.10.2   Defendant's safeguards

For the problem of self-incrimination which may arise, see *Rank Film Distribution v Video Information Centre* (1981) and the Supreme Court Act 1981, s 72. See *Crest Homes plc v Marks* (1987).

3.10.3   Self-incrimination

In *Columbia Picture Industries v Robinson* (1986), Scott LJ enumerated guidelines concerning the order, which included the following:

- The orders should not extend beyond what is necessary to achieve their purpose.
- Those who execute the order must provide details of what has been removed from defendant's premises.

- Material which is taken from the premises must be covered by the terms of the order.
- Seized material must be delivered as soon as possible to the defendant's solicitor.

See: *VDU Installations v Integrated Computer Systems* (1988); *Arab Monetary Fund v Hashim* (1989). In *Universal Thermosensors v Hibben* (1992), the following additional safeguards relating to the execution of the order were suggested:

- The order should be executed only on working days.

- An injunction restraining those on whom the order is served telling others of the order should be for a limited period, not as long as a week.

- The order should provide that it be served at business premises only in the presence of a company representative unless there is good reason not to do so.

- There should be consideration of some method of preventing plaintiff's conducting a thorough search of competitors' documents when the order is executed.

Equitable Remedies

Equitable remedies are available in all courts exercising jurisdiction in civil causes: Supreme Court Act 1981, s 49.

Nature of equitable remedies

Essentially these are discretionary and available only in the absence of an appropriate and adequate common law remedy.

Specific performance is an order of the court instructing a party to an agreement to perform his obligations according to the terms of the agreement.

Specific performance

Damages may be awarded instead of or in addition to specific performance. See Supreme Court Act 1981, s 50.

Contracts *specifically* enforceable include: contracts for sale or purchase of land or grant of a lease; contracts concerning personal property. See Sale of Goods Act 1979, s 52. Contracts *not specifically* enforceable include: contracts made for no consideration; contracts involving a loan and payment of money; contracts for personal services. See *Page One Records v Britton* (1968).

Defences to an action: proof that a contract is illegal, that the plaintiff has failed to come to equity with clean hands; unnecessary delay by the plaintiff. See Law of Property Act 1925, s 41; Misrepresentation Act 1967.

Equity has the power to rectify a written document which does not accurately express the agreement between parties. See *Craddock Bros v Hunt* (1923). Rectification is of the instrument recording agreement, not of the agreement itself. See Administration of Justice Act 1982, s 20.

Rectification

The essentials for the grant of rectification include: prior completed agreement; clear evidence of mistake common to both parties; no appropriate alternative remedy. See *Walker Property Investments v Walker* (1947).

The grounds for refusal of remedy include: unilateral mistake; alternative suitable remedy; excessive delay; acquiescence. See *Fredensen v Rothschild* (1941).

Rescission is the right to set aside a contract and be restored to the former position. Availability of the remedy depends on the possibility of *restitutio in integrum*. All property must be returned and accounts taken.

Rescission

Remedy may be available in cases of fraud, misrepresentation, fundamental mistake. See also Misrepresentation Act 1967, ss 1, 2.

Delivery up and cancellation is available in the case of many types of document, which, although seemingly valid, may, in fact, be void.

Other remedies

Other remedies include: the appointment of a receiver, where preservation of property is endangered (see *Ford v Rackham* (1853)); the court may order account so that sums due from one party to another may be investigated; an injunction, which is an order of the court directing a party to perform, or refrain from performing, an action.

Injunctions

The grant of an injunction is discretionary and is based on established principles. A breach is a contempt of court: see *Times Newspapers v A-G* (1991) and Supreme Court Act 1981, s 37.

Injunctions may be prohibitory; mandatory; interlocutory (until trial of action); perpetual (following trial); *quia timet* (restraining a threatened activity). Note the important principles concerning interlocutory injunction set out in *American Cyanamid Co v Ethicon Ltd* (1975). An unreasonable delay, construed as acquiescence, may result in a refusal of injunction.

A Mareva injunction (see *Mareva Compania Naviera SA v International Bulk Carriers SA* (1980)) prevents foreign parties from causing assets to be removed from the jurisdiction to avoid risk of having to satisfy judgment.

An Anton Piller order (see *Anton Piller KG v Manufacturing Processes Ltd* (1976)) is an interlocutory injunction designed to prevent the defendant concealing, removing or destroying evidence, eg, documents.

See *Third Chandris Shipping Corporation v Unimarine SA* (1979); *Columbia Picture Industries v Robinson* (1986).

Chapter 4

Essence of the Private Trust

Assume that S conveys Blackacre to T and directs T that he (T) is to hold Blackacre 'on trust' for B. Fundamental to a transaction of this nature is the *confidence* reposed in T by S and the resulting *obligation* which binds T to a course of action. A transaction of this nature is in essence a *trust*: it is built upon an obligation involving the administration of property placed under T's control for the benefit of B.

S is known as the *settlor*, T is the *trustee*; B is the *beneficiary* (or *cestui que trust*), because of his beneficial interest in the ownership of Blackacre, the *trust property*.

T will not be allowed, in general, to deviate from the terms of his undertaking. B's interest is an 'equitable interest' or estate or right, so-called because its recognition was confined originally to the courts of equity.

4.1   Fundamental concept and terminology

The trust has been defined, or described, by several jurists, and, recently, by statute. Among these definitions and descriptions are the following:

4.2   The trust defined

'I should define a trust in some way as the following - When a person has rights which he is bound to exercise upon behalf of another or for the accomplishment of some particular purpose he is said to have those rights in trust for that other and for that purpose and he is called a trustee.'

Maitland

4.2.1   Maitland

'All that can be said of a trust ... is that it is the relationship which arises whenever a person called the trustee is compelled in Equity to hold property, whether real or personal, and whether by legal or equitable title, for the benefit of some persons (of whom he may be one and who are termed *cestui que trust*) or for some object permitted by law, in such a way that the real benefit of the property accrues, not to the trustees, but to the beneficiaries or other objects of the trust.'

Keeton

4.2.2   Keeton

'The word 'trust' refers to the duty or aggregate accumulation of obligations that rest upon a person described as trustee. The responsibilities are in relation to property held by him, or under his control. That property he will be compelled by a court in its equitable jurisdiction to administer in the manner lawfully prescribed by the trust instrument, or where there be no specific provision written or oral, or to the extent that such provision is invalid or lacking, in accordance with equitable

4.2.3   Lewin

principles. As a consequence the administration will be in such a manner that the consequential benefits and advantages accrue, not to the trustee, but to the persons called *cestui que trust*, or beneficiaries, if there be any; if not, for some purpose which the law will recognise and enforce. A trustee may be a beneficiary, in which case advantages will accrue in his favour to the extent of his beneficial interest.'

Lewin

4.2.4   Underhill

'A trust is an equitable obligation binding a person (who is called a trustee) to deal with property over which he has control (which is called the trust property), for the benefit of persons (who are called beneficiaries or *cestui que trust*), of whom he may himself be one, and any one of whom may enforce the obligation. Any act or neglect on the part of a trustee which is not authorised or excused by the terms of the trust instrument, or by law, is called a breach of trust.'

Underhill

4.2.5   Recognition of Trusts
         Act 1987

'For the purposes of this Convention, the term 'trust' refers to the legal relationship created - *inter vivos* or on death - by a person, the settlor, when assets have been placed under the control of a trustee for the benefit of a beneficiary or for a specified purpose. A trust has the following characteristics - (a) the assets constitute a separate fund and are not a part of the trustee's own estate; (b) title to the trust assets stands in the name of the trustee or in the name of another person on behalf of the trustee; (c) the trustee has the power and the duty, in respect of which he is accountable, to manage, employ or dispose of the assets in accordance with the terms of the trust and the special duties imposed upon him by law. The reservation by the settlor of certain rights and powers, and the fact that the trustee may himself have rights as beneficiary, are not necessarily inconsistent with the existence of a trust.'

Recognition of Trusts Act 1987
Schedule, s 1

4.2.6   An American
         description

The American 'Restatement of the Law of Trusts' (1959) noted:

'A trust ... when not qualified by the word "charitable", "resulting" or "constructive", is a fiduciary relationship with respect to property, subjecting the person by whom the property is held to equitable duties to deal with the property for the benefit of another person, which arises as a result of a manifestation of an intention to create it'.

4.3   Development of the trust

In early times the transfer of land by will was rarely allowed. The idea of a person holding land 'to the use of' another grew and the following arrangement became common. A tenant, X, transferred land by the process of common law recovery, to a transferee, Y, who undertook to hold it 'to the use of' (ie, on behalf of) Z. Y was known as the *feoffee to uses* (ie, the party to whom a *feoffment* - a conveyance - had been made); Y was known as *cestui que use* - he to whose use the conveyance had been made.

Under common law the *cestui que use* had no rights over the land conveyed. The Chancellors intervened, however, to protect him against a *feoffee* who ignored the instructions of the *feoffor*.

'Dual ownership' of land grew: the *feoffee to uses* had legal ownership protected by common law; *cestui que use* had equitable ownership protected by the Chancellors in the court of equity. The result was a considerable growth in the employment of the 'use'.

The Statute of Uses 1535 'executed the use' and removed common law seisin from the *feoffee*. In *Jane Tyrrel's Case* (1557) it was held that, in the case of a use upon a use, the second use was not 'executed' by the Statute. The second use became known as 'a trust'. The phrase *cestui que trust* was used to refer to the beneficiary under a trust.

There is controversy as to the nature of the equitable interest arising as the result of the creation of a trust. Does it involve a right *in rem* (available against 'the world at large', ie, persons generally) or a right *in personam* (that is, against a specific person)?	**4.4** **Nature of the beneficiary's interest**
The traditional view suggests that the beneficiary's interest involves a right *in personam*. Maitland argues that to hold a contrary view is to ignore the important rule that an equitable interest does not prevail against a *bona fide* purchaser for value of the legal estate without notice of the trust. See *Pilcher v Rawlins* (1872) (at 1.5.4).	4.4.1 The traditional view
The so-called 'realist view' suggests that the right is *in rem*. Thus, a beneficiary who follows trust property (see Chapter 21) is exercising a proprietary right allowing him to follow the property into the hands of a trustee or of any person receiving property from the trustee other than by purchase for value without notice. See *Re Hallett's Estate* (1880); *Archer-Shee v Garland* (1931); *Parker-Tweedale v Dunbar Bank* (1990) (under basic principles of equity it is the trustee who has the rights and duties to protect the trust property, and a beneficiary has no cause of action against a third party).	4.4.2 The realistic view
Hanbury argues that the equitable interest of the beneficiary might be in the nature of a *hybrid*, partaking of *both* the right *in personam* and the right *in rem*.	4.4.3 The hybrid view

4.5 The trust and other relationships

A variety of legal concepts exists which gives rise to superficial similarities between the trust and those concepts, eg, bailments, contracts. It is important to recognise the singular nature of the trust.

4.5.1 Trusts and contract

It is suggested that the trust originated as a type of contract and that both are closely related. But it should be noted that: contract developed under the common law, the trust is 'a creature of equity'; the essence of a contract is usually a bargain between parties, whereas the beneficiary under a trust is generally a 'volunteer'; valuable consideration is generally necessary to a contract, whereas in the case of a completely constituted trust it need not have been given.

The rule in contract is that it cannot usually be enforced by one who is not a party to it. But in the case of a trust, the beneficiary, who is rarely a party to the instrument creating the trust, may be entitled to enforce it.

Per Lord Haldane in *Dunlop Pneumatic Tyre Co v Selfridge Ltd* (1915):

'Our law knows nothing of a *jus quaesitum tertio* arising by way of contract. Such a right may be conferred by way of property as, for example, under a trust, but it cannot be conferred on a stranger to a contract as a right to enforce the contract *in personam*.'

See now Law of Property Act 1925, s 56(1). Note that a person entitled to the benefit of a contract can subsequently establish a trust of that benefit for a third party by declaring himself trustee of it.

4.5.2 Trusts and bailment

Bailment involves a delivery of goods on the condition that they are to be restored by the bailee to the bailor as soon as the object for which they were bailed is achieved: *Coggs v Barnard* (1703). Bailment applies to personal property only; the trust applies to all kinds of property. The bailor does not, as such, divest himself of ownership; the settlor may cease to have any rights in the trust property.

4.5.3 Trusts and agency

Both contract and agency rest on a fiduciary relationship; a principal may exercise against the agent remedies of the type exercised by a beneficiary against a trustee; neither agent nor trustee may delegate responsibility; both are liable for profits made from that which has been entrusted to them. But the trustee has title to the trust property, whereas the agent has no title to his principal's property; the agent represents the principal, whereas the trustee does not represent *cestui que trust*; the agent is subject to the principal's control, whereas the trustee is not necessarily subject to the control of *cestui que trust*;

agency involves consent between agent and principal, whereas the trust involves no such consent between settlor and trustee or *cestui que trust*.

A power of appointment is a power (usually conferred under a trust or settlement) given to a person which enables him to dispose of real or personal property which is not his. A general power (eg, 'to X for life, remainder as he may appoint') enables X, the appointor (or donee of the power) to appoint in favour of any person including himself. A special power ('... as he may appoint among the children of Z') allows him to appoint only with reference to members of a particular class (the 'objects of the power').

4.5.4   Trusts and powers of appointment

A power is discretionary; a trust is imperative. See *Vestey v IRC* (1979). Hence a trust to divide property among a class will be enforced by the court, whereas the exercise of a power will not be so enforced. In general, the lack of some person to compel the performance of a trust may be fatal to its validity, whereas the validity of a power does not depend on the existence of some person able to compel its exercise: see *Brown v Higgs* (1803).

A 'power in the nature of a trust' (or 'trust-power') exists where the donor of the power has demonstrated a clear intention that the property is to pass to the objects of the power in any event: see *Re Hay's ST* (1981). Whether a power in the nature of a trust has been created or not is a matter of 'intention or presumed intention to be derived from the language of the instrument': *per* Evershed MR in *Re Scarisbrick's WT* (1951). The test is based on the following principles:

- Only a special power of appointment may take effect as a trust-power. See *Bond v Pickford* (1983).
- If there is a gift over in default of appointment (and for no other event), the power is a mere power, and this is so even if the gift over is void for some reason: see *Re Mills* (1930). Note *Re Beatty* (1990) in which the testatrix bequeathed personal chattels to trustees, stating that they 'shall ... distribute the chattels among such persons as they think fit within two years of death', and that any remaining property should fall into the residuary estate. It was held that these clauses would have been valid powers of appointment if they had been contained in a settlement; distribution under those clauses was valid.
- If there is a residuary gift in favour of the donee, this will not be considered as a gift over in default of appointment and the power will not necessarily lose the character of a trust: see *Re Brierley* (1894).

- Where there is no gift over in default of appointment, the power may be held to be a trust power; this will depend on the settlor's intention, to be ascertained by reference to the actual words used. See Administration of Justice Act 1982, s 21.

4.5.5 Classification of powers

Note *Mettoy Pension Trustees v Evans* (1990) in which Warner J suggested the following classification of powers: powers given to a person to determine the destination of trust property without that person being under any obligation to exercise that power (eg, special power of appointment with trust in default of appointment); any powers conferred on a person as a trustee of the power itself ('fiduciary powers') which cannot be released; any discretion which is really a duty to form a judgment as to the existence or otherwise of particular circumstances giving rise to particular consequences; discretionary trusts, ie, where a person is under a duty to select from among a class of beneficiaries those who are to receive and their shares.

4.5.6 The problem of certainty

In general, in the case of a private trust, the objects had to be certain or capable of being ascertained. In *IRC v Broadway Cottages Trust* (1955), it was held that a trust was void for uncertainty because the class could not be ascertained at any given time, ie, it was impossible to list all the beneficiaries when the trust came into operation. In the case of a power, it was held, in *Re Gulbenkian's Settlements* (1970), that the requirement of certainty was met if it were possible to ascertain whether any given postulant was, or was not, a member of the class. See also *Re Manisty's Settlement* (1974).

The facts of *McPhail v Doulton* (1971) are as follows: the settlor executed a deed in 1941 which provided that a the fund was to be held upon certain trusts in favour of the staff of a company, their relatives and dependants. The settlement provided, in clause 9(a), that 'the trustees shall apply the net income ... in making at their absolute discretion grants to or for the benefit of any of the officers and employees or ex-officers or ex-employees of the company or to any relatives or dependants of any such persons in such amounts at such times and on such conditions (if any) as they think fit ...'. Other clauses provided that the trustees should not be bound to exhaust the income of any one year and that no person should have a right to an interest other than pursuant to the exercise of the trustees' discretion.

The House of Lords held that clause 9(a) constituted a trust, not a power (as the Court of Appeal had held). The case

was to be remitted to the Chancery Division for determination of whether it was void for uncertainty. (Its validity was later upheld.) The test for certainty in trusts was the same as that for powers, namely, whether it could be said with certainty that any given person was or was not a member of the class (which was the test in *Re Gulbenkian's Settlements* (1970)).

Per Lord Shaw in *Lord Strathcona SS Co v Dominion SS Co* (1926):

> 'The scope of the trusts recognised in equity is unlimited. There can be a trust of a chattel or of a chose in action, or of a right or obligation under an ordinary legal contract, just as much as a trust of land.'

All property, legal or equitable, real or personal, with some few exceptions, may be made the subject of a trust. Property which is inalienable cannot be the subject-matter of a trust, for example, salaries or pensions given to enable persons to perform duties connected with the public service. See *Grenfell v Dean and Canons of Windsor* (1840).

4.6   Subject matter of the trust

Who may create a trust, be a beneficiary, or act as a trustee?

In general, any person who has the capacity to hold and dispose of a legal or equitable estate may create a trust in respect of it. Exceptions include:

4.7   Capacity of parties to a trust

- An infant may not hold a legal estate in land (see Law of Property Act 1925, s 1(6)) and cannot, therefore, make a settlement of a legal estate. In the case of other property he may make a settlement which is voidable. Where the infant is too young to understand the nature of his act, his purported creation of a trust will be void; if the property has been transferred, the transferee will hold for the infant upon a resulting trust.

- Persons of unsound mind may not create a valid testamentary trust or a trust *inter vivos*. See the Mental Health Act 1983, ss 94, 96.

- Corporations: municipal corporations require government consent to create trusts of their property; trading companies incorporated under the Companies Acts may issue debenture stock secured by trust deed.

Any person capable of holding an interest in property can be a beneficiary under a trust.

In general, the capacity to be a trustee exists where there is the capacity to take or hold property. This is discussed in Chapter 14.

| 4.8 | **Classification of trusts** | There is no statutory classification of trusts. A traditional classification is as follows: |

| 4.8.1 | Trusts imposed by statute | Trusts may be imposed by statute: see, eg, Administration of Estates Act 1925, s 33, under which an intestate's property vests in his personal representatives upon trust for sale; Law of Property Act 1925, s 19, under which the purported conveyance of a legal estate in land to an infant, jointly with one or more persons of full age, vests that estate in the other person(s) on the statutory trusts. |

| 4.8.2 | Express (or 'declared') trusts | Express (or 'declared') trusts created by the intentional and express declaration of the settlor, eg, as where X devises Blackacre to Y 'in trust for Z'. See *Comiskey v Bowring-Hanbury* (1905). See, further, Chapter 5. |

| 4.8.3 | Implied or resulting and constructive trusts | Implied or resulting, and constructive trusts are more fully dealt with in Chapters 8 and 9. Note this summary: |

- Implied trust

  An *implied trust* arises from the settlor's presumed but unexpressed intentions. Example: X agrees with Y, for value to convey an estate to him. X is then deemed by equity to be a trustee of that estate for Y.

- Resulting trust

  A *resulting trust* (*resultare* = to spring back) exists as a result of a reversion of property to the settlor by operation of equity. Example: X conveys property to Y on trust for Z who is, unknown to both, dead. There is a resulting trust of the beneficial estate to X: *Re Tilt* (1896).

- Constructive trust

  A *constructive trust* is 'imposed by law whenever justice and good conscience require it': *per* Lord Denning in *Hussey v Palmer* (1972). It is imposed irrespective of the express or presumed intentions of the parties: see, eg, *Bristol and West BS v Henning* (1985).

| 4.8.4 | Further classifications | Further classifications include the following: |

- Fixed and discretionary trusts

  The *fixed trust* involves an instrument stating the interest each beneficiary is to take; the *discretionary trust* reflects the discretion to be exercised by trustees, eg, as to who will benefit, nature of the benefits. See further Chapter 7.

- Executed and executory trusts

  The importance of the *executed* and *executory trusts* has diminished as a result of the abolition of the rule in

Shelley's Case (1581) (by the Law of Property Act 1925, s 131 and ss 60, 130 of that Act). The *executed trust* is one in which the settlor has declared and perfected in the trust instrument the limitations of the estate of trustees and beneficiaries, so that no further instrument is required to define those interests. The settlor has 'acted as his own conveyancer'. See *Egerton v Brownlow* (1853). The *executory trust* is one in which the trustee has not put into words the precise nature of the limitations. 'He has said in effect: "Now there are my intentions, do your best to carry them out".': *per* Jessel MR in *Miles v Harford* (1879).

- Completely and incompletely constituted trusts

  The *completely constituted trust* is one in which the trust property has been vested completely in the trustees. Where the trust property has not been so vested, the trust is *incompletely constituted*.

- Simple and special trusts

  The *simple trust* is one in which the trustee has no active duties to perform; he is known as a 'passive' or 'bare' trustee. A *special trust*, involving an 'active' trustee, arises where the trustee is appointed to carry out a scheme designated by the settlor.

- Private and public trusts

  A *private trust* exists for the benefit of an individual or class. A *public* (or *'charitable'*) *trust* has as its objective the promotion of some aspect of the public welfare. See Chapter 11.

- Trusts 'in the higher' and 'in the lower' sense

  The phrase *trusts in the higher sense* has been used to refer to, eg, a government duty which is *not enforceable* in the courts. A *trust in the lower sense* is based on an equitable obligation which is fully enforceable in the courts. See *Tito v Waddell (No 2)* (1977): the use of the word 'trust' in relation to the Crown in connection with a transaction to which the Crown is party does not necessarily create a trust in the sense of imposing some obligation of a fiduciary nature upon the Crown, as opposed to a governmental obligation which is unenforceable in the courts; *Town Investments Ltd v Department of the Environment* (1978).

Essence of the Private Trust

Suppose S conveys Blackacre to T, directing T to hold it 'on trust' for B. S is the settlor; T is the trustee; B is the beneficiary (*cestui que trust*).

Fundamentals

T must not deviate from the terms of his undertaking. B's interest is of an equitable nature.

Note Maitland's definition of the trust as 'when a person has rights which he is bound to exercise upon behalf of another or for the accomplishment of some particular purpose he is said to have those rights in trust for that other or for that purpose and he is called a trustee'.

The trust developed from the 'use', which bestowed equitable ownership and was protected by the Chancellors.

There is controversy over the nature of the beneficiary's interest. The traditional view suggests that it gives rise to a right *in personam*. The realist view argues that the right is *in rem*. See *Pilcher v Rawlins* (1872); *Archer-Shee v Garland* (1931). Hanbury argues that the right is probably of a hybrid nature.

Trust and contract. These developed separately. Note, too, that the beneficiary of a trust, who is not a party to the instrument creating it, may enforce it. See Law of Property Act, s 56(1).

The trust and other relationships

Trust and bailment. Bailment applies to personal property only - unlike the trust. See *Coggs v Barnard* (1703).

Trust and agency. Both rest on a fiduciary relationship. The agent represents his principal; the trustee does not represent *cestui que trust*. The trustee has title to the trust property; the agent has no title to his principal's property.

Trusts and powers of appointment. The power is generally discretionary; the trust is imperative. See *Vestey v IRC* (1979). Note that the test for 'certainty' in trusts is that for powers, namely, whether it can be said with certainty that a person is or is not a member of the class in question. See *McPhail v Doulton* (1971).

The scope of trusts recognised in equity is unlimited. Almost all property may be made the subject of a trust.

Subject matter of the trust and the problem of capacity

Any person who has the capacity to hold and dispose of a legal or equitable interest may create a trust in respect of it. An infant may not hold a legal estate in land (see Law of Property Act 1925, s 1(6)) and cannot make a settlement of a legal estate.

Any person capable of holding an interest in property can be a beneficiary under a trust.

The capacity to take or hold property is necessary for a person to be a trustee.

Classification of trusts

The nomenclature used here is discussed further at appropriate points in other chapters. It is important to note that there is no statutory classification. A summary is as follows:

Trusts imposed by statute, eg, Administration of Estates Act 1925, s 33.

Express or declared trusts. See *Comiskey v Bowring-Hanbury* (1905).

Implied (or resulting) and constructive trusts. The implied trust arises from the settlor's presumed intentions. The constructive trust is imposed by law whenever justice and good conscience require it.

Fixed and discretionary trusts. The former generally involves the terms of an instrument; the latter reflects discretion to be exercised by trustees.

Executed and executory trusts. In the former, the settlor has 'acted as his own conveyancer'; in the latter the precise nature of the limitations has not been put into words. See *Miles v Harford* (1879).

Completely and incompletely constituted trusts. In the former, the trust property is vested completely in the trustees; in the latter, this task remains to be done.

Simple and special trusts. The former calls for no active duties from the trustee; the latter demands his involvement in tasks designated by the settlor.

Private and public trusts. A private trust exists for the benefit of a class or individual; a public (or 'charitable' trust) involves promotion of some aspect of public welfare.

Trusts in the higher and lower senses. A trust 'in the higher sense' is not enforceable in the courts (it usually refers to government duties); a trust 'in the lower sense' is fully enforceable in the courts. See *Tito v Waddell (No 2)* (1977).

Chapter 5

Express Private Trusts

An express private trust is one which is created intentionally by the *express declaration of the settlor* by deed, will or other form of writing, or by parol, and which is intended by him to be for the benefit of some individual or class.	**5.1 Essence of the private trust**

It should be noted that the phrase 'express trust' covers not only the express private trust, but also the express public ('charitable') trust (see Chapter 11). Additionally, protective and discretionary trusts (see Chapter 7) may be included in the phrase. In this chapter we consider the express private trust only.

Examples of the express private trust are evident where, eg, X devises property to Y in trust for Z, or where X grants freehold land unto and to the use of Y, directing Y to apply that property for the benefit of Z, or where X by a valid will passes title in property to Y absolutely in the knowledge that during his (X's) lifetime he has communicated to Y his wish that Y shall hold the property on certain specified trusts and that Y has agreed to carry out that wish.

Where *pure personalty* is involved, a trust may be created validly by a settlor, who is legally entitled, either orally, or by writing or, in some cases, by conduct. Where *land* is involved, however, certain statutory requirements, some of which are considered here, must be taken into account.	**5.2 Statutory provisions related to the creation of the express trust**
Under s 2 of Law of Property (Miscellaneous Provisions) Act 1989, a contract for the sale or other disposition of an interest in land can *only* be made in writing and *only* by incorporating all the terms which the parties have expressly agreed in one document or, where contracts are exchanged, in each. The terms may be incorporated in a document either by being set out in it or by reference to some other document. The document incorporating the terms or, where contracts are exchanged, one of the documents incorporating them (but not necessarily the same one) must be signed by or on behalf of each party to the contract.	**5.2.1 Law of Property (Miscellaneous Provisions) Act 1989, s 2**

- The Law of Property Act 1925, s 40, ceases to have effect.

- 'Disposition' has the meaning given in the Law of Property Act 1925 (see s 205(1)(ii)). (' "Disposition" includes a conveyance and also a devise, bequest, or an appointment of property contained in a will; and "dispose of" has a corresponding meaning.')

- Nothing in the section affects the creation or operation of resulting, implied or constructive trusts.

5.2.2	Law of Property Act 1925, s 53(1)(b)

Law of Property Act 1925, s 53(1)(b):

'A declaration of trust respecting any land or any interest therein must be manifested and proved by some writing signed by some person who is able to declare such trust or by his will.'

(Signature by an agent seems not provided for.) The writing must be clear, unambiguous and contain all the terms of the trust. In the absence of writing the trust is unenforceable, and not necessarily void.

5.2.3	Law of Property Act 1925, s 53(1)(c)

Law of Property Act 1925, s 53(1)(c):

'A disposition of an equitable interest or trust subsisting at the time of the disposition must be in writing signed by the person disposing of the same, or by his agent thereunto lawfully authorised in writing or by will.'

The disposition must be in writing; parol assignment supported by written evidence is insufficient.

In *Grey v IRC* (1960) the House of Lords considered whether oral directions given by the settlor, Grey, to trustees, requiring them to hold on new trusts, were a 'disposition' within s 53(1)(c). It was held that the directions *were* dispositions. Because they were not written they were initially ineffective, but they were rendered effective on the execution of later deeds. See *Vandervell v IRC* (1967); *Re Danish Bacon Co Staff Pension Trusts* (1971). In that case, employees of a company were given the right to nominate a person to receive benefits accrued under the company's pension fund in the event of death occurring prior to qualification for a pension. X, an employee, had nominated his wife, the approved form having been used and X's declaration having been witnessed and signed. Later, X wrote to the company and changed the nomination. It was held that the documents together did supply the necessary writing under s 53(1)(c).

A failure to comply with the sub-section renders the disposition void.

5.2.4	Law of Property Act 1925, s 55

Nothing in s 53 shall invalidate dispositions by will or affect any interest validly created before 1926 or affect the right to acquire an interest in land by virtue of taking possession: Law of Property Act 1925, s 55.

Where the settlor intends that a trust of property shall arise on his death, creation of that trust must be by *will or codicil* executed under s 9 of the Wills Act 1837 as substituted by the Administration of Justice Act 1982. The will must be in writing, signed by the testator or by some other person in his presence and by his direction and the signature of the testator must be made or acknowledged in the presence of two or more witnesses present together at the same time. No form of attestation is necessary.

5.2.5   Wills Act 1837, s 9

The court will not allow the statutory provisions outlined above to be utilised in the service of a fraudulent intention. In *Hodgson v Marks* (1971), plaintiff had transferred premises to Evans; it was agreed orally between her and Evans that the premises would remain hers although they were in Evans' name. The Court of Appeal stated: 'Quite plainly Mr Evans could not have placed any reliance on s 53, for that would have been to use the section as an instrument of fraud.' See *Re Densham* (1975).

5.3   Equity will not allow a statute to be used as an instrument of fraud

Fundamental to the obligation from which the express trust is constituted is the requirement of *certainty*. In general, the creation of a trust necessitates three certainties: certainty of *words*, of *subject-matter*, and of *objects*.

5.4   Certainty in the creation of an express trust

Per Lord Langdale in *Knight v Knight* (1840):

'As a general rule, it has been laid down that, when property is given absolutely to any person, and the same person is, by the giver who has power to command, recommended, or entreated, or wished, to dispose of that property in favour of another, the recommendation, entreaty or wish shall be held to create a trust, *firstly*, if the words were so used that upon the whole they ought to be construed as imperative; *secondly*, if the subject of the recommendation or wish be certain; and, *thirdly*, if the objects or persons intended to have the benefit of the recommendation or wish be also certain.'

Equity looks at the intention rather than the form. In general, precise technical language is usually unnecessary for the creation of an express trust. Although phrases such as 'in trust for' and 'upon trust to' are commonly employed, they are not necessary; indeed, the word 'trust' need not be used. *Per* Megarry J in *Re Kayford* (1975):

5.5   Certainty of words

'It is well settled that a trust can be created without using the word "trust" or "confidence" or the like: the question is whether in substance a sufficient intention to create a trust has been manifested.'

In general, where an intention to create a trust is apparent, then an express trust may arise. See *Alimand Computer Systems v Radcliffes & Co* (1991).

5.5.1   Precatory words

Precatory (*precari* = to entreat) words are those words of prayer, entreaty, desire, etc, which suggest, when used within the context of a transfer or bequest of property, that the transferor or testator had in mind the creation of a trust. Examples: 'I will and desire that ...'; 'I most heartily beseech'. See, eg, *Comiskey v Bowring-Hanbury* (1905); *Re Eyre-Williams* (1923).

5.5.2   The old rule

Where a gift was made in absolute terms, accompanied by a hope, desire, recommendation, etc, that the donee would use it in a specified way, it was held that a trust was attached to the gift: *Malim v Keighley* (1795). In *Harding v Glyn* (1739), X gave property to Y, his wife, by will, and did 'desire Y at or before her death to give such leases, houses, furniture ... unto and amongst such of his own relations as she should think most deserving and approve of'. It was held that a trust had been created by the use of these words.

5.5.3   The modern attitude

The change in the approach of the courts to precatory words is considered by some commentators to date from *Lambe v Eames* (1871), in which a testator had given property to his widow 'to be at her disposal in any way she may think best for the benefit of herself and her family'. It was held that no trust had been created. The words were considered to have been intended as 'a hint' to the widow, which was not intended to be obligatory upon her. The tendency today seems to be against the ready inference of a trust. Certainty of intention to create a trust is vital.

Per Romer J in *Re Williams* (1897):

'The rule you have to observe is simply this: in considering whether a precatory trust is attached to any legacy, the court will be guided by the intention of the testator apparent in the will, and not by any particular words in which the wishes of the testator are expressed.'

Per Lopes J in *Re Hamilton* (1891):

'It seems to me perfectly clear that the current of decisions with regard to precatory trusts is now changed and the result is that the court will not allow a precatory trust to be raised unless on the consideration of all the words employed it comes to the conclusion that it was the intention of the testator to create a trust.'

Per Cotton LJ in *Re Adams and Kensington Vestry* (1884):

'We must not extend the old cases in any way or rely on the mere use of any particular words, but, considering all the words which are used, we have to see what is their true effect, and what was the intention of the testator as expressed in his will. In my opinion, here he has expressed his will in such a way as not to show an intention of imposing a trust on the wife, but, on the contrary, in my opinion, he has shown an intention to leave the property, as he says he does, to her absolutely.'

(The testator had given all his estates to his wife absolutely 'in full confidence that she would do what was right as to the disposal thereof among his children'. It was held that the widow took an absolute interest and that there was no trust in favour of the children.)

In *Re Steele's WT* (1948), testatrix stated in her will: 'I give my diamond necklace to my son to go and be held as an heirloom by him and by his eldest son on his decease and to go and descend to the eldest son of such eldest son and so on, ... as far as the rules of equity will permit, and I request my said son to do all in his power by his will or otherwise to give effect to this, my wish'. It was held that the necklace was held upon the trusts of the will and that where there is an earlier decision that a trust was created by the use of a particular form of words, a trust would today be created by the use of identical words.

In *Comiskey v Bowring-Hanbury* (1905), X, by the terms of his will, gave all his property to Y, his wife, 'absolutely in full confidence that she will make such use of it as I would have made myself, and that at her death she will devise it to such one or more of my nieces as she may think fit'. It was held by the House of Lords that the words 'in full confidence' did create a trust.

Note *Re Johnson* (1939), in which the testator gave his estate equally between his mother and X, stating in his will: 'I request that my mother on her death leave the property or what remains of it ... to my sisters. I request that the said X will leave her property to my sisters.' It was held that the gifts to the mother and X were absolute; the testator was merely expressing a wish, not imposing a trust. See *Tito v Waddell* (1977); *Swain v The Law Society* (1982).

The general rule is that the property upon which the trust is based and the interests which are to be taken must be 'sufficiently certain': see *Horwood v West* (1823).	**5.6 Certainty of subject-matter**
The following examples of uncertainty relating to trust property should be noted:	5.6.1 Uncertainty relating to trust property

• *Sprange v Barnard* (1789)

  The testatrix gave £300 to her husband for his own use, and directed that, at his death, 'the remaining part of what is left, that he does not want for his own wants and use, shall be divided between A, B and C.' It was held that there was no trust since there could be no certainty as to what would be left at the husband's death. He was absolutely entitled, therefore, to the £300.

- *Palmer v Simmonds* (1854)

  The testatrix gave residuary property under her will to X 'for his own use and benefit, as I have full confidence in him, that if he should die without lawful issue he will leave the bulk of my said residuary estate unto Y and Z.' *Per* Kindersley VC:

  'I am bound to say that the testatrix has not designated the subject as to which she expresses her confidence; and I am therefore of opinion that there is no trust created; that X took absolutely.'

5.6.2   Uncertainty relating to beneficiaries' interests

Examples of uncertainty relating to beneficiaries's interests are as follows:

- *Curtis v Rippon* (1820)

  The testator left property to his wife 'trusting that she would, in fear of God, and love of the children committed to her care, make such use of it as should be for her own and their spiritual and temporal good, remembering always, according to circumstances, the Church of God and the poor'. It was held that the wife was absolutely entitled to the property since there was no ascertained part of it for the children, the Church or the poor.

- *Boyce v Boyce* (1849)

  The testator devised to trustees on trust two houses, one to be conveyed to X, 'whichever she may think proper to choose or select', the other to go to Y. In the event, X predeceased the testator. It was held that Y did not have a valid claim.

- *Re Golay's WT* (1965)

  The testator directed executors to allow X to enjoy one of his flats during her lifetime and 'to receive a reasonable income' from his other properties. *Per* Ungoed-Thomas J:

  'In my view the testator intended by "reasonable income" the yardstick which the court could and would apply in quantifying the amount so that the direction in the will is not in my view defeated by uncertainty.'

5.7   Certainty of objects

'Objects' does not refer to objectives; it refers to the persons intended to have the benefit of the trust. *Per* Evershed MR in

Re Endacott (1960): 'No principle has greater sanction or authority behind it than the general proposition that a trust by English law, not being a charitable trust, must have ascertained or ascertainable beneficiaries.' See *Re Barlow's WT* (1979).

In *Sale v Moore* (1827), a recommendation 'to consider the near relations' was held not to constitute a binding trust, since it could not be discovered how the 'near relations' might be ascertained. In *Re Ball* (1947), a gift 'to dependants' was not upheld because it was considered too vague.

Following *McPhail v Doulton* (1971) (see Chapter 4) a trust is valid in this context if it can be said with certainty that a given individual is or is not an 'object', ie, a member of the class of beneficiaries.

The test of 'administrative unworkability' was applied in *R v District Auditor ex p W Yorks Metropolitan CC* (1986), in which it was held that a trust under which trustees were 'to apply and expend the trust fund for the benefit of any or all or some of the inhabitants of the County of W Yorks' could not take effect as a private trust because the definition of the beneficiaries was so 'hopelessly wide' as to be incapable of forming anything like a class.

In general, the effect of uncertainty is as follows:

- *Uncertainty of words*

  The donee takes the property beneficially: see *Re Conolly* (1910). (No trust was created by a gift by will which stated: 'I specifically desire that the sums hereby bequeathed shall ... be specifically left by the legatees to such charitable institutions ... as my sisters may select.')

- *Uncertainty of subject-matter*

  Should the nature of the actual trust property be uncertain, the transaction fails in its entirety. Should the beneficial interests intended to be taken by the beneficiaries be uncertain, the property may be held on resulting trusts for the settlor (see Chapter 8), or, should he be dead, for the residuary legatee or devisee, or for those entitled on intestacy. On the basis of the maxim 'equality is equity', the court may divide the beneficial interest equally among the beneficiaries: see *Doyley v A-G* (1735).

- *Uncertainty of objects*

  If the words are sufficiently certain to have created a trust, but the objects are uncertain, the property will be held on a resulting trust (see Chapter 8) for the settlor or his estate. See *Re Endacott* (1960).

5.8   Absence of the certainties

5.9   Secret trusts

Assume that X gives property by his will to Y absolutely and that, during his lifetime, he has indicated to Y that the property is to be used for the benefit of Z, and that Y has agreed, expressly, or impliedly by his silence, to use it in that manner. In such a case there exists a secret trust. 'The whole theory of the formation of a secret trust is that the Wills Act 1837 has nothing to do with the matter': *per* Danckwerts J in *Re Young* (1951). In order to establish the existence of a secret trust, which is regarded as within the jurisdiction of equity, the standard of proof will be the ordinary civil standard of proof necessary to establish an ordinary trust: *Re Snowden* (1979).

5.9.1   The fully-secret trust

The fully-secret trust arises in the circumstances outlined above, ie, where the will or other instrument does not disclose the existence of the trust or its terms. It is dealt with on the basis that 'the testator has died, leaving the property by his will in a particular manner on the faith and in the reliance upon an express or implied promise by the legatee to fulfil his wishes': *per* Lord Davey in *French v French* (1902).

In *Ottaway v Norman* (1972), Brightman J enunciated the essential elements of the secret trust which must be shown to exist:

- The intention of the testator to subject the primary donee to an obligation in favour of the secondary donee; and

- Communication of that intention to the primary donee. (The communication must have taken place either before or after the making of the will, but during the testator's life: see *Moss v Cooper* (1861)); and

- The acceptance of that obligation by the primary donee either expressly or by acquiescence. (Silence might be taken as implied assent.)

Examples of the principles relating to the fully-secret trust are as follows:

- X bequeaths a legacy to Y and, during X's lifetime, Y promises that he will hold it on trust for Z. Z can enforce the trust: *McCormick v Grogan* (1869).

- X leaves property to Y and Z as *tenants in common*. Only Z has agreed to hold the property on trust for A. Z is bound, but Y is not. X leaves property to Y and Z as *joint tenants*. Only Z has agreed to hold the property in trust for A. Where Z's promise is made *after* the execution of the will, only Z is bound; where it is made *before* the will, both Y and Z are bound: *Re Stead* (1900).

- In *Re Gardner* (1920) a wife left her estate to her husband, 'knowing that he will carry out my wishes'. Evidence was given that soon after the execution of the will she had stated in his presence that, after his death, the property should be divided among certain named individuals. It was held that the husband had accepted a secret trust by which he was bound.

X gives property under his will to Y. There is a direction in the will that it is to be held on trust, but the existence of the trust is not apparent from the will (or any other instrument). The direction reads: property to Y 'on the trust I have discussed with him'. This is a half-secret trust, ie, one where a will or other instrument discloses the existence of a trust, but not its detailed terms. The essence of the half-secret trust is as follows:

5.9.2   The half-secret trust

- The instrument should declare that property has been left on trust *and* that the trust has been communicated to the trustee.

- The trust should be communicated to the trustee before, or at the time of, making of the will. If communicated after the making of the will, its effectiveness is doubtful.

- Where the testator has handed to the trustee a sealed letter marked 'Not to be opened until after my death', and the trustee is aware that the envelope contains terms of a trust, which he agrees to carry out, such a communication suffices to create a half-secret trust. See *Re Bateman's WT* (1970).

- Individuals named as trustees in a half-secret will may not take beneficially: *Re Rees* (1950).

- In the event of failure of a half-secret trust, the trustees hold on trust for the residuary devisee or legatee if there is a residuary gift. If there is no such gift, they hold for those entitled on intestacy.

In *Re Cooper* (1939), X bequeathed £5,000 to Y and Z as trustees 'upon trusts already communicated to them'. Y and Z accepted before the will was executed. At a later date X executed a codicil increasing the legacy to £10,000, but the increase was not communicated to Y and Z. It was held that the trusts were effective in relation to the first £5,000, but that they failed in relation to the second £5,000 given under the codicil.

In *Blackwell v Blackwell* (1929), a testator bequeathed by codicil a legacy to five persons upon trust to invest at their discretion and 'to apply the income ... for the purposes indicated by [the testator] to them'. Before execution of the codicil the objects of the trust had been communicated in outline form to four of the legatees, and to the fifth in detail. All accepted the trust. The legatee to whom the detail had been communicated made a memorandum of his instructions a few hours after execution of

5.10   Consideration of the secret trust by the House of Lords

the codicil. The residuary legatees claimed a declaration that no valid trust had been created in favour of the objects communicated to the five persons, on the ground that no parol evidence was admissible in order to establish the testator's purpose. The House of Lords held that such evidence was admissible and proved a *valid secret trust* for those named by the testator in his instructions to the legatees.

Per Viscount Sumner:

'A testator cannot reserve to himself a power of making future unwitnessed dispositions by merely naming a trustee and leaving the purposes of the trust to be supplied afterwards, nor can a legatee give testamentary validity to an unexecuted codicil by accepting an indefinite trust, never communicated to him in the testator's lifetime ... To hold otherwise would indeed be to enable the testator to "give the go-by" to the requirements of the Wills Act because he did not choose to comply with them.'

'It is communication of the purpose to the legatee, coupled with acquiescence or promise on his part, that removes the matter from the provisions of the Wills Act and brings it within the law of trusts as applied in this instance to trustees, who happen also to be legatees.'

Express Private Trusts

An express private trust is one created intentionally by the settlor's express declaration in a deed, will or other form of writing, or by parol, intended by him to be for the benefit of an individual or class. Example: S devises Blackacre to T in trust for B.

Essence of the private trust

A trust for pure personalty may be created validly by writing, or orally or even by conduct. In the case of land, there are certain statutory requirements which must be observed:

- *Law of Property (Miscellaneous Provisions) Act 1989*

  A contract for the sale or other disposition of land can be made in writing only. Law of Property Act 1925, s 40, is now ineffective. Nothing in this section affects the creation or operation of resulting, implied or constructive trusts.

- *Law of Property Act 1925, s 53(1)(b)*

  A declaration of trust concerning land must be proved by writing signed by a person able to declare that trust or by his will.

- *Law of Property Act 1925, s 53(1)(c)*

  A disposition of equitable interest must be in writing. See *Grey v IRC* (1960).

- *Wills Act 1837, s 9 as amended*

  A will or codicil must be in accordance with the requirements of the Act.

  Equity will not allow a statute to be used as an instrument of fraud

  See *Hodgson v Marks* (1971); *Re Densham* (1975).

See Lord Langdale's formulation of 'the three certainties' in *Knight v Knight* (1840). They must be present at the creation of an express trust.

The three certainties

- *Certainty of words*

  Precise, technical language is not necessary. The intention to create the trust must be made manifest. Precatory words will be construed with this requirement in mind. See *Re Steele's WT* (1949).

- *Certainty of subject-matter*

  The property and the interests to be taken must be sufficiently certain. See *Re Golay's WT* (1965).

- *Certainty of objects*

  'Objects' does not mean 'objectives'; it refers to persons intended to have the benefit of the trust. Beneficiaries must be ascertained or ascertainable. Note the test of 'administrative unworkability' in relation to ascertaining of beneficiaries. See *Re Endacott* (1960).

Absence of the certainties

Where there is uncertainty of words: the donee takes the property beneficially. Where there is uncertainty of subject-matter: the trust may fail in its entirety, or the beneficial interest may be divided among beneficiaries. Where there is uncertainty of objects: if the words are sufficiently certain to have created a trust, the property may be held on resulting trust for the settlor or his estate.

Fully-secret trusts

A fully-secret trust arises where the will or other instrument does not disclose the existence of the trust or its terms. Example: S gives property by his will to T absolutely; but during S's lifetime he has indicated to T that the property is to be used for B's benefit, and T has agreed. See *Re Gardner* (1920). In general, T would be bound.

Half-secret trusts

A half-secret trust arises where the will or other instrument discloses the existence of a trust, but not the details. See *Re Bateman's WT* (1970). If the trust is communicated after the making of the will, its effectiveness is doubtful. Individuals named as trustees in a half-secret will may not take beneficially.

Chapter 6

Completely and Incompletely Constituted Trusts

Whether or not beneficiaries may be able to enforce a trust will often depend on whether the trust has or has not been 'completely constituted'. If it *has*, then it can be enforced by the beneficiaries against the trustees and binds all save a *bona fide* purchaser of the legal estate for value. If it *has not*, it will not operate as a trust and can be enforced only as a contract or covenant to create a trust; but to be thus enforceable, the beneficiaries must have given value ('equity will not assist a volunteer').

6.1 **Essence of the distinction**

The *completely constituted trust* is one which has been 'perfectly created', ie, the settlor has done everything in his power necessary to transfer his interest in the trust property to a trustee for the benefit of the intended beneficiaries, or has declared himself a trustee of that property. The *incompletely constituted trust* is one which requires some further action by the settlor before it can be said to be 'perfectly created'.

6.1.1 Definitions

T bequeaths £200,000 to A and B on trust for the purchase of property to be settled on C and the children of C. The trust property has been vested in trustees on trust for the beneficiaries; the trust is *completely constituted*. What had to be done has been done. Note, in comparison, *Milroy v Lord* (1862), the basic facts of which are set out in para 6.1.3 below. A purported trust, relating to share certificates, was held to be *incompletely constituted* because of a failure to transfer shares in the legally necessary manner. Requirements of the appropriate mode of transfer had not been fulfilled.

6.1.2 Examples

In the case of executed and executory trusts, the trust property has been vested (in both cases) in trustees, so that trusts of this type are completely constituted.

6.1.3 Comparison with executed and executory trusts

In *Milroy v Lord* (1862), the settlor, X, executed a voluntary deed which purported to transfer fifty bank shares to Y to be held in trust for Z. X later handed the share certificates to Y. At that time Y held a general power of attorney entitling him to transfer X's shares. The shares could be transferred only by registration of the transferee in the bank's books; this was not done. It was held that no trust existed because the shares had never legally vested in Y.

6.2 Creation of the completely constituted trust

Per Turner LJ:

'I take the law of this court to be well settled, that, in order to render a voluntary settlement valid and effectual, the settlor must have done everything which, according to the nature of the property comprised in the settlement, was necessary to be done in order to transfer the property and render the settlement binding upon him. He may, of course, do this by actually transferring the property to the persons for whom he intends to provide, and the provision will then be effectual, and it will be equally effectual if he transfers the property to a trustee for the purposes of the settlement, or declares that he himself holds it in trust for those purposes; and if the property be personal, the trust may, as I apprehend, be declared either in writing or by parol; but in order to render the settlement binding one or other of these modes must, as I understand the law of this court, be resorted to, for there is no equity in this court to perfect an imperfect gift. The cases, I think, go further to this extent: that if the settlement is intended to be effectuated by one of the modes to which I have referred, the court will not give effect to it by applying another of those modes. If it is intended to take effect by transfer, the court will not hold the intended transfer to operate as a declaration of trust, for then every imperfect instrument would be made effectual by being converted into a perfect trust.'

The *Milroy* principle was qualified later in *Re Rose* (1952). The donor executed two valid transfers of shares in a company and handed them to the donee, together with the necessary certificates. Under the articles of association in force, the company directors had discretionary powers allowing them to register, or reject, a transfer. In the event, registration was refused until after the donor's death. The Court of Appeal held that the donor had done all in his power, according to the nature of the property which constituted the settlement, which was necessary to be done by him so as to vest the legal estate in the donee, and that the *Milroy* doctrine had no application.

The result is that *Milroy* is effectively qualified: a gift of shares is valid in equity if the transferor has executed the transfer in the manner required by the company's articles, *and* has done everything else necessary for him to do in order that the transfer shall be binding on him.

Per Evershed MR:

'I agree that if a man purporting to transfer property executed documents which are not apt to effect that purpose, the court cannot then extract from those documents some quite different transaction, and say that they were intended merely to operate as a declaration of trust, which *ex facie* they were not; but if a document is apt and proper to transfer the property - is in truth the appropriate way in which the property must be transferred - then it does not seem to me to follow from the statement of Turner LJ in *Milroy* that, as a result, either during some limited period or otherwise, a trust may not arise, for the purpose of giving effect to the transfer ... And, for my part, I do not think that *Milroy* is an authority which compels this court to hold that in this case - where, in the terms of Turner LJ's judgment, the settlor did everything which, according to the nature of the property comprised in the settlement, was necessary to be done by him in order to transfer the property - the result necessarily negatives the conclusion that, pending registration, the settlor was a trustee of the legal interest for the transferee.'

In *Letts v IRC* (1956) a father had intended to make a gift of shares to his children. He was entitled to have the shares allotted to him as fully paid up, and directed the company to allot them directly to his children. It was held that his direction perfected the gift, since he had done all that he could do to effect the transfer of shares.

So that a trust might be completely constituted, the settlor must convey the property to be held on trust by trustees. Where the settlor is the legal and equitable owner of the property, a conveyance to trustees must pass the legal interest effectively. Where he possesses only an equitable interest, he may create a trust which will be completely constituted by his assigning his interest to trustees: see *Re McArdle* (1951). In this case, A and his brothers and sisters were entitled under their father's will, to a house upon the death of their mother. A and his wife, B, lived with the mother in the house. B made considerable improvements to the house. Later, A and his brothers and sisters signed a document, addressed to B, stating their agreement that, in consideration of the improvements made to the house, they agreed to the executors repaying £488 to B from the estate when it was distributed. The court held that the intending donors had not done all in their power to make the purported gift complete. They had not authorised the executors to pay, so that the gift was imperfect.

Per Jenkins LJ:

'A voluntary equitable assignment, to be valid, must in all respects be complete and perfect, so that the assignee is entitled to demand payment from the trustee or holder of the fund, and the trustee is bound to make payment to the assignee, with no further act on the part of the assignor remaining to be done to perfect the assignee's title.'

(The assignment of an equitable interest must be in writing: Law of Property Act 1925, s 53(1)(c).)

6.3 Transfer by conveyance of property to trustees

6.3.1   Appropriateness of mode of transfer

The effectiveness of the transfer of title depends upon the nature of the property; the appropriate mode of transfer must be employed. Thus: in the case of *land* a deed is essential (see Law of Property Act 1925, s 52(1)); in the case of *personal chattels* capable of passing by delivery, deed or delivery is required (see *Jaffa v Taylor* (1990)); in the case of *registered shares*, by proper transfer under the Stock Exchange (Completion of Bargains) Act 1976, as amended by the Companies Act 1985 (see s 184).

In *Re Cole* (1964), a husband bought a house in London and furnished it for members of his family who were then living elsewhere. When his wife subsequently visited the house he said to her: 'It's all yours'. The husband was later declared bankrupt and the wife claimed that the furniture in the house belonged to her. It was held that a gift of chattels cannot be perfected by merely showing them to the purported donee and speaking words of gift. An unequivocal act of delivery or change in possession must be shown; the wife had been unable to do this.

6.4   Transfer by declaration of trust

A trust is completely constituted by the settlor's declaring himself a trustee of the property for the *cestui que trust*. This is so whether the settlor's interest is legal or equitable.

6.4.1   The declaration

The following points should be noted:

- No special form of words is essential. The settlor 'need not use the words, "I declare myself a trustee", but he must do something which is equivalent to it, and use expressions which have that meaning; for however anxious the court may be to carry out a man's intention, it is not at liberty to construe words otherwise than according to their proper meaning': *per* Jessel MR in *Richards v Delbridge* (1874).

- The court must be satisfied that 'a present irrevocable declaration of trust has been made': *per* Neville J in *Re Cozens* (1913).

- The declaration need not be communicated to the *cestui que trust*: *Standing v Bowring* (1885).

- Should the declaration concern *land*, it must be evidenced in writing: Law of Property Act 1925, s 53(1)(b).

In *Jones v Lock* (1865), X, who had a son aged nine months, said to the boy's nurse that he intended to make the child a present. He produced a cheque for £900, drawn in his favour, and said: 'I give this to baby ... It is for him and I am going to put it away for him ...' He then put the cheque in his safe. A few days later he died and one of the executors obtained payment of the cheque in favour of the estate. It was held that there had been *no* gift to the baby; *no* valid declaration of trust in its favour could be deduced from X's statement or actions.

Per Lord Cranworth:

'This is a special case in which I regret to say that I cannot bring myself to think that, either on principle or on authority, there has been any gift or any valid declaration of trust ... The case turns on the very short question whether [X] intended to make a declaration that he held the property in trust for the child; and I cannot come to any other conclusion than that he did not. I think it would be a dangerous example if loose conversations of this sort, in important transactions of this kind, should have the effect of declaration of trust ... It was all quite natural, but the testator would have been very much surprised if he had been told that he had parted with his £900 and could no longer dispose of it. It all turns on the facts, which do not lead me to the conclusion that the testator meant to deprive himself of all property in the note, or to declare himself a trustee of the money for the child.'

See *Paul v Constance* (1977); *Swiss Bank Ltd v Lloyds Bank Ltd* (1980).

Equity will not assist a volunteer nor will it perfect an imperfect gift. A volunteer is unable, therefore, to enforce an incompletely constituted gift. In some few cases, which are exceptions to the general rule, an apparently imperfect gift may be rendered effective: these exceptions are of a statutory and equitable nature.	**6.5 Perfecting an imperfect gift**

The following are examples of statutory exceptions:	6.5.1 Statutory exceptions

- Under the Law of Property Act 1925, ss 1(6), 19(4), an infant may not hold a legal estate in land. An attempted transfer of a legal estate to an infant operates as an agreement for value by the grantor to execute a settlement in favour of the infant and, in the meantime, to hold the land in trust for him.

- Under the Settled Land Act 1925, s 4(1), the settlement of a legal estate in land *inter vivos* requires a vesting deed and a trust instrument. Under s 9, an instrument which does not comply with the requirements of s 4 will be deemed to be a trust instrument. 'As soon as practicable after a settlement, or an instrument which for the purposes of the Act is deemed to be a trust instrument, takes effect as such, the trustees of the settlement may, and on the request of the tenant for life or statutory owner, shall, execute a principal vesting deed ...' so that the settlement is perfected.

6.5.2	Equitable exceptions	Equitable exceptions include: equitable estoppel; the rule in *Strong v Bird* (1874); *donationes mortis causa*.

6.6   Equitable estoppel

The doctrine of estoppel operates so as to prevent X acting in a manner which is inconsistent with his representations to Y, in reliance of which Y has acted to the detriment of his own interests. 'The whole point of estoppel ... as I understand it is that if a man has been induced to act to his detriment, he ought to be protected': *per* Lord Widgery in *Norfolk CC v Secretary of State for the Environment* (1973). At common law X was estopped from denying matters the truth of which he had previously affirmed. In equity two doctrines have emerged (although Lord Scarman, in *Crabb v Arun DC* (1976) denied their separate nature): promissory and proprietary estoppel.

6.6.1   Promissory estoppel

Where X, by his words or conduct, makes to Y an unambiguous representation, by assurance or promise concerning his (X's) future actions, which is intended to affect the legal relationship between X and Y, so that Y alters his position in reliance on that representation, to his disadvantage, X will not be allowed to act inconsistently with his representation. See *Pacol v Trade Lines* (1982); *Ajayi v Briscoe Ltd* (1964).

6.6.2   Proprietary estoppel

X may be estopped from denying Y's rights in X's property in certain circumstances, eg, as where Y has incurred expenditure on the property, or where Y acted in a belief encouraged by X that he (Y) has an interest in the property sufficient to justify his expenditure on it, or where X has stood by, knowing of Y's mistaken belief and has allowed Y to incur expenditure. (But where the enforcement of the right claimed by Y will result in contravention of a statute, no equity arises.) See *Berg Homes v Grey* (1979).

In *Dillwyn v Llewellyn* (1862), a testator, T, placed his son, S, in possession of land, but no formal conveyance was executed. T, however, did sign a memorandum declaring that his purpose was to furnish S with a dwelling house. S later expended a large sum on the house, with T's full knowledge and agreement. It was held that S was entitled to call for a conveyance of the fee simple.

Per Lord Westbury:

'If A puts B in possession of a piece of land and tells him, "I give it to you that you may build a house on it", and B, on the strength of the promise, with the knowledge of A, expends a large sum of money in building a house accordingly, I cannot doubt that the donee acquires a right from the subsequent transaction to call on the donor to perform that contract and complete the imperfect donation which was made'.

Note *Inwards v Baker* (1965). Defendant wished to build a bungalow but found that sites in the neighbourhood were too expensive. His father said, 'Why don't you build on my land?' Defendant built the bungalow on his father's land and lived there. After the father's death, the trustees attempted to recover possession from the son. The court held that the son could remain there for as long as he required the bungalow as his home. The trustees, who were the father's successors in title, were bound by the equity.

See also *Dodsworth v Dodsworth* (1973); *Pascoe v Turner* (1979).

An exception to the general rule that equity will not perfect an imperfect gift is seen in *Strong v Bird* (1874). In this case, defendant, X, borrowed £1,000 from his stepmother, Y, with whom he shared a house. Y paid £200 per quarter for her board, and agreed that the debt was to be paid off by a deduction of £100 from the quarterly payments. On the third quarter day she decided to pay the full amount of £200, and continued to do so each quarter day until her death four years later. X was the executor of Y's will. Y's next of kin claimed that X owed the balance of the debt to Y's estate. It was held that the appointment of X as executor was evidence of Y's continuing intention to release the debt which, therefore, was extinguished.

6.7   The rule in *Strong v Bird* (1874)

The rule may be stated thus: a present intention to make a gift or release a debt, which intention continues unchanged until the death of the donor or creditor, will become effective by appointing the donee or debtor as executor or by his becoming administrator or trustee of the property.

The rule does *not* apply to a promise to make a gift in the future; it will apply only where there is an intention of a present gift: see *Re Innes* (1910).

The intention required for purposes of the rule will be negatived by the subsequent taking of security for the debt or by the donor treating the property as his own. See *Re Eiser's WT* (1937); *Re Wale* (1956).

There must be evidence of a continuing intention to make the gift: *Re Gonin* (1979).

In *Re Freeland* (1952), testatrix had promised to give plaintiff a motor car at a future date. She never gave the car, and, on her death, plaintiff became her executrix. The court did not apply the rule in *Strong v Bird* because the gift had never been made absolute.

In *Ralli's WT* (1964), testator left residuary estate on trust for his wife for life, then for his daughters, Helen and Irene, absolutely. Helen covenanted by marriage settlement to settle after-acquired property in favour of Irene's children. On the death of the testator's widow and of Helen, Irene's husband (the plaintiff) was the sole surviving trustee of the will trusts and the marriage settlement. Helen's share of the residuary estate was, therefore, vested in him. Did plaintiff hold on trust for those persons interested under Helen's will or on the trusts of her marriage settlement? It was held that he held Helen's share of the residuary estate upon the trusts of her marriage settlement; it was immaterial that the property came to him in his capacity as trustee.

> *Per* Buckley J:
>
> 'The question is: For whom, if anyone, does [plaintiff] hold the fund in equity? ... It is for the defendants to invoke the assistance of equity to make good their claim to the fund. To do so successfully they must show that the plaintiff cannot conscientiously withhold it from them. When they seek to do this, he can point to the covenant which, in my judgment, relieves him from any fiduciary obligation he would otherwise owe to the defendants as Helen's representatives ... he is relying upon the combined effect of his legal ownership and his rights under the covenant.'

(Helen's imperfect gift to the trustee of the settlement was completed when he acquired the legal estate in a different capacity - essentially an extension by analogy of the *Strong v Bird* rule.)

6.8 Donationes mortis causa

A *donatio mortis causa* is a gift of property made by the donor in contemplation of his death within the near future. Its relevance here is that 'the principle of not assisting a volunteer to perfect an incomplete gift does *not* apply to *donatio*': *per* Lindley LJ in *Re Dillon* (1890).

In *Re Beaumont* (1902), Buckley J described the *dmc* as 'of an amphibious nature, being a gift which is neither entirely *inter vivos* nor testamentary. It is an act *inter vivos* by which the donee is to have the absolute title to the subject of the gift, not at once, but if the donor dies. If the donor dies the title becomes absolute not under but as against his executor. In order to make the gift valid it must be made so as to take complete effect on the donor's death'.

6.8.1 Requisites for a *dmc*

The requisites for a *dmc* were enunciated recently by Nourse LJ in *Sen v Headley* (1991):

> 'The three general requirements for such a gift may be stated very much as they are stated in Snell's *Equity* (29th edition). *First*, the gift must be made in contemplation, although not necessarily in expectation, of impending death. *Secondly*, the gift must be made upon the condition that it is to be absolute and perfected only on the donor's death, being revocable

until that event occurs and ineffective if it does not. *Thirdly*, there must be a delivery of the subject-matter of the gift, or the essential indicia of title thereto, which amounts to a parting with dominion and not merely physical possession over the subject-matter of the gift ...'

- **The property must be capable of passing by *donatio***

  In general, anything capable of transfer by mere delivery may be the subject-matter of a *dmc*; or, if it cannot pass in that way, by the delivery of an appropriate document, etc.

  Examples of property represented by documents and held capable of passing by *donatio*: a bond (*Gardner v Parker* (1818)); an insurance policy (*Amiss v Witt* (1863)); post office savings bank book (*Re Weston* (1902)); mortgage of land (*Duffield v Elwes* (1827)).

  It has been held that there cannot be a *donatio* of: a certificate of building society shares (*Re Weston* (1902)); a promissory note drawn by the donor (*Re Leaper* (1916)).

  In *Sen v Headley* (1991), the Court of Appeal held that land is capable of passing by way of a *dmc*.

- **The gift must be made in contemplation of death within the near future**

  The donor must have contemplated his death at the time of the gift; the test is probably subjective. It matters not that the death occurs from some cause other than the disease from which the donor was suffering: see *Wilkes v Allington* (1931) - gift given in contemplation of death from cancer, but donor died of pneumonia.

- **The gift must have been made conditional on the donor's death**

  The appropriate condition is that the gift shall be complete only on the donor's death; it is, therefore, revocable during his lifetime.

  The condition need not be expressly stated; it is usually implied from the very fact of the donor's illness at the time of the gift: *Re Lillingston* (1952).

  In the absence of such a condition, the gift will take effect as a gift *inter vivos* or will fail in its entirety: see *Tate v Hilbert* (1793).

  Revocation of a *dmc* may be express (eg, as where the donor resumes dominion over the property: see *Bunn v Markham* (1816)), or automatic (as where the donor recovers from his illness: see *Staniland v Willott* (1852)). A purported revocation by will does not suffice, since the donee's title will have been completed on the death of the donor: see *Jones v Selby* (1710).

- **Delivery is essential**

  'Delivery' is effected by delivery of the actual property, or, eg, keys, or something which represents the property, and must be made to the donee or to someone on his behalf.

  In *Bunn v Markham* (1816) the donor sealed property in three parcels, writing on each the intended donee's name. He declared that the parcels were intended for the donees and that they were to receive them after his death. The parcels were placed in a locked chest; the donor kept the key. It was held that this *did not* constitute a sufficient act of delivery.

  Where the gift is of a chose in action, the donor should deliver to the donee a document which is evidence of title: see *Re Weston* (1902), *Re Wasserberg* (1915).

  The test concerning the nature of the appropriate document to be delivered is 'whether the instrument amounts to a transfer, as being the essential indicia or evidence of title, possession or production of which entitles the possessor to the money or property purported to be given': *Birch v Treasury Solicitor* (1951).

  In *Sen v Headley* (1991), it was held that a delivery of title deeds (kept in a steel box, the key to which had been given by X to Y during one of her visits to the hospital during X's final illness) amounted to X's parting with dominion over his house.

  In *Woodard v Woodard* (1992), X's father, Y, suffering from a terminal illness told X to keep the keys to Y's car, which X used regularly, saying 'I won't be using them any more.' It was held that there had been an *effective dmc*. The fact that spare keys and documents had not been handed to X was not important because they were not prerequisites to the making of the gift; this was a matter of evidence only.

6.9 Volunteers and settlements for value

The concept of the 'volunteer' mentioned earlier involves the following rule: if X makes a promise to Y that he will create a trust, and fails to do so, or creates an imperfect trust only, Y can compel performance of the trust *only* if he is not a 'volunteer', ie, only if he has given valuable consideration, or if he is within a marriage consideration: see *Re D'Angibau* (1880).

'Good consideration', eg, consideration of generosity or moral duty will *not* suffice. Therefore a settlement supported only by consideration of this type is held to be 'voluntary'. Valuable consideration, eg, money, money's worth, marriage, is essential.

If marriage is to create a settlement for value, it must follow a settlement executed in consideration of it, or be followed by a settlement executed in pursuance of an ante-nuptial agreement: *Re Holland* (1902). A settlement executed *after* marriage without any ante-nuptial agreement is 'voluntary' in nature.

Persons within the marriage consideration include husband, wife, issue of the marriage and grandchildren: see *De Mestre v West* (1891).

In *Re Plumptre's Settlement* (1910), there was a covenant in a marriage settlement to settle the wife's after-acquired property on trusts for the wife and husband for life, then for their issue, with ultimate trust for the wife's next of kin. The husband bought stock in the wife's name, but it was never properly settled. The wife died without issue. It was held that the next of kin could not enforce the covenant against the husband; they were strangers to the marriage consideration and, therefore, no more than volunteers.

Per Eve J:

> 'What is the position of the next of kin here? They are not, in my opinion, *cestuis que trust* under the settlement ... for nothing therein amounts to a declaration of trust, or to anything more than an executory trust on the part of the husband and wife ... The collaterals are no parties to the contract; they are not within the marriage consideration and cannot be considered otherwise than as volunteers, and in this respect it makes no difference that the covenant sought to be enforced is the husband's, and that the property sought to be brought within it comes from the wife.'

In *Re Cook's ST* (1965), by agreement in 1934, followed by a settlement of family property made between X, Y (his son) and the trustees, certain very valuable oil paintings became Y's absolute property. Y covenanted for valuable consideration that, should any of the paintings be sold in his lifetime, proceeds of the sale would be paid to the trustees to hold upon trust for Y's children. In 1962, Y gave to his wife, Z, a Rembrandt painting, which she wished to sell. The children of Y's *previous marriage* claimed that the gift to Z was ineffective. It was held that they were not to be considered as parties to the covenant; they were mere volunteers who could *not* enforce it.

Completely and Incompletely Constituted Trusts

Completely constituted trust: the settlor has done all in his power and all that was necessary to do so as to render the settlement binding. *Incompletely constituted trust*: some further action is required (eg, an appropriate transfer of property) before it can be said to be 'perfectly created'.

Where trust property is registered land; the trust is completely constituted when the settlor signs the appropriate transfer which he passes with the land certificate to the trustees. Where trust property comprises company shares; if the settlor fails to execute an appropriate share transfer form, the trust is incompletely constituted.

Definitions and examples

In all cases an appropriate mode of transfer must be employed. See, eg, Law of Property Act 1925, s 52(1).

Note *Re Cole* (1964) - an unequivocal act of delivery or change in possession must be shown so as to establish a gift of chattels. See *Re Cozens* (1913) ('a present irrevocable declaration of trust').

Conveying property to trustees

Equity will not assist a volunteer, nor will it perfect an imperfect gift. An incompletely constituted gift will not be enforced, therefore, as a general rule. There are exceptions of a statutory and equitable nature, to this rule.

Perfecting the imperfect gift

The following are examples of statutory exceptions:

Statutory exceptions

- Law of Property Act 1925, ss 1(6), 19(4). An attempted transfer of a legal estate to an infant will operate as an agreement to execute a settlement in his favour; in the meantime the land will be held in trust for him.

- Settled Land Act 1925, ss 4(1), 9. Under s 9, an instrument which does not comply with the requirements of s 4 concerning the settlement of a legal estate in land, *inter vivos*, may be deemed to be an appropriate trust instrument.

The doctrine of equitable estoppel operates so as to prevent X acting in a manner which is inconsistent with his representations to Y, in reliance on which Y has acted to his detriment. In the case of *promissory* estoppel, X's representations to Y are intended to affect their legal

Equitable exceptions

relationship (see *Pacol v Trade Lines* (1982)). In the case of *proprietary* estoppel, Y has been encouraged by X to act on the basis that he (Y) has an interest in the property sufficient, say, to justify expenditure on it (see *Berg Homes v Grey* (1979). See also *Dillwyn v Llewellyn* (1862).

The rule in *Strong v Bird*

A present intention to make a gift or release a debt, which intention continues unchanged until the death of the donor or creditor, will become effective by appointing the donee or debtor as executor or by his becoming administrator or trustee of the property.

There must be evidence of a continuing intention to make the gift. The intention required for purposes of the rule will be negatived by the subsequent taking of security for the debt.

The rule does not apply to a promise to make a gift in the future. See *Re Innes* (1910).

Donatio mortis causa

(Gift in contemplation of death.) The principle of not assisting a volunteer to perfect an incomplete gift does not apply to *dmc*. See *Re Beaumont* (1902).

Requisites for a *dmc*: the gift must be made in contemplation of impending death; the gift is perfected only on the donor's death and is revocable until that event; delivery of subject-matter is essential (parting with dominion over the subject-matter is necessary).

Property capable of passing as *dmc* includes bonds, insurance policies, land (*Sen v Headley* (1991)). Property incapable of passing includes building society shares and a promissory note drawn by the donor.

Volunteers and settlements for value

If X promises Y that he will create a trust, and fails to do so, Y can compel performance only if he is not a volunteer, ie, only if he has given valuable consideration or if he is within a marriage consideration. See *Re D'Angibau* (1880).

'Good consideration' (eg, consideration of moral duty) will not suffice.

Persons within the marriage consideration include husband, wife, issue of the marriage, grandchildren. See *Re Plumptre's Settlement* (1910).

Chapter 7

Protective and Discretionary Trusts

Trusts of this type are often intended to have as their objectives the reduction of tax liability or the protection of some beneficiaries against the negative consequences of their undue extravagance.

The *protective trust* is usually a trust for life or some lesser period, which is intended to be determinable on the happening of specified events, eg, the beneficiary's bankruptcy, upon which the trust income will be applied at the absolute discretion of the trustees for the support of the beneficiary and his family. Example: 'Life interest to X until he shall attempt to alienate the same, or shall be judged bankrupt.'

The *discretionary trust* (in the specific sense used here) is a trust under which trustees are allowed the exercise of a discretion to pay or apply income for beneficiaries, but no beneficiary may claim as of right that any part or all of the capital or income is to be paid to him or applied in any way specifically for his benefit.

Example of the protective trust: see *Re Westby* (1950); of the discretionary trust: see *Re Allen-Meyrick's WT* (1966).

It is not possible, in general, to create a perfect trust which, at one and the same time, has as its objective the granting of a complete interest, and the fettering of the effective disposition of that interest by, eg, the attaching of a condition prohibiting its alienation.

A condition which is attached to a gift to X, which states, in effect, that his interest shall determine prematurely ('to X on the condition that he shall not be adjudged bankrupt'), is generally void.

As a contrast to the grant to X (upon condition subsequent) is the determinable interest, which may be valid, eg, as in the case of a grant of a life interest to Y 'until he becomes bankrupt'. In the case of the gift to X, there is a conditional interest, ie, an interest which can be defeated by a separate condition (bankruptcy). But in the case of the grant to Y, the interest contains the determining event within the limitation itself: see *Re Dugdale* (1888).

Brandon v Robinson (1811) is a leading case in this area. The testator, T, had devised and bequeathed property to the defendant trustees on trust for sale, proceeds for those of his children living at the time of his death, in equal shares. T directed that the shares 'of such of the legatees as at the time of T's decease should have attained the age of 21 should be considered as vested interests'. The share of his son, X, was to be invested in named securities, and the income 'as the same became due and payable, should be paid from time to time into his own proper hands, or on his proper order and receipt, subscribed with his own proper hand, to the intent the same should not be grantable, transferable, or otherwise assignable, by way of anticipation of any unreceived payment, or any part thereof'.

After attaining 21, and following T's death, X became bankrupt. The plaintiff, the surviving assignee in bankruptcy, filed a bill for the trusts of the will to be executed, and requested the share to which he, as assignee, was entitled.

It was held that the assignee *could* claim the income. T had created a life interest with a condition that it was not to be alienated; such a condition was *void*.

Per Lord Eldon:

> 'There is no doubt that property may be given to a man until he shall become bankrupt. It is equally clear, generally speaking, that if property is given to a man for his life, the donor cannot take away the incidents to a life estate; and, as I have observed, a disposition to a man until he shall become bankrupt, and after his bankruptcy over, is quite different from an attempt to give it to him for life, with a proviso that he shall not sell or alienate it. If that condition is so expressed as to amount to a limitation, reducing the interest short of a life estate, neither the man nor his assignees can have it beyond the period limited.'

A determinable interest may not be utilised by a settlor in an attempt to defeat a claim of his trustee in bankruptcy. Should he, therefore, attempt to settle property upon himself 'until bankruptcy', then, on occurrence of that event, the property will generally vest in his trustee in bankruptcy: see *Re Burroughs-Fowler* (1916).

In *Re Detmold* (1889), a marriage settlement of the settlor's own property allowed income to be made payable to himself during his life 'or until he shall become bankrupt, or shall ... suffer something whereby [that income] or some part thereof would ... by operation or process of law, if belonging absolutely to him, become vested in or payable to some other person', and, upon determination of the trust in his favour, upon trust to pay the income to his wife.

In July 1888, a judgment creditor of the settlor was appointed to receive income, and, some two months later, the settlor was declared bankrupt.

It was held that the settlor's wife *was entitled* to the income. *Per* North J:

> 'The limitation of the life interest to the settlor was validly determined by the fact that, in consequence of the order appointing the receiver, [the settlor] ceased to be entitled to receive the income. This took place before the bankruptcy, and, therefore, the forfeiture is valid against the trustee in bankruptcy.'

The protective trust utilises the principle of the determinable interest, so that a life interest may be made determinable upon the occurrence of a stated event (bankruptcy, alienation, etc), on which the interest is forfeited and is then followed by discretionary trusts in favour of the life tenant and his family. See *Gibbon v Mitchell* (1990). Such a trust may be created expressly or by incorporating the Trustee Act 1925, s 33. Reference to 'the protective trusts' will suffice: in *Re Wittke* (1944), a gift 'upon protective trusts for the benefit of my sister' was held to suffice.

7.3   The protective trust

Under the Trustee Act 1925, s 33, where income is directed to be held on protective trusts for the benefit of a person ('the principal beneficiary') for the period of his life or any less period, then during that period the income is to be held subject to the trusts set out in this section.

7.3.1   The Trustee Act 1925, s 33

Income will be held on trust for the principal beneficiary until 'he does or attempts to do or suffers any act or thing, or until any event happens ... whereby if the income were payable during the trust period to the principal beneficiary absolutely ..., he would be deprived of the right to receive the same or any part thereof'.

Should the interest terminate, the income will be held on trust for the maintenance or support of the principal beneficiary, the spouse, and their issue, or if there is neither spouse nor issue, it will be held for the principal beneficiary and those persons who, if he/she were actually dead, would be entitled to the property or income thereof.

The section must be read subject to the Family Law Reform Act 1987, s 19(3), under which, in determining 'children' or 'issue', no account is to be taken of legitimacy.

Nothing in s 33 operates to validate any trust which would, if contained in the instrument creating the trust, be liable to be set aside: s 33(3).

The general effect of the utilisation of s 33 (or its essential features stated expressly) is that trusts are considered to be engrafted on the life interest; in the event of the life interest being extinguished, the engrafted trusts are also considered as extinguished.

In *Re Allsopp's Marriage ST* (1959), an express protected trust was created in 1916 by a marriage settlement, with discretionary trusts to arise on forfeiture. The marriage was dissolved in 1928 and the court ordered a variation of the settlement by extinguishing the husband's rights. It was held that the husband's life interest having been extinguished, the discretionary trust, which was linked very closely with that interest, was considered as being destroyed.

7.3.2	Events held to have caused a forfeiture	The principal beneficiary's bankruptcy, or alienation, will generally result in forfeiture of the life interest. In *Re Walker* (1939), it was held that this would be so even if the bankruptcy had occurred prior to the trust coming into operation. It is necessary to construe carefully the terms of a forfeiture provision so as to decide whether a particular event has caused a forfeiture. Examples of events causing a forfeiture are as follows:

- *Re Balfour's Settlement* (1939)

  Income was payable to X for life or until he should 'do or suffer something whereby the same or some part thereof would through his act or default or by operation or process of law or otherwise if belonging absolutely to him become vested in or payable to some other person', with discretionary trust over. During a period of three years the sole trustee advanced part of the capital to X at his request. This was a breach of trust, and, later, X was adjudicated bankrupt. A part of X's income was impounded so as to make good the breach. It was held that X's interest had been determined.

- *Re Baring's ST* (1940)

  A wife had a protected life interest, with income payable to her 'until some event should happen whereby the income would become payable to .... some other person', with discretionary trust over. A sequestration order was obtained by her husband against her when she refused to return her children to the jurisdiction of the court. The order was temporary only but, nevertheless, it was held that the life interest was forfeited. The settlement was based on the settlor's intention that 'there should be a continuous benefit to the beneficiaries so that either the tenant for life should be in a position to have the income, or the discretionary trust should arise': *per* Morton J.

- *Re Dennis' ST* (1942)

  The settlor's son was given a protected life interest under a family settlement of 1923, when he was an infant, 'until any act or event should happen whereby the income would become vested in some other person'. On attaining his majority in 1935, a supplementary deed was executed under which the trustees were to pay to him only part of the income and accumulate the balance for him over the next six years. It was held that this caused a forfeiture.

- *Re Richardson's WT* (1958)

  Testator gave £2,000 to trustees to hold income on protective trusts for the benefit of his grandson, X, during his life and until he reached the age of 35, in accordance with the terms of the Trustee Act 1925, s 33. If, on reaching that age, X had not attempted to do any act, or no event had occurred, whereby he would have been deprived then, or thereafter, of the right to receive the capital or income, he would receive the capital absolutely. If this were not so, he was to receive the income on protective trusts for his life. At a later date, X's wife obtained a decree of divorce against him, and, one year later, an order was made, charging his interest with an annual payment to her of £50. In that same year he reached the age of 35 and, ten months later, was adjudicated bankrupt. It was held that the bankruptcy had created a forfeiture. 'I have come to the conclusion that in the events which happened in this case, by the time that [X] became bankrupt, his interest under the will had been forfeited ...': *per* Danckwerts J.

The following are illustrations of events held not to have caused a forfeiture:

7.3.3 Events held not to have caused a forfeiture

- *Re Tancred's Settlement* (1903)

  The principal beneficiary was entitled to income for life 'until he should dispose or attempt to dispose of the income or do something whereby the income would become payable to or vested in some other person'. He later assigned his interest to the trustees of his marriage settlement, appointing them his attorneys and authorising them to charge to the fund their expenses arising out of receiving the income. It was held that there was no forfeiture.

- *Re Westby's Settlement* (1950)

  The tenant for life under a protective trust was of unsound mind and fees became payable from his estate under the Lunacy Act 1890, s 148(3) (see now the Mental Health Act 1983, s 106(6)). It was held that the payments were in the nature of management expenses, so that there was no forfeiture.

- *Re Oppenheim's WT* (1950)

  Tenant for life under a protective trust was certified as of unsound mind. It was held that the appointment of a receiver did not cause a forfeiture. *Per* Harman J:

  I think that a man who has a statutory agent, as this man has, can give by his agent a personal discharge no less than ... if he were at the top of Mount Everest, his banker could give a personal discharge on his behalf. It seems to me also that the forfeiture was not intended to operate in a case of this kind where no one else will be entitled to the benefit of the income in the event which has happened. It was intended to prevent the income from getting into other hands. That does not occur in the present case.'

- *Re Longman* (1955)

  X was entitled to income subject to forfeiture if he were to 'commit any act whereby any part of the income became vested in or payable to any other person'. X authorised trustees to pay his creditors from a dividend which was due to him from a company. In the event, the company failed to declare a dividend. It was held that this did not occasion a forfeiture. 'It seems to me that the authorities given by the son were completely nugatory, and that there was nothing on which they could operate and they never did operate on anything': *per* Danckwerts J.

7.3.4   General effects of a forfeiture

Until the trustees receive notice of an act which effectively amounts to a forfeiture, they are justified in paying income to the principal beneficiary. Upon forfeiture the life interest of the beneficiary is determined and the discretionary trusts are brought into operation. In such an event the trustees may not retain the income; their duty is to apply it for whatever purposes are stated in the discretionary trusts.

In *Re Gourju's WT* (1943), X was a protected life tenant under the will of her husband. She was residing in a part of France occupied by the Germans and, under the Trading with the Enemy Act 1939 and subsequent Orders, she lost entitlement to receive income from the fund so that her protected life interest was forfeited. Discretionary trusts came into operation.

The trustees intended to accumulate income and pay it to X when the war ended. It was held that they were not able to do so; they had a duty to pay members of the discretionary class.

7.4   The discretionary trust

A discretionary trust may arise when a life interest under a protective trust is determined, or as the result of its being specially created. Such a trust may be: *exhaustive*, ie, the trustees must distribute the entire income, but must exercise a discretion in relation to the way in which the distribution will be made as between the objects of the trust; or *non-exhaustive*, ie, the trustees have a discretion which relates not only to *how* the distribution will be made, but *whether* it will be made: see *Gartside v IRC* (1968). See *Re Trafford* (1985).

In general, only the trustees may exercise the discretion which has been vested in them.

Trustees may not surrender that discretion to the court. In *Re Allen-Meyrick's WT* (1966), the testatrix gave residue to trustees to apply the income in their absolute discretion for the maintenance of the husband. Subject to the exercise of the discretion, the residue was given in trust to two godchildren. The trustees made payments to the husband (who had been declared bankrupt); they could not agree whether to apply any further income in this fashion, and wished to surrender discretion to the court. The court would not accept a general surrender of discretion; it would assist in the resolution of specific problems, but no more than that.

If discretion is not exercised within a reasonable time (and the interpretation of 'reasonable' will depend on the individual case) it may be lost.

Trustees who have an absolute and uncontrolled discretion but who fail to distribute trust income in accordance with the settlement may, notwithstanding their delay, be permitted by the court to distribute accrued income among beneficiaries as they think fit: see *Re Locker's Settlement* (1978). 'The discretion of the trustees ought to be exercised promptly, if at all, where its exercise is optional, just as it ought to be exercised promptly in every case where its exercise is obligatory': *per* Goulding J.

Until the trustees exercise their discretion in his favour, the discretionary beneficiary possesses no interest in the trust fund. Hence, should he die before the exercise of that discretion, no rights concerning the trust will pass to his estate.

Where a person has a right to be regarded as a potential beneficiary, he may apply to the court if the trustees exercise their discretion improperly or if they refuse to exercise it.

In *Tempest v Lord Camoys* (1882), the court considered the following matter arising from the will of X. Y and Z, the trustees, possessed the power 'at their absolute discretion' to sell land and to apply the purchase money in the purchase of other land. Money could be raised by mortgage for that purpose. Some family members desired to purchase Bracewell Hall for £60,000; £30,000 of available money was to be used in

7.4.1 Exercise of the discretion

7.4.2 The discretionary beneficiary

the purchase, the balance to be raised by a mortgage. Y agreed with the plan; Z opposed it. Y brought a petition to the court asking that the purchase be ordered.

The court held that it was not willing to interfere with a trustee's *bona fide* exercise of his discretion.

Per Jessel MR:

'It is settled law that when a testator has given a pure discretion to trustees as to the exercise of a power, the court does not enforce the exercise of the power against the wishes of the trustees, but it does prevent them from exercising it improperly. The court says that the power, if exercised at all, is to be properly exercised. This may be illustrated by the case of persons having a power to appoint new trustees. Even after a decree in a suit for administering the trusts has been made they may still exercise the power, but the court will see that they do not appoint improper persons. But in all cases where there is a trust or duty coupled with the power, the court will then compel the trustees to carry it out in a proper manner and within a reasonable time. In the present case there was a power which amounts to a trust to invest the fund in question in the purchase of land. The trustees would not be allowed by the court to disregard that trust, and if Z had refused to invest the money in land at all the court would have found no difficulty in interfering. But that is a very different thing from saying that the court ought to take from the trustees their uncontrolled discretion as to the particular time for the investment and the particular property which should be purchased.'

A discretionary beneficiary has the right to obtain information concerning the trust.

Where the object of a discretionary trust is adjudged bankrupt or assigns his interest, neither the trustee in bankruptcy nor the assignee is entitled to receive any payment from the fund.

Where trustees have paid a discretionary beneficiary *after* they have received notice of bankruptcy or assignment, they may be liable to the trustee in bankruptcy or to the assignee for the sums they have paid: *Re Neil* (1890).

Where trustees have been directed to apply the trust fund for the sole benefit of a specified person, then, although the precise method of application is within their discretion, if that person is of full age and *sui juris*, he may terminate the trust and demand payment of the fund: *Saunders v Vautier* (1841). See also *Napier v Light* (1974).

In *Re Smith* (1928), a fund was held by trustees on trust 'to pay or apply the whole or any part of the annual income thereof or if they shall think fit from time to time any part of the capital thereof unto or for the maintenance and personal support and benefit of X ... remainder after death to be held in trust for her children'. X and her children mortgaged their interests in the trust to an insurance company. The problem arose as to whether the trustees had to pay the income of the trust to the mortgagees, or whether they retained a discretion to pay it to X. The court held that the mortgage was valid, and that the insurance company, as mortgagees, should receive the income from the trustees.

Per Romer J:

'What is to happen where the trustees have a discretion whether they will apply the whole or only a portion of the fund for the benefit of one person, but are obliged to apply the rest of the fund, so far as not applied for the benefit of the first named person, to or for the benefit of a second named person? There, two people together are the sole objects of the discretionary trust and, between them, are entitled to have the whole fund applied to them or for their benefit. It has been laid down by the Court of Appeal (in *Re Nelson* (1928)) that in such a case you treat all the people put together just as though they formed one person, for whose benefit the trustees were directed to apply the whole of a particular fund.'

Protective and Discretionary Trusts

The protective trust is intended to be determinable on the happening of specified events, upon which the trust income will be applied at the absolute discretion of the trustees for the support of the beneficiary and his family. Example: 'Life interest to B until he shall attempt to alienate the same, or shall be adjudged bankrupt'.

The discretionary trust is one under which trustees are allowed a discretion to pay or apply income for beneficiaries, but no beneficiary may claim as of right that capital or income is to be paid to him.

A condition attached to a gift to X which states, in effect, that his interest may determine prematurely, is generally void. Example: 'to X on the condition that he shall not be adjudged bankrupt'. A grant of a life interest to Y 'until he becomes bankrupt', the interest contains the determining event within the limitation itself and is valid. See *Re Dugdale* (1888).

A determinable interest may not be utilised by a settlor in an attempt to defeat a claim of his trustee in bankruptcy. See *Re Burroughs-Fowler* (1916).

These utilise the principle of determinable interests. A life interest may be made determinable upon the occurrence of a stated event, upon which an interest is forfeited, to be followed by discretionary trusts.

Trustee Act 1925, s 33, states that where income is directed to be held on protective trusts for the period of a beneficiary's life or any less period, the income is to be held subject to the trusts set out in the section.

A reference in an instrument to 'the protective trusts' will suffice: *Re Wittke* (1944).

The effect of utilisation of s 33: trusts are considered as engrafted on the life interest; if the life interest is extinguished, engrafted trusts are extinguished.

The principal beneficiary's bankruptcy, or alienation, will generally result in the forfeiture of a life interest. Examples: the impounding of the beneficiary's income to make good the result of breach of trust; a sequestration order against the beneficiary. See *Re Balfour's Settlement* (1938). Examples of events which did not result in forfeiture: payments on behalf

Definitions and examples

Determinable interests

of a beneficiary in the nature of management expenses; proposed payment of creditors from company dividends which, in the event, were not declared. See *Re Longman* (1955).

Trustees must apply the income for whatever purposes as are set out in the discretionary trusts. See *Re Gourju's WT* (1943).

Discretionary trusts

Discretionary trusts may arise when a life interest under a protective trust is determined, or as the result of their being specially created.

In the case of an exhaustive discretionary trust, the trustees must distribute the entire income, exercising a discretion as to the way in which distribution will be made; in the case of a non-exhaustive trust, the trustees have a discretion as to whether a distribution will be made. See *Re Trafford* (1985).

Trustees may not delegate the exercise of their discretion to the court. The discretion must be exercised within a reasonable time.

Discretionary beneficiaries have the right to obtain information concerning the trust.

Where trustees are directed to apply the trust fund for X's benefit, then although the exact method of application of the fund is within their discretion, X, if of full age and *sui juris* may terminate the trust and demand payment of the fund. See *Saunders v Vautier* (1841).

Chapter 8

Implied and Resulting Trusts

It should be noted that a number of 'resulting trusts' which arise because of the settlors' presumed intentions are often described as 'implied trusts'. Additionally, the descriptions, 'resulting' and 'constructive' trusts, tend to be used conterminously.

In *Hussey v Palmer* (1972), X, an elderly widow, was invited to live with her daughter and son-in-law. She accepted, but found the accommodation too small and an extra bedroom was built, X paying the construction costs. Following arguments, X left the house and claimed the cost of the bedroom, based on a resulting trust.

Per Lord Denning:

'Although plaintiff alleged that there was a resulting trust, I should have thought that the trust in this case, if there was one, was more in the nature of a constructive trust; but that is more a matter of words than anything else. The two run together. By whatever name it is described, it is a trust imposed by law whenever justice and good conscience require it. It is a liberal process, founded upon large principles of equity, to be applied in cases where the legal owner cannot conscientiously keep the property for himself alone, but ought to allow another to have the property or the benefit of it or a share in it. The trust may arise at the outset when the property is acquired, or later on, as the circumstances may require. It is an equitable remedy by which the court can enable an aggrieved party to obtain restitution ... I have no doubt that there was a resulting trust, or, more accurately, a constructive trust for [X], and I would so declare.'

The following definitions are to be kept in mind in this chapter:

An *implied trust* is one which will be enforced by the court as a result of surrounding circumstances, or the language of the parties, so that effect can be given to their implied, although unexpressed, intentions. Thus: X purchases property in Y's name. There is a presumption in equity that X intended Y to hold that property in trust for him: see *Re Howes* (1905).

A *resulting trust* is one which arises in circumstances where the beneficial interest in property 'comes back' (*resultare* = to spring back) to the person or his representatives who transferred the property to the trustee or who provided the means of obtaining that property. Thus: X transfers funds to trustees to be held on the trusts of a marriage settlement; the marriage is later declared void *ab initio*. The fund will be held for X on a resulting trust: see *Re Ames' Settlement* (1946). See also *Hodgson v Marks* (1971); *Simpson v Simpson* (1989); *Tinsley v Milligan* (1993).

8.2	**Types of implied and resulting trusts**	The types of implied/resulting trusts to be discussed below are related to: mutual wills; purchases in the name of another (and analogous cases); failure to dispose of the beneficial interest; trusts declared illegal.
8.2.1	Mutual wills	The term 'mutual wills' is used in this context to refer to wills made as the result of an agreement between persons to create irrevocable interests in favour of ascertainable beneficiaries. Should one testator revoke his will after the death of the other, who has not revoked his will, the interests created by the agreement are enforceable in equity. See *Re Dale* (1993).

Per Lord Camden in *Dufour v Pereira* (1769):

'The parties by the mutual will do each of them devise, upon the engagement of the other, that he will likewise devise in manner therein mentioned. The instrument is the evidence of the agreement and he that dies first does by his death carry the agreement on his part into execution. If the other then refuses, he is guilty of fraud, can never unbind himself, and becomes a trustee, of course. For no man shall deceive another to his prejudice. By engaging to do something that is in his power, he is made a trustee for the performance, and transmits that claim under him.'

Assume that A and B agree that each will execute a will giving the other a life estate in their respective properties, with remainder to C. Should the survivor alter his will, his personal representative takes the property subject to the implied trust: *Re Green* (1951).

C's interest will arise as soon as either A or B dies. Should C die before the survivor, C's interest will not lapse: it will form a part of his estate and will be payable to his personal representatives.

In *Re Hagger* (1930), a husband (H) and wife (W) executed a joint will under which they gave all the property they possessed at the death of the first to the survivor for life, remainders over. H and W agreed that there should be neither revocation nor alteration save by mutual agreement. W died first; H took the income of the estate until he died. Three beneficiaries under the joint will survived W; all died before H. It was held that, from W's death, the property which H possessed was subject to a trust. The beneficiaries took vested interests in remainder, hence, their deaths, before that of H, did not result in any lapse of the shares which had accrued to them; the shares were payable to their personal representatives.

Per Clauson J:

'To my mind, *Dufour v Pereira* decides that where there is a joint will such as this, on the death of the first testator the position as regards that part of the property which belongs to the survivor is that the survivor will be treated in this court as holding the property on trust to apply it so as to carry out the effect of the joint will. As I read Lord Camden's judgment in *Dufour* that would be so, even though the survivor did not signify his election to give effect to the will be taking benefits under it. But in any case it is clear that Lord Camden has decided that if the survivor takes a benefit conferred on him by the joint will he will be treated as a trustee in this court, and he will not be allowed to do anything inconsistent with the provisions of the joint will. It is not necessary for me to consider the reasons on which Lord Camden based his judgment. The case must be accepted in this court as binding. Therefore I am bound to hold that from the death of the wife the husband held the property, according to the tenor of the will, subject to the trusts thereby imposed upon it, at all events if he took advantage of the provisions of the will. In my view he did take advantage of those provisions ...'

An implied trust will arise only where the wills of A and B are made in accordance with an arrangement. Such an arrangement will not be presumed from the coincidental execution of identical wills. Independent evidence of an agreement by A and B to create an interest for C is essential: *Re Oldham* (1925).

A will is always revocable. Before the death of a party to the agreement, either party may withdraw from the arrangement: *Stone v Hoskins* (1905). Notice of revocation must be given to the other party: see *Dufour v Pereira* (1769). Where the first party to die has revoked his will, the survivor who, on the death of that party, has notice of the revocation, cannot claim to have the later will of the deceased set aside (or indirectly enforced): *Stone v Hoskins* (1905).

The application of the doctrine of mutual wills was considered recently in *Re Dale* (1993). The court held that the doctrine was not to be confined to cases where the second testator to die benefited under the will of the testator who was the first to die when the aim of the principle underlying the doctrine was to prevent the latter individual from being defrauded. From this, it followed that the doctrine would apply also to those cases in which the two testators had left their property not to each other but to particular beneficiaries.

(i) Morritt J stated that the doctrine was to the effect that where two persons had agreed as to the disposal of their property and had executed mutual wills in pursuance of the agreement, then on the death of the first testator (T1), the property of the surviving testator (T2) (which was the subject matter of the agreement), was held on an implied trust for the beneficiary who had been named in the wills of T1 and T2. Because a will is inherently revocable, the survivor might thereafter alter it; but in such an event, his personal representatives would take the property subject to the trust. This fundamental doctrine was not in dispute.

(ii) The doctrine that no man shall deceive another to his prejudice (discussed in *Dufour v Pereira* (1769)) remained important in considering mutual wills. The doctrine applied when T2 benefited under the will of T1. It should not be any the less a fraud on T1 if the agreement was that each testator should leave his or her property to particular beneficiaries, such as their children, rather than to each other. It should be assumed that they had good reason for doing so; but, in any event it was that for which they had bargained. In each case a binding contract existed. In each case it had been performed by T1 on the faith of T2's promise. In each case T2 would have deceived T1 to the latter's detriment if T2 were allowed to go back on the agreement into which he had entered.

(iii) A fraud upon T1 should include those cases in which T2 derived benefit; yet there was no reason as to why the principle ought to be confined to cases of this nature. To hold that the principle should not be so confined was consistent with the authorities and was in furtherance of equity's original jurisdiction to intervene in cases of fraud.

8.2.2   Purchases in the name of another and analogous cases

Per Eyre CB in *Dyer v Dyer* (1788):

'The clear result of all the cases, without a single exception, is that the trust of a legal estate, whether freehold, copyhold, or leasehold; whether taken in the names of the purchasers and others jointly, or in the names of others without that of the purchaser; whether in one name or several; whether jointly or successive, results to the man who advances the purchase-money. This is a general proposition supported by all the cases, and there is nothing to contradict it; and it goes on a strict analogy to the rule of common law, that where a feoffment is made without consideration, the use results to the feoffor.'

The general principle (the underlying presumption of which is rebuttable) applies to land and pure personalty: see *The Venture* (1908). Where the result will be contrary to public policy, the principle will not be applied: *Groves v Groves* (1829). In this case the presumption of a trust did not operate where a person purchased an estate in the name of another so as to enable the nominal purchaser to vote at a parliamentary election. (The person in whom the property was vested held beneficially.)

'Where a man buys land in another's name and pays money, it will be in trust for him that pays the money, though no deed declaring the trust, for the Statute of Frauds [see now the Law of Property Act 1925, s 53(2)] does not extend to trusts raised by operation of the law': (1683) 2 Ventr 361. Hence: A purchases real or personal property in B's name; B will be presumed in equity to hold for A on a resulting trust. See *Gascoigne v Thwing* (1686).

A purchases real or personal property in the joint names of A and B. A and B are presumed in equity to hold on a resulting trust for A: *Benger v Drew* (1721). (Note, should A be B's husband, the presumption of advancement may apply.)

A and B purchase real or personal property in B's name. A resulting trust arises in favour of A as a proportionate beneficiary (in relation to the sum he has advanced). See *Wray v Steele* (1814); *Burns v Burns* (1984). In *Sekhon v Alissa* (1989), it was held that where mother and daughter both contributed to the purchase of property conveyed into the sole name of the daughter, there was a presumption of a resulting trust in favour of the mother, *unless* evidence could be established to show that the money was in the nature of a gift or a personal interest-free loan not intended to give rise to an interest. The mother had an interest in the property and the extent of that interest was determined by the amount of her contribution.

If the purchase is made by X and Y in unequal shares and the conveyance is made to X and Y jointly, then in the event of X's death Y is legally entitled to the entire property. He must hold X's share on trust for X's estate: *Cobb v Cobb* (1955). (But this has no application where the purchase was made in equal shares: *Lake v Gibson* (1729).) Where X and Y have jointly advanced money on mortgage in their joint names, and X dies, then whether the money was advanced in equal or unequal shares, Y will hold X's share on trust for X's estate: see *Morley v Bird* (1798).

Assume that X makes a voluntary transfer of his property to Y (a gift without consideration).

- In the case of a voluntary transfer of *personalty*, there is a presumption of a resulting trust for the transferor. In *Re Vinogradoff* (1935), X gratuitously transferred stock into the joint names of herself and her infant granddaughter. It was held that the stock was held upon a resulting trust for X's estate. 'The stock was not the property of the infant, but formed a part of the estate of the testatrix': *per* Farwell J.

- In the case of *realty*, the situation is covered by the Law of Property Act 1925, s 60(3): 'In a voluntary conveyance a resulting trust for the grantor shall not be implied merely by reason that the property is not expressed to be conveyed for the use or benefit of the grantee.'

| 8.2.3 | Failure to dispose of the beneficial interest |

A resulting trust will arise in favour of the donor or his representative where the trust does not disclose the method by which the beneficial interest should be applied, *or where it* directs application of the interest for a purpose which in the event does not exhaust the property, or where an express trust cannot be made effective. See *King v Denison* (1913).

In *Re Abbott Fund Trusts* (1990), money had been subscribed to a fund for the support of two handicapped ladies; no provision was made for its disposal on the death of the survivor. It was decided that the fund was to be held upon a resulting trust for the subscribers. *Per* Stirling J:

'The ladies are both dead, and the question is whether so far as this fund has not been applied for their benefit, there is a resulting trust for the subscribers. I cannot believe that it was ever intended to become the absolute property of the ladies so that they should be in a position to demand a transfer of it to themselves, or so that if they became bankrupt the trustee in bankruptcy should be able to claim it. I think that the trustee or trustees were intended to have a wide discretion as to whether any, and if any, what, part of the fund should be applied for the benefit of the ladies and how the application should be made. That view would not deprive them of all right in the fund, because if the trustees had not done their duty - if they either failed to exercise their discretion or exercised it improperly - the ladies might successfully have applied to the court to have the fund administered according to the terms of the circular [concerning subscriptions]. In the result, therefore, there must be a declaration that there is a resulting trust of the moneys remaining unapplied for the benefit of the subscribers to the fund.'

In *Re Gillingham Bus Disaster Fund* (1958) a fund was raised by subscription for the benefit of victims of an accident and for other causes. The trust failed as a charity (see Chapter 11); it was held that the surplus was to be held on a resulting trust for the donors, although many were anonymous. *Per* Harman J:

'The general principle must be that where money is held upon trust and the trusts declared do not exhaust the fund, it will revert to the donor or settlor under what is called a resulting trust. The reasoning behind this is that the settlor or donor did not part with his money absolutely but only *sub modo* to the intent that his wishes as declared by the declaration of trust should be carried into effect. When, therefore, this has been done any surplus belongs to him. This doctrine does not, in my judgment, rest on any evidence of the state of mind of the settlor, for in the vast majority of cases, no doubt, he does not expect to see his money back; he has created a trust which so far as he can see will absorb the whole of it. The resulting trust arises where that expectation is for some unforeseen reason cheated of fruition, and is an inference of law based on after-knowledge of the event.'

Where trustees hold property absolutely for a beneficiary who is alive when the trust is created, and who later dies intestate, leaving no person entitled on his intestacy, there is *no* resulting trust; in such a case the property goes to the Crown as *bona vacantia*: see Administration of Estates Act 1925, ss 45, 46.

In the case of the intentional creation of a trust for an illegal purpose, a resulting trust in favour of the settlor may be implied if that illegal purpose has not been executed or the result of permitting the trustee to keep the property will not involve the protection of a fraudulent activity: see *Law v Law* (1735); *Ayerst v Jenkins* (1873).	8.2.4 Trusts declared illegal

In *Chettiar v Chettiar* (1962), a Malayan father conveyed 40 acres of his rubber plantations to his son, so as to evade regulations concerning the ownership of those who owned more than 100 acres. In fact, he had no intention of giving the land to his son. The Privy Council held that the father would have to rebut the presumption of advancement and that this would necessitate his disclosing illegal conduct of which the court would be bound to take notice. The legal estate would lie, therefore, where it fell. ('Plaintiff stating that he had been guilty of a fraud upon the law ... and coming to equity to be relieved against his own act, and the defence being dishonest, between the two species of dishonesty the court would not act, but would say, "Let the estate lie where it falls".': *per* Lord Eldon in *Muckleston v Brown* (1801). 'Those who violate the law must not apply to the law for protection': *per* Lord Truro in *Benyon v Nettlefold* (1850).)

In *Rowan v Dann* (1992), X, a farmer, fearing that his creditors might take possession of his land, granted tenancies to D, with whom he was discussing a joint business venture.

No rent was paid because X remained entitled to shooting rights, which were not worth anything like the rents. The trial judge found that the leases were a sham, and that on the failure of the joint venture there was a resulting trust entitling X to have back his land free from tenancies. D appealed, arguing that a resulting trust ought not to be available to X because he did not have 'clean hands'. The Court of Appeal held that X was entitled to have back the land free of tenancies because the 'equitable balance' came down in his favour. The improper purpose was common to both sides. D had not suffered any disadvantage and X was entitled to withdraw from a transaction entered into for an improper purpose where that purpose had not been carried out.

8.3 **Presumption of advancement**	The general principle is that where a voluntary conveyance has been made to the wife or child of the donor or to a person to whom he stands *in loco parentis*, there will arise a presumption that a gift was intended.

Per Jessel MR in *Bennet v Bennet* (1879):

'The doctrine of equity as regards presumption of gifts is this, that where one person stands in such a relation to another that there is an obligation on that person to make a provision for the other, and we find either a purchase or investment in the name of the other, or in the joint names of the person and the other, of an amount which would constitute a provision for the other, the presumption arises of an intention on the part of the person to discharge the obligation to the other; and therefore, in the absence of evidence to the contrary, that purchase or investment is held to be in itself evidence of a gift. In other words, the presumption of gift arises from the moral obligation to give. That reconciles all the cases upon the subject but one, because nothing is better established than this, that as regards a child, a person not the father of the child may put himself in the position of one *in loco parentis* to the child, and so incur the obligation to make provision for the child ... A person *in loco parentis* means a person [see 8.3.3 below] taking upon himself the duty of a father of a child to make a provision for that child. It is clear that in that case the presumption can only arise from the obligation, and therefore in that case the doctrine can only have reference to the obligation of a father to provide for his child, and nothing else. But the father is under that obligation from the mere fact of his being the father, and therefore no evidence is necessary to show the obligation to provide for his child, because that is part of his duty. In the case of a father, you have only to prove the fact that he is the father, and when you have done that the obligation at once arises; but in the case of a person *in loco parentis* you must prove that he took upon himself the obligation.'

Assume that a husband buys property and that he has it conveyed to his wife, or that it is conveyed to both jointly. In the first circumstance it is considered *prima facie* as a gift to the wife; in the second, both hold, *prima facie*, as beneficial joint tenants. Should an intending husband buy property in his intended wife's name, then the presumption of a gift will arise if the marriage takes place: *Wirth v Wirth* (1956).

8.3.1   Presumption in relation to a wife

In general, where property is purchased by a father in the name of his child, then, *prima facie*, it is a gift to the child. See *Dyer v Dyer* (1788).

8.3.2   Presumption in relation to a child

A person *in loco parentis* is one who has taken on responsibilities for providing for a child in the way a parent would provide. 'I cannot put the doctrine so high as to hold that if a person educates a child to whom he is under no obligation either morally or legally the child is therefore to be provided for at his expense': *per* Page-Wood VC in *Tucker v Burrow* (1865).

8.3.3   Presumption in relation to a person acting *in loco parentis*

It is possible to rebut presumptions in relation to a resulting trust, advancement, and fraudulent or illegal purposes.

8.4   Rebutting the presumptions

The presumption of a resulting trust does not generally operate in the face of the presumption of advancement. It may be rebutted, additionally, by showing evidence of intention to benefit. Oral evidence may be admitted so as to establish the nature of the transaction in question: see Law of Property Act 1925, s 53(2).

8.4.1   Resulting trust

Note *Standing v Bowring* (1885), in which X transferred stock into the joint names of herself and Y, her godson, with the express intention that Y, should he survive her, was to have the stock, but that, during her life, she should retain the dividends. It was held that the presumption of a resulting trust had been rebutted effectively. *Per* Cotton LJ:

'The rule is well settled that where there is a transfer by a person into his own name jointly with that of a person who is not his child, or his adopted child, then there is *prima facie* a resulting trust for the transferor. But that is a presumption capable of being rebutted by showing that at the time the transferor intended a benefit to the transferee, and in the present case there is ample evidence that at the time of the transfer, and for some time previously, the plaintiff intended to confer a benefit on her late husband's godson [Y].'

8.4.2   Advancement

The presumption of advancement may be rebutted by evidence of actual intention.

Per Viscount Simonds in *Shephard v Cartwight* (1955):

'It must then be asked by what evidence can the presumption be rebutted, and it would, I think, be very unfortunate if any doubt were cast ... upon the well-settled law on the subject. It is, I think, correctly stated in substantially the same terms in every textbook that I have consulted and supported by authority extending over a long period of time. I will take, as an example, a passage from Snell's *Equity* (24th edition): "The acts and declarations of the parties before or at the time of purchase, or so immediately after it as to constitute a part of the transaction, are admissible in evidence either for or against the party who did the act or made the declaration ... But subsequent declarations are admissible as evidence only against the party who made them, and not in his favour." The burden of authority in favour of the broad proposition as stated in the passage I have cited is overwhelming and should not be disturbed.'

8.4.3   Fraudulent or illegal purpose

The presumption may not be rebutted by evidence that the transfer in question was made for a fraudulent or illegal purpose.

See, eg, *Re Emery's Investment Trusts* (1959) - the purpose of advancement was the evasion of tax.

In *Gascoigne v Gascoigne* (1918), a husband, H, took a lease of property in the name of his wife, W. H used W's name with her full knowledge; his intention was to protect the property from creditors. He argued that W held the property on a resulting trust for him, and attempted to rebut the presumption of advancement by evidence of his scheme intended to defraud creditors. *Per* Lush J:

'The findings of fact [by the county court judge] must be taken to mean that plaintiff, with his wife's knowledge and connivance, concocted the scheme of putting his property in her name, while retaining the beneficial interest, for the purpose of misleading, defeating, and delaying present or future creditors. This was the whole basis of plaintiff's case, and it could not be put in any other way consistently with his claim to be owner of the property. It was the reason he himself gave for his conduct. Now, assuming that there was evidence to support the finding that the defendant was a party to the scheme which plaintiff admitted, but without deciding it, what the learned judge has done is this: he has permitted plaintiff to rebut the presumption which the law raises by setting up his own illegality and fraud, and to obtain relief in equity because he has succeeded in proving it. Plaintiff cannot do this; and whether the point was taken or not in the county court, this court cannot allow a judgment to stand which has given relief under such circumstances as that.'

To whom the property results will differ according to whether the trust arises under an instrument *inter vivos* or a will.

8.5   To whom the property results

Under an instrument *inter vivos*, the beneficial interests result to the settlor. See *Symes v Hughes* (1870). (*Per* Lord Romilly: 'Where the purpose for which the assignment was given is not carried into execution, and nothing is done under it, the mere intention to effect an illegal object when the assignment was executed does not deprive the assignor of his right to recover the property from the assignee who has given no consideration for it'.)

8.5.1   Instrument *inter vivos*

Under a will, to whom the property results depends on the nature of the property in question.

8.5.2   Will

If the property is *realty*, it will result to those who are entitled to the testator's real property.

If the property is *personalty*, it results to those entitled to the testator's personal property. See *Curteis v Wormald* (1878).

The rule in *Lassence v Tierney* (1849) states, *per* Lord Davey:

'If you find an absolute gift to a legatee in the first instance, and trusts are engrafted or imposed on that absolute interest which fail, either from lapse or invalidity or any other reason, then the absolute gift takes effect so far as the trusts have failed to the exclusion of the residuary legatee or next-of-kin, as the case may be.'

In *Hancock v Watson* (1902), T gave property by his will to X. At a later point in the will he stated: 'But it is my will and mind that [the property] allotted to X shall remain in trust for her for life'. The remainder was left on trusts, but, in the event, they were void through remoteness.

It was held that, because the trusts in remainder had effectively failed, X would take the property *absolutely*.

Summary of Chapter 8

Implied and Resulting Trusts

It should be noted that 'implied' and 'resulting' are often used conterminously in this context.

Definitions and examples

An implied trust is enforced by the court as the result of surrounding circumstances, and language of the parties, so that effect may be given to implied, unexpressed intentions. Example: X purchases property in Y's name; there is an equitable presumption that X intended Y to hold the property in trust for him.

Implied trust

(*Resultare* = to spring back.) The resulting trust arises where the beneficial interest in property results to the person (or his representatives) who transferred the property to the trustee. Example: X transfers funds to trustees to be held on trusts of a marriage settlement and the marriage is later declared void *ab initio*. The fund is held on resulting trust for X.

Resulting trust

'Mutual wills' refers to wills made by agreement between persons to create irrevocable interests in favour of ascertainable beneficiaries. Should one testator revoke his will after the death of the other, who has not revoked his will, the interests created by the agreement may be enforceable in equity.

Mutual wills

Where A and B agree that each is to execute a will giving the other a life estate in their respective properties, remainder to C, and should the survivor alter his will, his personal representative takes subject to the implied trust: see *Re Green* (1951).

Before the death of a party to the agreement, either party may withdraw from the arrangement: *Stone v Hoskins* (1905).

Where A purchases real or personal property in B's name, B is presumed in equity to hold for A on resulting trust.

Purchase in the name of another, etc

Where A purchases real or personal property in the joint names of A and B, then, in equity, A and B are presumed to hold on resulting trust for A.

Where A and B purchase real or personal property in B's name, a resulting trust arises in favour of A as a proportionate beneficiary (in relation to the sum he has advanced). See *Sekhon v Alissa* (1989).

Where a purchase is made by X and Y in unequal shares and a conveyance is made to X and Y jointly, in the event of X's death, Y is entitled to the entire property, but he must hold X's share on trust for X's estate. See *Cobb v Cobb* (1955); *Lake v Gibson* (1729).

Failure to dispose of beneficial interest

A resulting trust arises in favour of the donor or his personal representative where the trust does not disclose the method by which the beneficial interest should be applied, or where it directs the application of the interest for a purpose which fails to exhaust the property, or where the express trust cannot be made effective. See *Re Abbott Fund Trusts* (1900).

Trusts declared illegal

In the case of the intentional creation of a trust for an illegal purpose, a resulting trust may be implied in the settlor's favour if the illegal purpose has not been executed, or the result of permitting the trustee to keep the property will not involve protecting a fraudulent activity. See *Ayerst v Jenkins* (1873).

Presumption of advancement

Where a voluntary conveyance has been made to the wife or child of the donor or to a person to whom he stands *in loco parentis*, there is a presumption that a gift was intended. Thus, where property is purchased by a father in the name of his child, then, *prima facie*, it is a gift to the child: see *Dyer v Dyer* (1788). The presumption may be rebutted by evidence of actual intention.

To whom property results

Where the trust arises under an instrument *inter vivos*: the beneficial interests result to the settlor.

Where the trust arises under will and the property is realty: the property results to those entitled to the testator's real property. Where the trust arises under will and the property is personalty: the property results to those entitled to the testator's personal property.

Chapter 9

Constructive Trusts

The term 'constructive' is used in this context to mean 'inferred, presumed from circumstances, arising from the construing of facts'. A constructive trust is one which is imposed by the courts irrespective of the express or presumed intentions of the parties, in the interests of conscience and justice. Thus: X, a stranger, knowingly receives trust property, being aware that it has been transferred to him in breach of trust; X holds that property for the beneficiaries upon a constructive trust: see *Lee v Sankey* (1873).

Per Cardozo J in *Beatty v Guggenheim Exploration Co* (1919):

'A constructive trust is the formula through which the conscience of equity finds expression. When property has been acquired in such circumstances that the holder of the legal title may not in good conscience retain the beneficial interest, equity converts him into a trustee.'

The essence of the constructive trust is, therefore, that although title may be in X, the beneficial interest is in Y, as a result of the operation of the rules of equity, and this will be so irrespective of the intentions of either X or Y. The doctrine will not apply to a transaction involving an express declaration of trust: *Pink v Lawrence* (1977). The Court of Appeal considered, in this case, circumstances arising where a house was conveyed to plaintiff and defendant as joint tenants in law and equity. Subsequently, plaintiff claimed that defendant had been joined on the transfer only to satisfy the mortgagees, having contributed nothing to the price, so that the property was held on a constructive trust for plaintiff's benefit alone. Plaintiff sought an order requiring defendant to transfer all his interest in the property. Defendant claimed an interest on the ground of having paid £500 towards the purchase price. A ruling by the Master stated that defendant could not establish an interest unless he proved that he had paid £500 and that the sum was paid towards the purchase price. Defendant's appeal was allowed: in the absence of rescission by reason of mistake or fraud or a claim to rectify the transfer, the express declaration of trust contained in the transfer precluded any implication of a constructive trust.

Per Lord Herschell in *Bray v Ford* (1896):

'It is an inflexible rule of a Court of Equity that a person in a fiduciary position ... is not, unless otherwise expressly

9.1 Essence of the constructive trust

9.2 Profits made by a person in a fiduciary position

provided, entitled to make a profit; he is not allowed to put himself in a position where his interest and duty conflict. It does not appear to me that this rule is, as has been said, founded upon principles of morality. I regard it rather as based on the consideration that, human nature being what it is, there is danger, in such circumstances, of the person holding a fiduciary position being swayed by interest rather than by duty, and thus prejudicing those whom he was bound to protect. It has, therefore, been deemed expedient to lay down this positive rule. But I am satisfied that it might be departed from in many cases, without a breach of morality, without any wrong being inflicted, and without any consciousness of wrong-doing. Indeed, it is obvious that it might sometimes be to the advantage of the beneficiaries that their trustee should act for them professionally rather than a stranger, even though the trustee were paid for his services.'

The fiduciary relationship may arise, eg, where X entrusts property to Y, relying on Y to deal with it for X's benefit or for purposes authorised by X and in no other way: see *Reading v A-G* (1951). X, a soldier serving in Egypt, assisted criminals to smuggle drugs to places in Cairo; his task was to accompany the criminals' vehicles, wearing his army uniform so that they might not be subject to police search. He was arrested; the Crown seized money in his bank account. X brought a petition of right to recover that money. The House of Lords held that money acquired by X, as a result of a use of his uniform in breach of his duty to the Crown could be retained by the Crown as money had and received to its use, so that X's petition failed.

Per Lord Porter:

'Any official position, whether marked by a uniform or not, which enables the holder to earn money by its use gives his master a right to receive the money so earned even though it was earned by a criminal act. "You have earned", the master can say, "money by the use of your position as my servant. It is not for you, who have gained this advantage, to set up your own wrong as a defence to my claim.".'

The rule applies to *all* persons in a fiduciary position, not merely to trustees. It operates for the protection of the person to whom the duty is owed and that person alone may relax it: see *Boulting v ACTAT* (1963).

9.2.1   Lessee

In *Keech v Sandford* (1726), the lessee of profits of a market devised the lease to a trustee for an infant. The trustee obtained a renewal of the lease for himself, and the court held that the lease was to be held in trust for the infant, and that an account of profits made since the renewal was to be given. *Per* Lord King:

'I must consider this as a trust for the infant, for I very well see, if a trustee, on the refusal to renew, might have a lease to himself, few trust estates would be renewed to *cestui que use*. Though I do not say there is fraud in this case, yet he should rather have let it run out than to have had the lease to himself. This may seem hard, that the trustee is the only person of all mankind who might not have the lease, but it is very proper that the rule should be strictly pursued, and not in the least relaxed; for it is very obvious what would be the consequences of letting trustees have the lease on refusal to renew to *cestui que use*.'

The rule was later extended to those who have a partial interest in a lease, eg, tenant for life (*Randall v Russell* (1817)), tenant in common (*Hunter v Allen* (1907)). Where the lessee can establish that he has not abused his position, the presumption that the renewed lease is held on constructive trust may be rebutted and he may be allowed to keep the lease for his own benefit.

In *Re Biss* (1903), X carried on a business in premises leased to him for a seven-year period. X continued as a yearly tenant on expiration of the lease. He died later and his widow and son, S, applied for renewal of the lease, but it was refused. At a later date a new lease was granted to S. It was held that S was *not* in breach of a fiduciary duty and could hold the lease beneficially.

Significant extracts from the decision of the Court of Appeal (*per* Collins MR) are set out below:

(i)   'In the present case the appellant is simply one of the next of kin of the former tenant, and had, as such, a possible interest in the term. He was not, as such, a trustee for the others interested, nor was he in possession. The administratrix [the widow] represented the estate and alone had the right to renew, and she unquestionably could renew only for the benefit of the estate. But is the appellant in the same category? Or is he entitled to go into the facts to show that he has not, in point of fact, abused his position, or in any sense intercepted an advantage coming by way of accretion to the estate? He did not take under a will or settlement with interests coming after his own, but simply got a possible share upon an intestacy in case there was a surplus of assets over debts.'

(ii) 'It seems to me that his obligation cannot be put much higher than that of any other tenant in common against whom it would have to be established, not as a presumption of law but as an inference of fact, that he had abused his position. If he is not under a personal incapacity to take a benefit, he is entitled to show that the renewal was not in fact an accretion to the original term, and that it was not until there had been an absolute refusal on the part of the lessor, and after full opportunity to the administratrix to procure it for the estate if she could, that he accepted a proposal of renewal made to him by the lessor.'

(iii) 'These questions cannot be considered or discussed when the party is by his decision debarred from keeping a personal advantage derived directly or indirectly out of his fiduciary or quasi-fiduciary position; but when he is not so debarred I think it becomes a question of fact whether that which he has received was in his hands an accretion to the interests of the deceased, or whether the connection between the estate and the renewal had not been wholly severed by the action of the lessor before the appellant accepted a new lease. This consideration seems to get rid of any difficulty that one of the next of kin was an infant. The right or hope of renewal incident to the estate was determined before the plaintiff intervened.'

In *Protheroe v Protheroe* (1968), it was held that the trustee of a lease could not under any circumstances purchase the freehold for his own benefit. *Per* Lord Denning:

'There is a long established rule of equity from *Keech v Sandford* downwards that if a trustee who owns the leasehold gets in the freehold, that freehold belongs to the trust, and he cannot take the property for himself.'

9.2.2   Directors

'Directors of a limited company are the creatures of statute. In some respects they resemble trustees; in others they do not': *per* Lord Russell in *Regal (Hastings) Ltd v Gulliver* (1942). The rule in *Keech v Sandford* does apply to them and they are accountable for any profits made by them based on knowledge acquired as directors.

The facts in *Regal (Hastings) Ltd* were as follows:

R Ltd established a subsidiary, A Ltd, so as to acquire leases of two cinemas. A Ltd had an authorised share capital of some 5,000 £1 ordinary shares. The cinema owner agreed to the lease, conditional upon the share capital of A Ltd being completely subscribed for. In fact, the resources of R Ltd allowed it to subscribe for only 2,000 of the 5,000 shares. It was arranged and agreed that the directors of R Ltd should subscribe for the remaining 3,000 shares. The directors did this and, later, when the business of R Ltd was transferred to new controllers, the directors derived a profit from their holdings in A Ltd. The new controllers of R Ltd caused the company to bring an action against the former directors of R Ltd to account for that profit which, they claimed, had been made from their office. It was held that the directors had made the profit from their position as directors of the firm, and, because there had been no approval of their action by shareholders, they were under a duty to account.

Directors may not take advantage of their position to enter into contracts with their company.

A director with an interest in a contract with the company must disclose it to the whole board and not just to a directors' committee. If he fails to do so he will be a constructive trustee of the benefits transferred: *Guinness v Saunders* (1990). In this case, two defendants and a director of the X company, agreed to pay the second defendant £5m for his assistance and advice in a take-over bid which plaintiffs were making. X company, having paid the sum, later claimed recovery, arguing that the second defendant was in breach of his fiduciary duty as a director in that he had not disclosed his interest in the agreement to the directors of X company. ('It is the duty of a director of a company who is in any way, whether directly or indirectly, interested in a contract or proposed contract with the company to declare the nature of his interest at a meeting of the directors of the company': Companies Act 1985, s 317(1).) The House of Lords dismissed an appeal from the decision of the Court of Appeal, holding that the second defendant was not entitled to any of the money, whether on a *quantum meruit* basis, or as an equitable allowance. He was in breach of his fiduciary duty to avoid a conflict of personal interest and duty to the company. Section 317 stressed the significance which the legislature places upon the principle that a company must be protected against a director involved in a conflict of interests.

9.2.3 Agents

Where property is handed to an agent for sale, safe custody or investment, he is considered as a trustee of that property: *Burdick v Garrick* (1870). A solicitor to whom funds are handed for investment, or who receives money arising from the exercise of a client's power of sale is a trustee: *Dooby v Watson* (1888).

In *Boardman v Phipps* (1966), X, a solicitor, and Y, a director of P Ltd, arranged to acquire shares in, and control of, L Ltd. L Ltd owned a block of shares in P Ltd. The shares in L Ltd were owned by a trust. X acted as solicitor for the trust, and he and Y made a very large profit as a result of the dealings. This was done with the knowledge of the trustees and beneficiaries. However, one of the beneficiaries, Z, claimed not to have understood the scope of the dealings and not to have the received the expert advice necessary in the circumstances. Were X and Y to be regarded as constructive trustees for Z of the proportion of the profit which could be attributed to Z's share of the trust holding? *Per* Lord Hodson:

'The problem of law involved in this case is that no person standing in a fiduciary position, when a demand is made on him by the person to whom he stands in the fiduciary relationship to account for profits acquired by him by reason of his fiduciary position and by reason of the opportunity and the knowledge, or either, resulting from it, is entitled to defeat the claim on any ground save that he made profits with the knowledge and assent of the other person.'

The House of Lords held that X and Y had been enabled to make a profit by reason of a fiduciary relationship and were liable to account for it. But having acted with complete honesty throughout the dealings they were entitled to payment 'on a liberal scale' for their work and skill.

Per Lord Cohen:

'I desire to repeat that the integrity of the appellants is not in doubt. They acted with complete honesty throughout and the respondent is a fortunate man in that the rigour of equity enables him to participate in the profits which have accrued as the result of the action taken by the appellants ... in purchasing the shares at their own risk ... The trial judge evidently shared this view. He directed an inquiry as to what sum is proper to be allowed to the appellants or either of them in respect of his work and skill in obtaining the said shares and the profits in respect thereof. The trial judge concluded by expressing the opinion that payment should be on a liberal scale. With that observation I respectfully agree.'

9.3 Vendor under a contract for sale of land

Where there is a specifically enforceable contract for the sale of land, the purchaser becomes the owner of the land in equity, and 'the vendor of the estate is, as from the time of his contract, considered as trustee for the purchaser': *per* Lord Hardwicke in *Green v Smith* (1738). Until completion the vendor retains a beneficial interest in the property; he may occupy it and enjoy rent and profits until completion. He must maintain the property with the care required from a trustee and, should he wilfully damage the property he is liable in damages for breach of trust. See *Cumberland Consolidation Holdings v Ireland* (1946).

9.4 Mortgagee exercising the power of sale

A mortgagee who has exercised the statutory power of sale and is in possession of mortgage money is a trustee for that money. 'The money which is received by the mortgagee, arising from the sale, after discharge of prior incumbrances to which the sale is not made subject, if any, or after payment into court under this Act of a sum to meet any prior incumbrance, shall be held in trust by him ...': Law of Property Act 1925, s 106. See also *Cuckmere Brick Co v Mutual Finance* (1971).

Where a person has acquired property as a direct consequence of his fraudulent conduct towards another, he is considered in equity as a constructive trustee for the person injured as a result of that conduct: see *Sellack v Harris* (1708). In *Bulkeley v Wilford* (1834), the testator's solicitor, who was also his heir-presumptive, advised him to perform an act which, unknown to the testator, was an effective revocation of the will. It was held that the heir was a constructive trustee for the devisees. See also *Bannister v Bannister* (1948).

9.5   Property acquired by fraud

In *Re Crippen* (1911), C murdered his wife who had died intestate. C was hanged and, in his will, left property to his mistress, X. X was not entitled to the wife's estate because C was never beneficially entitled to it. A constructive trust was imposed for those entitled. See also *Re Giles* (1971) (a person guilty of killing another, although suffering from diminished responsibility may not profit under that other's will or intestacy); Forfeiture Act 1982, allowing the court to modify the public policy rule preventing a person who has unlawfully killed another from acquiring a benefit from that death, where the justice of the case so requires, having regard to the conduct of the offender, or the deceased, or other material circumstances.

9.6   Property acquired as the result of an unlawful killing

A stranger who knowingly receives trust property and knows also that it has come to him in breach of trust will hold that property upon constructive trust for the beneficiaries: *Rolfe v Gregory* (1865). See *Nelson v Larholt* (1948). Even though the stranger has received the trust property innocently, if he deals subsequently with it in a manner not consistent with the performance of the trust of which he has become aware, he holds upon constructive trust: *Lee v Sankey* (1873). It is immaterial that the stranger has gained no personal advantage: *Carl-Zeiss Stiftung v Herbert Smith & Co (No 2)* (1969).

9.7   Stranger receiving trust property

A person who knowingly assists in a 'fraudulent design' by the trustees, even though he receives no trust property, becomes a constructive trustee: *Eaves v Hickson* (1861).

Note *Agip v Jackson* (1991): where an employee has practised fraud on his employer with the assistance of a third party, that party is liable in equity as a constructive trustee for funds of which they had disposed and which could be traced.

Per Ungoed-Thomas in *Selangor Rubber Estates Ltd v Cradock (No 3)* (1968):

'Knowledge is interpreted thus: The knowledge required to hold a stranger liable as constructive trustee in a dishonest and fraudulent design is knowledge of circumstances which would indicate to an honest, reasonable man that such a design was being committed or would put him on enquiry, which the stranger failed to make, whether it was being committed.'

In *Karak Rubber Co v Burden (No 2)* (1972), K Ltd was a dormant company with a large bank balance with the X Bank. B bought the company and arranged for payment of the shares in a way which resulted in the company's own money being used for their purchase. The company later went into liquidation. It was held that the bank was liable in negligence in that it failed to perform its duty with reasonable care, and that the X Bank and B were constructive trustees of the money.

In *Baden Delvaux* (1992), Gibson J considered the categories of 'knowledge' which would be sufficient to found liability in a case in which a third party knowingly assists trustees to commit a breach of trust (thereby becoming himself a constructive trustee). The categories were: actual knowledge; wilfully closing one's eyes to the obvious; wilfully and recklessly failing to make such enquiries as an honest and reasonable person would make; knowledge of circumstances which would indicate the facts to a reasonable and honest man; knowledge of circumstances which would put a reasonable and honest man on enquiry.

In *Re Montagu's ST* (1987) it was held that it is unlikely that there could ever be 'imputed knowledge' in relation to the imposition of a constructive trust. See also *Lipkin Gorman v Karpnale Ltd* (1989); *Eagle Trust v SBC Securities* (1991) - it is not possible for a person to become a constructive trustee for 'knowing assistance' in a fraudulent design if he had no actual knowledge of the fraudulent nature of the design, if it were not possible for a reasonable man to infer such knowledge from the circumstances, and the person had acted without any dishonesty or lack of probity.

The phrase 'dishonest and fraudulent design' was considered in *Selangor Rubber Estates Ltd v Cradock (No 3)* (1968) in which it was held not to be a term of art. The words, *per* Ungoed-Thomas J:

'are to be understood according to the plain principles of a court of equity ... which in this context at any rate are just plain, ordinary commonsense. I accept that "dishonest and fraudulent", so understood, is certainly conduct which is morally reprehensible; but what is morally reprehensible is best left open to identification and not to be confined by definition.'

9.8   Trustee *de son tort*

Where a person who is not a trustee and who has no authority from a trustee takes upon himself to intermeddle with trust matters or to carry out acts which are characteristic of the office of trustee, he makes himself a trustee *de son tort* (trustee 'of his own wrongdoing') and is held to be a constructive trustee. See, eg, *Re Barney* (1892) (in order to be considered a trustee *de son tort*, a person ought to have the trust property vested in him); *Mara v Browne* (1896).

Per Bennett J, in *Williams-Ashman v Price and Williams* (1942):

'*Mara v Browne* seems to me to be a decision that an agent in possession of money which he knows to be trust money, so long as he acts honestly, is not accountable to the beneficiaries interested in the trust money unless he intermeddles in the trust by doing acts characteristic of a trustee and outside the duties of an agent.'

See also *Re Bell's Indenture* (1980).

In English law the constructive trust is seen as a special variety of trust, ie, a *substantive relationship* between trustee and beneficiary. This is in contrast to the view in the USA, where the constructive trust is viewed as a *remedy*, available to a person entitled to restitution. Thus, in *Hussey v Palmer* (1972), Lord Denning spoke of the constructive trust in terms which seemed to lean towards the American interpretation: '[The constructive trust] is an equitable remedy by which the court can enable an aggrieved party to obtain restitution'. In *Re Sharpe* (1980), Lord Denning's view was criticised by Browne-Wilkinson J, who noted that the court must first discover a right that has been infringed in order to provide a remedy. See also *Baumgartner v Baumgartner* (1988).	**9.9 Right or remedy**

Problems of establishing an interest in the family home may emerge from disputes which arise when a marriage has broken down or when a relationship involving an unmarried couple ends. The doctrine of constructive trusts has been utilised in this area of dispute. See also the Matrimonial Proceedings and Property Act 1970 and the Matrimonial Causes Act 1973.	**9.10 The constructive trust and the family home**

In *Hussey v Palmer* (1972), Lord Denning suggested that whether a trust is resulting or constructive is merely a matter of words. The two run together and are imposed 'when justice and good conscience require it'. (He had reached this conclusion by reference to the judgment of Lord Diplock in *Gissing v Gissing* (1971) which, in relation to a matter concerning interests in the family home, stated that it was unnecessary 'for present purposes' to distinguish between a resulting, implied and constructive trust.)

Lord Denning held that he was able to impose a constructive trust whenever this was required in the interests of justice and conscience; intention of the parties was of no relevance.

In *Eves v Eves* (1975) the court considered the case of a single woman who had entered into a relationship with a married man. She took his name and had two children by him. He bought a house which he promised to put into their joint names. Because she was not yet 21, he told her, he would do this later. At a later date he deserted her. She had not made any financial contribution but had done much work in the house and garden and had cared for the children. She was awarded a one-quarter share in the property. *Per* Lord Denning:

'In view of [Mr Eves'] conduct it would, I think, be most inequitable for him to deny her any share in the house. The law will impute or impose a constructive trust by which he was to hold it in trust for them both.'

Lord Denning stated further: 'Equity is not past the age of child-bearing. One of her latest progeny is *a constructive trust of a new model*. Lord Diplock brought it into the world and we have nourished it.'

These views were challenged vigorously: see, eg, *Carly v Farrelly* (1975); *Muschinski v Dodds* (1985) (which criticised the leaving open to the court, in accordance with Lord Denning's concept of the 'new model', consideration of 'a formless void of individual moral opinion').

9.11   The significance of common intention

Lord Denning's approach is no longer accepted. There must now be demonstrated a *common intention* that the party claiming an interest in the family home should have a beneficial interest in it.

In *Burns v Burns* (1984), X and Y lived together but did not marry. In 1963 X bought a house which was conveyed into his name. Y did not contribute directly to the purchase price or mortgage payments. She looked after the house and the children, paid rates and telephone bills. In 1980 the relationship ended and Y claimed a beneficial interest in the house. *Per* Fox LJ:

'If the plaintiff is to establish that she has a beneficial interest in the property, she must establish that the defendant holds the legal estate upon trust to give effect to that interest. That follows from *Gissing v Gissing* (1971). For present purposes I think that such a trust can only arise (a) by express declaration or agreement *or* (b) by way of a resulting trust where the claimant has directly provided part of the purchase price *or* (c) from the common intention of the parties.'

Points (a) and (b) did not apply and Y's case rested upon her being able to demonstrate a common intention that she should have a beneficial interest in the property. Nothing had occurred between the parties at the time of the acquisition of the house and thereafter to raise an equity which would prevent X denying Y's claim. Y had not been able to establish any trust in her favour. (See also *Windeler v Whitehall* (1990).)

In *Grant v Edwards* (1986), X and Y, who were not married, set up house together. X purchased a house in the joint names of X and his brother. X told Y that her name had not been placed on the title to the house because such an act would have adversely affected divorce proceedings pending against Y's husband. X paid the deposit and mortgage instalments; Y contributed substantially to the upkeep of the home. Following their separation, Y claimed a beneficial interest in the home.

The court held that Y would have to show, in order to establish a constructive trust, a common intention and also that 'she did act to her detriment on the faith of the common intention between her and the defendant that she was to have some sort of proprietary interest in the house': *per* Nourse LJ. This was shown and Y was held entitled to a half share in the house.

In *Lloyds Bank v Rosset* (1990), H purchased a semi-derelict property for himself and his wife, Y, which was intended as a matrimonial home for them. The purchase money was provided by H, and the house was conveyed into H's name. W carried out restoration work on the house. The couple later separated and W claimed a beneficial interest under a constructive trust.

The House of Lords decided that W had no beneficial interest. There was no evidence of any express agreement as to how a beneficial interest was to be held; indeed, there was no evidence of such an agreement. A common intention might be inferred from a direct contribution by W to the purchase price. Further, the work done by W on the restoration of the property was insufficient to establish a common intention that H and W were to hold jointly. W, therefore, held no interest in the property.

In *Ungurian v Lesnoff* (1989), X, a Polish citizen, gave up her career, nationality, and flat in Poland, to live with Y who bought a house in London in his name. X and Y lived in the house as man and wife, and X carried out significant improvements to the property. She remained in the house after the relationship ended and claimed a beneficial interest in the property.

It was held that there was a common intention that X would have the right to reside in the property for life. The house was to be considered as settled land, and X was a tenant for life in accordance with the Settled Land Act 1925. She was entitled to call for a vesting deed, appoint trustees, and sell the house, reinvesting the proceeds in another house.

Constructive Trusts

A constructive trust is one imposed by the courts, irrespective of the express or presumed intentions of the parties, in the interests of conscience and justice.

    Example: X, a stranger, knowingly receives trust property, being aware that it has been transferred to him in breach of trust. X will hold that property upon a constructive trust for the beneficiaries. See *Lee v Sankey* (1873).

Definition and example

A person in a fiduciary position is not entitled to make a profit and to put himself in a position where interest and duty conflict. See *Bray v Ford* (1896). This rule applies to all persons in fiduciary positions. See *Keech v Sandford* (1726). Thus, directors may not take advantage of their position to enter into contracts with their company. See *Boardman v Phipps* (1966).

    Where property is handed to an agent for sale, or safe custody, he is considered as a trustee of that property. See *Dooby v Watson* (1888)

Profit made by person in fiduciary position

The vendor of an estate is, as from the time of his contract, considered as a trustee for the purchaser.

Vendor under contract for sale of land

A mortgagee who has exercised the statutory power of sale and is in possession of mortgage money is a trustee for that money. See Law of Property Act 1925, s 106; *Cuckmere Brick Co v Mutual Finance* (1971).

Mortgagee exercising the power of sale

Where a person has acquired property as the direct consequence of his having behaved fraudulently to another, he is considered in equity as a constructive trustee for the other person who has suffered as a result of that fraud: *Sellack v Harris* (1708).

Property acquired by fraud

A person guilty of unlawfully killing another may not profit under that other's will or intestacy. See Forfeiture Act 1982. See *Re Crippen* (1911).

Property acquired as the result of an unlawful killing

One who knowingly receives trust property and is aware that he has received it as the result of a breach of trust holds it on constructive trust for the beneficiaries. It is immaterial that the stranger has gained no personal advantage.

Stranger receiving trust property

The knowledge required to hold a stranger liable is knowledge of the circumstances which would indicate to an honest, reasonable man that fraud was being committed.

It is unlikely that there could ever be 'imputed knowledge' in relation to the imposition of a constructive trust. See *Eagle Trust v SBC Securities* (1991).

Trustee *de son tort*

Where a person who is not a trustee and has no authority from a trustee takes it upon himself to intermeddle with trust matters he makes himself a trustee *de son tort* (trustee 'of his own wrongdoing'), and is held to be a constructive trustee.

The constructive trust and the family home

Where X and Y set up a home and there is a subsequent separation, and Y claims a beneficial interest in the property, a common intention that Y should have such an interest must be demonstrated. See *Gissing v Gissing* (1971); *Grant v Edwards* (1986); *Ungarian v Lesnoff* (1989).

Chapter 10

Unlawful and Voidable Trusts and Trusts of Imperfect Obligation

Unlawful trusts, ie, those which are illegal because they contravene statute or common law or are contrary to principles of public policy and general morality, are *not enforceable* by the courts. Not only are such trusts ineffective, but the courts will not assist a settlor to recover his property in such circumstances. *Voidable trusts* are exemplified by the Law of Property Act 1925, s 173(1), by which a voluntary disposition of land made with the intention of defrauding a purchaser is voidable at his instance. *Trusts of imperfect obligation* are intended for a non-charitable purpose and are characterised by their having no beneficiaries; with some important exceptions, trusts of this type are void.

10.1 Essence of trusts of these types

The following types of trust are included under the general heading of 'unlawful' and will be declared void.

10.2 Unlawful trusts

The rule against perpetuities attempts to make property inalienable by the settlor's insistence upon the passing of a very long period of time before the vesting of an interest. The common law rule states that where there is a possibility that a future interest in property might vest after the expiration of the 'perpetuity period', such an interest will be void. At *common law* the perpetuity period consists of lives in being at the time the instrument creating the interest becomes effective, *plus* 21 years and any gestation period.

10.2.1 Trusts which offend the rule against perpetuities

The rule is concerned not with probabilities and actual events, but with *possibilities*.

Under the Perpetuities and Accumulations Act 1964, s 1(1), the settlor may specify a perpetuity period not exceeding *eighty years*.

Under the 1964 Act, s 3, it is now possible to 'wait and see' whether or not an interest does actually vest within the perpetuity period; where it does not actually vest it is declared void.

Where a donor purports to make a gift which prevents capital and income being alienated for a period which exceeds the common law perpetuity period (ie, life in being plus 21 years), the trust is void. It should be noted that the rule has no application to charitable trusts (see Chapter 11).

10.2.2 Trusts which offend the rule against 'perpetual trusts'

10.2.3	Trusts which offend the rule against accumulations	The rule at law relating to the period for which income could be accumulated was linked to the rule against perpetuities. Changes were introduced by the Accumulations Act 1800 (enacted following *Thellusson v Woodford* (1798)), the Law of Property Act 1925, ss 164-166, the Perpetuities and Accumulations Act 1964, s 13, and the Family Law Reform Act 1969, Sch 3 para 7. Statutory periods determining accumulation depend upon whether the trust arises under an *inter vivos* settlement, or is created by will.

In the case of a *settlement inter vivos*, the settlor may not direct the accumulation of income for longer than any one (only) of the following periods: 21 years from the death of the settlor; 21 years from the date of the settlement; the settlor's life; the minority of a person who is living (or is *en ventre sa mère*) at the date of the settlor's death; the minority of a person living (or *en ventre sa mère*) at the date of the settlement; the minority of a person who, under the terms of the settlement, would, were he of full age, would be entitled to the income directed to be accumulated.

In the case of a *settlement created under a will*, the settlor may not direct the accumulation of income for longer than any one (only) of the following periods: 21 years from the death of the testator; the minority of any one living (or *en ventre sa mère*) at the testator's death; the minority of any person who, under the terms of the will, were he of full age, would be entitled to the income directed to be accumulated.

Where there is a direction to accumulate for a period in excess of the common law perpetuity period, such a direction is *void in toto*: *Curtis v Lukin* (1842). Where a direction does not infringe the general perpetuity period, but does exceed the appropriate statutory period, such a direction is *not void in toto*, but is void only in so far as it exceeds that statutory period: see *Griffiths v Vere* (1803).

An appropriate statutory period will be determined by the court, taking into account what period the settlor had in mind, or whichever approximates closest to his intentions: see *Lady Rosslyn's Trust* (1848).

Where the settlor's direction is void, the income passes to that person who would have been entitled had the direction to accumulate not have been given: see the Law of Property Act 1925, s 164(1).

10.2.4	Trusts in restraint of marriage	The general rule is that a trust in *total restraint* of marriage will be *void*, and this will be so even where the objective of the condition seems not to be the imposition of a total restraint if that is the probable result: see *Lloyd v Lloyd* (1852).

A clause restricting marriage with a particular person, or preventing a second marriage, is a *partial restraint* and may be valid: see *Jenner v Turner* (1880).

A trust until marriage, and then over, is valid: see *Morley v Rennoldson* (1843).

Should the settlor's intention be not restraint of marriage, but primarily to ensure some other objective, a gift over in the event of marriage may be upheld: see *Re Hewett* (1918).

In *Leong v Chye* (1955), Lord Radcliffe noted the differences concerning a particular restraint imposed on realty and personalty:

> 'For, whereas a condition subsequent in partial restraint of marriage was effective to determine the estate in the case of a devise of *realty* even without any new limitation to take effect on the forfeiture, so that a residuary devisee or heir came in of his own right, it was early determined and consistently maintained that a condition subsequent in partial restraint of marriage, when annexed to a bequest of *personalty*, was ineffective to destroy the gift unless the will in question contained an explicit gift over of the legacy to another legatee. And for this purpose a mere residuary bequest was not treated as a gift over.'

Trusts which have the effect of encouraging any weakening of the sanctity of the marriage bond, or which tend to interfere with parental duties, or encourage the separation of parent and child, are considered as contrary to public policy and will be void. See *Re Borwick* (1933).

10.2.5   Trusts designed to induce separation of husband and wife, or parent and child

A trust designed to become effective on a future separation of husband and wife will be held void. A trust based upon a separation which is already agreed on will be held valid: see *Re Caborne* (1943).

A condition that a married woman live apart from her husband was held void: *Wren v Bradley* (1848).

In *Re Thompson* (1939), the testator, T, gave an annuity to his daughter if still married 'to her present husband'; but she would receive the income of the entire estate should she be widowed or be remarried to some other person. It was held that the provision was *not* contrary to public policy, since T's real purpose was to prevent income falling into the hands of the husband who was considered by T to be a spendthrift.

10.2.6   Trusts for illegitimate children

The general rule was that a trust for an unborn illegitimate child was void, on the ground of public policy (which interpreted such a trust as likely to promote immorality).

Note the Family Law Reform Act 1969, s 15(7): 'Any rule of law that a disposition in favour of illegitimate children not in being when the disposition takes effect is void as contrary to public policy' is abolished. See the Family Law Reform Act 1987 which repealed and replaced the 1969 Act, s 15.

The old law continues to apply to dispositions made before 1st January, 1970.

| 10.2.7 | Trusts made illegal by statute |

The Race Relations Act 1976 declares unlawful any discrimination on grounds of colour, ethnic origins etc. A provision in a charitable instrument which provides for conferring benefits on persons of a class defined by reference to colour will be disregarded: see s 34(1). See also the Sex Discrimination Act 1975, s 43 (as amended by SI 1977/528).

| 10.2.8 | Trusts involving directions of a purely capricious nature |

See *Brown v Burdett* (1882) in which a direction that all the rooms in the house of the testatrix were to be blocked up for twenty years was held void.

| 10.2.9 | Trusts designed to encourage a breach of law |

A trust which was designed with the objective of encouraging a breach of the criminal law would be held void. See *Thrupp v Collett* (1858) (a trust to pay fines imposed on poachers was held void).

10.3   Voidable trusts

Trusts of this nature are often designed with the intention of defrauding the settlor's creditors. The appropriate legislation is to be found in the Insolvency Act 1986 and the Law of Property Act 1925.

| 10.3.1 | Transactions entered into at an undervalue |

The Insolvency Act 1986, ss 423-425, replaces the Law of Property Act 1925, s 172, which is repealed. Where a person has entered into a transaction at an undervalue with the intention of defeating the creditors' claims, the court may make orders restoring the *status quo ante* and protecting the interests of those prejudiced.

A 'transaction at an undervalue' takes place when X makes a gift to Y or he otherwise enters a transaction with Y on terms that provide for X to receive no consideration; or X enters into a transaction with Y in consideration of marriage; or X enters into a transaction with Y for a consideration the value of which, in money or money's worth, is significantly less than the value, in money or money's worth, of the consideration provided by X: s 423(1).

The court will make an order only if satisfied that X entered such a transaction for the purpose of putting assets beyond the reach of a person who is making, or may at some time make, a claim against him, or of otherwise prejudicing the interests of such a person in relation to the claim which he is making or may make: s 423(3).

A claim may be made by the official receiver, by the trustee of the debtor's estate (where the debtor has been adjudged bankrupt), or a victim of the transaction.

The court may make an order (see ss 423, 425) requiring, eg, that property transferred by X to Y shall be vested in any person either absolutely or for the benefit of all the persons on whose behalf the application for the order is made, or releasing or discharging (in whole or part) any security given by the debtor. No order may be made so as to prejudice any property which was acquired from a person other than the debtor and was acquired in good faith, for value and without notice of all the relevant circumstances, or prejudice any interest deriving from such an interest: s 425(2)(a).

Under the Law of Property Act 1925, ss 173(1), 173(2), which has application to land only: 'Every voluntary disposition of land made with intent to defraud a subsequent purchaser is voidable at the instance of that purchaser. For the purposes of this section, no voluntary disposition, whenever made, shall be deemed to have been made with intent to defraud by reason only that subsequent conveyance for valuable consideration was made, if such subsequent conveyance was made after June 28th, 1893.'

10.3.2 Voluntary disposition followed by conveyance for valuable consideration

The requirement of 'certainty of objects' (see Chapter 5) necessitates, save in the case of charitable trusts, the ascertainment of beneficiaries. The validity of a private trust necessitates that the trustees shall hold on trust for individuals who can be ascertained: see, eg, *Re Flavell's WT* (1969). (In this case, the testator gave one-third of his estate, following a life interest to his wife, 'to be retained by my trustees and be used by them for the formation of a superannuation and bonus fund for the employees of the X Company, such fund to be established and constituted in such manner as my trustees shall in their absolute discretion think fit'. The trust was held void.) Where there are no ascertainable beneficiaries the court cannot usually enforce the trust since there are no persons in whose favour performance can be decreed. Trusts of this nature are known as 'unenforceable' (or 'purpose') trusts.

10.4 Trusts of imperfect obligation

The principle of unenforceability has been applied in cases such as the following:

10.4.1 Unenforceable trusts

- *Re Astor's ST* (1952)
  Trusts for 'the maintenance of good understanding, sympathy and co-operation between nations ... the preservation of the independence and integrity of

newspapers ... the control, publication, financing or management of any newspapers, periodicals, books, pamphlets ...' were held invalid because *inter alia*, they were non-charitable trusts which no person could enforce. 'A court of equity does not recognise as valid a trust which it cannot both enforce and control. This seems to me to be good equity and good sense': *per* Roxburgh J. 'A gift on trust must have a *cestui que trust*': *per* Harman J in *Re Wood* (1949), cited in *Re Astor's ST* by Roxburgh J.

- *Re Shaw* (1957)

  George Bernard Shaw made a residuary gift under his will providing for the institution of an inquiry into how much time might be saved by the use of a new, 40-letter English alphabet, and for the persuasion of the government and public to adopt it. It was held that the trusts were void, *inter alia*, for lack of someone to enforce them.

10.4.2   Exceptions

Examples of the exceptions to the general principle of unenforceability include the following (this classification is based upon that given by *Morris and Leach* (1956) as cited in *Re Endacott* (1960) by Lord Evershed):

- Trusts for the erection and maintenance of monuments or graves. The trust is held valid (and of a charitable nature) if the tomb may be considered as part of the fabric of a church, or if the trust involves the maintenance of the churchyard: see *Hoare v Osborne* (1866); *Re Eighmie* (1935).

  A trust for the maintenance of a tomb 'for ever' offends the rule against perpetuities and is void: *Re Elliot* (1952).

  A trust for the erection of a monument to the testator or a member of his family is valid if it is not intended to continue outside the perpetuity period: *Re Hooper* (1932).

  In *Trimmer v Danby* (1856), a testator gave money to executors, directing them 'to lay out and expend the same to erect a monument to my memory in St Paul's, among those of my brothers in art'. The bequest was upheld.

  Per Kindersley V-C:

  'I do not suppose that there would be anyone who could compel the executors to carry out this bequest and raise the monument; but if the residuary legatees or the trustees insist upon the trust being executed, my opinion is that this court is bound to see it carried out. I think, therefore, that as the trustees insist upon the sum of £1,000 being laid out according to the directions in the will, that sum must be set apart for the purpose.'

- Trusts for the saying of masses in jurisdictions where such trusts are not regarded as charitable. See *Gilmour v Coats* (1949); *Re Hetherington* (1990) (at 12.4.4).

- Trusts for the maintenance of particular animals. A trust for the maintenance of animals in general may be charitable: *Re Wedgwood* (1915). A trust for the benefit of specific animals is not generally charitable, but if restricted to the perpetuity period it may constitute a valid 'unenforceable trust'.

- Trusts for the benefit of unincorporated associations. This matter is considered later.

- Miscellaneous cases. See *Re Thompson* (1934) in which the testator gave a legacy to a friend, L, to be applied in such a manner as he might think fit towards the promotion and furtherance of fox-hunting, with Trinity Hall as the residuary legatee. It was held that L and Trinity Hall could legally carry out the testator's wishes. Clauson J required an undertaking from the trustee to apply the legacy towards the testator's objective, while empowering the residuary legatees to apply to the court should the trustee not fulfil his undertaking.

An unincorporated association was described by Lawton LJ in *Conservative and Unionist Central Office v Burrell* (1982) as:

> 'two or more persons bound together for one or more common purposes, not being business purposes, by mutual undertakings each having mutual duties and obligations, in an organisation which has rules which identify in whom control of it and its funds rests and on what terms and which can be joined or left at will'.

It is not a 'legal person'; its purposes may be charitable or non-charitable and, therefore, in general, it may not be the subject of legal rights and obligations. A number of problems arise for consideration, two of which are now discussed.

How may a gift to a non-charitable unincorporated association be interpreted? A number of interpretations are suggested in *Re Recher's WT* (1972).

- As a gift to individual members of the association at the date of the gift for their benefit as joint tenants or tenants in common. The association would be, effectively, a 'label' which defined the class intended to take. It would seem, therefore, that each member would participate in a division of the gift, taking the share to which he was entitled. 'Cases

10.5 Problems of the unincorporated association

10.5.1 Interpretation

within this category are relatively uncommon': *per* Vinelott J in *Re Grant's WT* (1980). See *Leahy v A-G of New South Wales* (1959).

- As a gift to present and future members forever or for an indefinite period. Such a gift is prevented from failing under the general perpetuities rule by the Perpetuities and Accumulations Act 1964, which allows an effective gift in favour of those members ascertained within the perpetuity period.

- As a gift to trustees or officers of the association. Such a gift may fail for want of a beneficiary. See *Morice v Bishop of Durham* (1805); *Re Lipinski's WT* (1976).

    (i)   In *Morice v Bishop of Durham* (1804), a bequest had been made to the Bishop on trust for 'such objects of benevolence and liberality as the Bishop of Durham in his own discretion shall most approve of'. The court held that this did not constitute a charitable trust; as there were no ascertainable beneficiaries, the trust failed.

    Per Grant MR:

    'The only question is whether a trust upon which the residue of the personal estate is bequeathed, be a trust for charitable purposes. That it is upon some trust, and not for the personal benefit of the Bishop is clear from the words of the will; and is admitted by his Lordship who expressly disclaims any beneficial interest. That it is a trust, unless it be of a charitable nature, too indefinite to be executed by this court, has not been, and cannot be, denied. There can be no trust over the exercise of which this court will not assume a control; for an uncontrollable power of disposition would be ownership and not trust. If there be a clear trust, but for uncertain objects, the property that is the subject of the trust is undisposed of, and the benefit of such trust must result to those to whom the law gives ownership in default of disposition by the former owner. But this doctrine does not hold good with regard to trusts for charity. Every other trust must have a definite object. There must be somebody in whose favour the court can decree performance.'

    (ii)   In *Re Lipinski's WT* (1976), the testator bequeathed residuary estate to trustees on trust, one half to the Hull Maccabi Association in memory of his late wife to be used 'solely for the work of constructing the new buildings for the association and/or improvements to the said buildings'. The trust was held to be valid, it was essentially a trust for the members of the association, who were ascertained or ascertainable.

Per Oliver J:

'I do not really see why such a gift, which specifies a purpose which is within the powers of the association and of which the members of the association are the beneficiaries, should fail. Why are not the beneficiaries able to enforce the trust, or, indeed, in the exercise of their contractual rights, to terminate the trust for their own benefit? Where the donee association is itself the beneficiary of the prescribed purpose, there seems to me to be the strongest argument in common sense for saying that the gift should be construed as an absolute one ..., the more so where, if the purpose is carried out, the members can by appropriate action vest the resulting property in themselves, for here the trustees and the beneficiaries are the same persons.'

- As a gift to existing members beneficially, but on the basis that the subject-matter of the gift is given as an accretion to the funds which are the subject-matter of the *contract* which the members have made *inter se*. Such a construction would allow the gift to be considered valid. An individual member's share would accrue to other members of the association in the event of his resignation or death.

10.5.2 Distribution of surplus funds

How ought surplus funds to be distributed when an association is wound up? Should they be held on resulting trusts, for example?

When does a club, for example, cease to exist? Mere inactivity will not suffice to show non-existence, although it may be so prolonged that the only reasonable inference is that the club has been dissolved spontaneously: see *Re GKN Sports and Social Club* (1982). In this case it was held that, on dissolution, full members (who alone paid subscriptions) were entitled to receive shares in the surplus funds; division on an equal basis was ordered. (Dissolution of a club may result in accordance with the club's rules; by agreement of members; by order of the court; when the continued existence of the club appears to have no purpose.)

On dissolution it becomes necessary to ask whether distribution of assets is affected by statute (see *Ross v Lord Advocate* (1986)), by the club's own rules, or by implying into the *contract* which arises from the rules a term that, on dissolution, the club's funds shall go to members in equal shares.

In *Re Printers' Protection Society* (1899), the concept of a resulting trust was taken into account, so that members (at the date of dissolution) took on the basis of the amounts they had contributed.

In *Re Hobourn Distress Fund* (1946), following a resolution to wind up, the resulting trust concept was applied; the assets were distributed among past and present members in shares proportionate to their contributions.

In *Re Sick and Funeral Society of St John* (1973), a society had been formed among teachers and children of a Sunday school so as to provide sickness and death benefits for members. Subscriptions were based on a sliding scale determined by age. It was decided unanimously to wind up the society; no further subscriptions were to be made and surplus assets amounted to £4,000. Prior to distribution of the assets, four ex-members, whose membership had been terminated for failure to pay subscriptions, made a claim whereby they might pay up arrears and participate in the distribution. It was held that full shares would be ordered for full members, with half shares for child members. All ex-members were to be excluded.

Per Megarry J:

'I should be very slow to accept that a member of a society may disregard all his obligations as a member for several years, and then, when it appears that there is some advantage in resuming his membership, assert that he is still a member because the correct procedure under the rules to terminate his membership has not been followed. The question, of course, is not one of expulsion, or of the society snatching at some trivial or short-lived breach of rules by a member to deny him membership; it is a question of a voluntary disregard of the obligations of membership over a continuous period of years ... Yet if the contentions of the four members are right, either the society or the members concerned may, if it suits them, claim that the membership is still in being. Such members might find that the society is claiming many years' arrears of a substantial contribution, or the members might, as here, suddenly reassert their membership when some advantage turns up. I do not think that this can be right ...'

In *Re Bucks Constabulary Friendly Society* (1979), a fund was established, and appropriately registered, to provide from voluntary contributions by members, funds to relieve widows and orphans of deceased members of the Buckinghamshire Constabulary. Under statute, the property of such a society vested in trustees for the benefit of the society and its members. There were no rules to cover the distribution of assets on a dissolution of the society. Following such a dissolution, the question arose as to whether the assets should be distributed among those individuals who claimed membership at the time of the dissolution or whether the assets should pass as *bona vacantia* to the Crown. The court held that as there were members at the time of the dissolution, the assets belonged to them; any claim by the Crown should be excluded.

Per Walton J:

'The modern cases show that the members' entitlement is much more likely to be upon the basis of contractual rights. The distribution will be *per capita* and confined to those who were members at the time of the dissolution.'

Unlawful and Voidable Trusts and Trusts of Imperfect Obligation

Unlawful trusts are those which are illegal as contravening statute or common law or are not otherwise enforceable by the courts because they are contrary to public policy. Such trusts are ineffective.

Voidable trusts are exemplified by Law of Property Act 1925, s 173(1), by which a voluntary disposition of land made with the intention of defrauding a purchaser is voidable at his instance.

Trusts of imperfect obligation are designed for non-charitable purposes, and have no designated beneficiaries; with important exceptions they are void.

Characteristics of trusts of these types

The following are examples of unlawful trusts:

Unlawful trusts

- *Trusts which offend the rule against perpetuities.* This rule is directed against attempts to make property inalienable. The common law rule states that where there is a possibility that a future interest in property might vest after the expiration of the 'perpetuity period' (lives in being plus 21 years and any gestation period), the interest is void. See the Perpetuities and Accumulations Act 1964, allowing a perpetuity period not exceeding 80 years, and a 'wait and see' period.

- *Trusts which attempt to create 'perpetual trusts'.* A gift which prevents capital and income being alienated for longer than the common law perpetuity period is void.

- *Trusts which offend the rule against accumulations.* Settlors may no longer direct the accumulation of income for a period in excess of the common law perpetuity period.

- *Trusts in restraint of marriage or directed against the maintenance of family life.* Trusts in restraint of marriage and those directed against the maintenance of family life, eg, inducing the separation of husband and wife are generally void.

- *Trusts made illegal by statutes.* Trusts made illegal by statute, eg, where they are based on racial discrimination are void.

Voidable trusts are often designed so as to defraud the settlor's creditors. Note the Insolvency Act 1986. Examples are trusts based on transactions entered into at an undervalue (see the

Voidable trusts

1986 Act, ss 423-5), and voluntary dispositions followed by conveyances for valuable consideration. See Law of Property Act 1925, s 173(1), (2).

Trusts of imperfect obligation

Where there are no ascertainable beneficiaries, the court cannot usually enforce the trusts. See *Astor's ST* (1952). Exceptions include: trusts for the erection and maintenance of monuments or graves; trusts for the saying of masses; trusts for the maintenance of particular animals; trusts for the benefit of unincorporated associations.

Unincorporated associations

Two important problems have arisen in recent years in relation to unincorporated associations.

• How may a gift to a non-charitable unincorporated association be interpreted?

See *Re Recher's WT* (1972). Interpretations include: as a gift to individual members at the date of the gift for their benefit as joint tenants or tenants in common; as a gift to present and future members forever or for an indefinite period; as a gift to the association's trustees or officers; as a gift to existing members beneficially with the subject-matter of the gift construed as an accretion to funds which are the subject of the contract made by members *inter se*.

• How ought surplus funds to be distributed when an association is wound up?

See *Re Printers' Protection Society* (1899); *Re Bucks Constabulary Protection Society* (1979). In the latter case, the society's rules did not provide for distribution of assets on dissolution; it was held that the assets belonged to members in existence at the date of dissolution, to the exclusion of the Crown's claim based on *bona vacantia*.

Chapter 11

Charitable Trusts (1)

A charitable trust is one by the terms of which the income is to be applied *exclusively* for purposes of a charitable nature. There is no statutory definition of the concept of 'charity'; the 1989 White Paper, *Charities: a Framework for the Future* (Cm 694), stated that there would be few advantages, and many dangers, in attempting a 'redefinition' of the term. It may be that such a definition would prove unduly restrictive, since 'there is no limit to the number and diversity of the ways in which man will seek to benefit his fellow-men': *per* Viscount Simonds in *IRC v Baddeley* (1955).

Note, in relation to the Charities Act 1993, a 'charity' means 'any institution, corporate or not, which is established for charitable purposes and is subject to the control of the High Court in the exercise of the court's jurisdiction with respect to charities': s 96(1).

The scope of 'charity' today is a reflection of the many decisions derived from a consideration of the 'spirit and intendment' of the preamble of the Statute of Elizabeth 1601 (which is discussed later). 'Those purposes are charitable which that Statute enumerates or which by analogies are deemed within its spirit and intendment': *per* Grant MR in *Morice v Bishop of Durham* (1805).

The question as to whether a trust is or is not charitable is decided by the court; the opinions of the settlor or testator as to the nature or purpose of his gift are of little relevance: see *Royal Choral Society v IRC* (1943). Thus: in *Re King* (1923), a bequest for the erection of a stained glass window in a church to perpetuate the memory of the testatrix was held to be charitable; in *Incorporated Society of Law Reporting for England and Wales v A-G* (1971), a non-profit making organisation which has as its object the publication of law reports was held to be charitable within the spirit of the preamble to the Statute of Elizabeth. (*Per* Lord Russell: 'In a case such as the present ... I believe the proper question to ask is whether there are any grounds for holding it to be outside the equity of the Statute.')

To be valid, a charitable trust must be of a charitable nature, must be wholly and exclusively charitable, and must promote a public benefit.

11.1 **Nature of the charitable trust**

11.2   The Statute of Charitable Uses 1601

The preamble to the Statute of Charitable Uses 1601, referred to as the Statute of Elizabeth, sought to enunciate the most important and common charitable purposes of its time; it remains of much significance today.

The preamble (in modern style and spelling) refers to land, profits, goods, given and assigned:

> 'some for the relief of aged, impotent and poor people, some for maintenance of sick and maimed soldiers and mariners, schools of learning, free schools, and scholars in universities, some for repair of bridges, ports, churches, highways, some for education and preferment of orphans ... some for marriages of poor maids, some for supportation, aid and help of young tradesmen, handicraftsmen and persons decayed, and others for relief or redemption of prisoners and captives, and for aid and ease of any poor inhabitants concerning payment of fifteens [a tax on movable property].'

The Statute was *repealed* by the Mortmain and Charitable Uses Act 1888, but s 13(2) preserved the preamble. The 1888 Act, and with it the preamble, were repealed by the Charities Act 1960, s 38(1):

> 'Any reference in any enactment or document to a charity within the meaning, purview and interpretation of the Charitable Uses Act 1601, or the preamble to it, shall be construed as a reference to a charity within the meaning which the word bears as a legal term according to the law of England and Wales.'

The classification contained within the preamble remains a guide to the courts in their attempts to discover whether or not a gift is charitable.

Per Viscount Simonds in *Williams' Trustees v IRC* (1947):

> 'It is still the general law that a trust is not charitable and entitled to the privileges which charity confers, unless it is within the spirit and intendment of the preamble to the Statute of Elizabeth.'

The following comments in *Scottish Burial Society v Glasgow CC* (1968) should be noted:

(i)   *Per* Lord Upjohn:

> 'It may seem almost incredible to anyone not familiar with this branch of the English law that this should still be taken as the test; it is undoubtedly the accepted test, though only in a very wide and broad sense.'

(ii) *Per* Lord Reid:

> 'The courts appear to have proceeded first by seeking some analogy between an object mentioned in the preamble and the object with regard to which they had to reach a decision. Then they appear to have gone further, and to have been satisfied if they could

find an analogy between an object already held to be charitable and the new object claimed to be charitable.'

(iii) *Per* Lord Wilberforce:

'On this subject [the legal test of charitable purposes], the law of England though no doubt not very satisfactory and in need of rationalisation, is tolerably clear. The purposes in question, to be charitable, must be shown to be for the benefit of the public, or the community, in a sense of manner within the intendment of the preamble to the Statute of Elizabeth. The latter requirement does not mean quite what it says; for it is now accepted that what must be regarded is not the wording of the preamble itself, but the effect of decisions given by the courts as to its scope, decisions which have endeavoured to keep the law as to charities moving according as new social needs arise or old ones become obsolete or satisfied.'

11.3 Differences between charitable and non-charitable trusts

A private trust is designed and intended to benefit one person or a number of persons; a charitable trust is intended to benefit society or some part of it. The same rules which apply to private trusts generally apply to charitable trusts, but the charitable trust enjoys some advantages which are not available to the private trust.

11.3.1 Taxation privileges

The investment income of a charitable trust is exempt from income tax if applied *only* for charitable purposes. The trading income of a charitable trust is exempt from income tax if applied *only* for charitable purposes *and* if the purpose, or one of the principal purposes, of the charity is to carry on such work *or* if the trading is carried on mainly by the beneficiaries of the charity. See *IRC v Helen Slater Charitable Trust Ltd* (1982) (money donated by one charity to another was held to have been applied for charitable purposes, so that the donating trust was entitled to tax exemptions). Gifts to charities are generally exempt from capital gains tax: Taxation of Chargeable Gains Act 1992, s 257. For exemptions from VAT, see SI 1973/385, 1986/53.

11.3.2 Exemption from aspects of the rule against perpetuities

In general, the private and the charitable trust are subject to the rule against perpetuities (see Chapter 10). *Per* Lord Selborne in *Chamberlayne v Brockett* (1872):

'If the gift in trust for charity is itself conditional upon a future and uncertain event, it is subject to the same rules and principles as any other estate depending for its coming into existence upon a condition precedent. If the condition is never fulfilled, the estate never arises; if it is so remote and indefinite as to transgress the limits of time prescribed by the rules of law against perpetuities, the gift fails *ab initio*.'

Note the application of the 'wait and see' rule in the Perpetuities and Accumulations Act 1964, s 3 (see Chapter 10).

The rule has no application in the case of a gift to one charity with gift over to some other charity on the occurrence of an event which may be outside the perpetuity period: see *Re Tyler* (1891). This exception has no application to a gift over from a charity to an individual: see *Re Bowen* (1893).

11.3.3	Exemption from aspects of the rule against perpetual trusts

The rule against perpetual trusts (see Chapter 10) does not apply to a charitable trust, for its objects may continue in perpetuity. In the case of trusts for the maintenance of tombs, the following points should be noted:

- A trust limited to the perpetuity period may be valid but unenforceable: *Trimmer v Danby* (1856).

- A gift for the upkeep as a whole of the churchyard which includes the tomb is held to be a charitable gift: *Re Eighmie* (1935).

- A gift to one charity with gift over to another if the tomb is not kept in repair is valid: *Christ's Hospital v Grainger* (1849).

11.3.4	Exemption from some rules relating to trustees

In the case of a *private trust* the trustees must act unanimously. (See Chapter 15.) In the case of a *charitable trust* the majority of trustees may bind the minority: *Re Whiteley* (1910).

11.4 The certainty rule

A charitable trust will not fail provided there is certainty of intention to give the property to charity and that such intention is exclusively charitable.

In order that a trust might be considered as possessing a valid charitable nature, its objective must be the furtherance of purposes which are *wholly charitable*, ie, its essential nature will be held to be within the courts' interpretation of the Statute of Elizabeth.

11.4.1	Problems

Problems have arisen where a testator has directed that a gift be used for 'charitable or deserving', 'charitable or benevolent', 'charitable or other' objects to be selected by his executor. 'Or' has been interpreted as introducing an alternative (ie, 'or' is considered as being used disjunctively), so that the gifts could be applied to a purpose which was not charitable; hence the gifts were held to be *not charitable*: see *Re Eades* (1920).

A gift created by the use of the phrase *charitable or educational or religious purposes* would be held valid since each of the separate heads is charitable: *Re Ward* (1941).

Use of *charitable and benevolent; charitable and philanthropic* and similar phrases will not necessarily invalidate a gift, since the word following the conjunction 'and' is considered not to vitiate the exclusive charitable purpose, but rather to restrict the type of charity the testator had in mind: *Re Sutton* (1885).

In *A-G of the Bahamas v Royal Trust Co* (1986), X left an estate to be held on trust for '... the education and welfare of Bahamian children and young people ...' The trustees of the estate asked the court to determine whether the gift was validly charitable or not. It was held that the gift was not charitable. The words 'education and welfare' were to be construed disjunctively; thus the gift had two purposes, rather than the sole purpose of educational welfare. A trust which was solely for the welfare of a certain class did not possess the capacity of being charitable. The trusts within that clause were held void, and the funds involved fell into residue.

Under the Charitable Trusts (Validation) Act 1954, where an imperfect trust is couched in terms such that the property which is the subject of the trust could be used either exclusively for charitable or non-charitable purposes, *retrospective validation may be possible*. As a result, certain gifts which might otherwise have been held to have failed will be saved so as to be made available for charitable purposes.

11.4.2   The Charitable Trusts (Validation) Act 1954

 ̄ The Act was passed following the decision of the House of Lords in *Chichester Diocesan Fund v Simpson* (1944). A testator had directed his executors to apply the residue of his estate 'for such charitable institution or institutions or other charitable or benevolent object or objects in England as they might in their absolute discretion select'. It was held that the phrase 'or benevolent' suggested an alternative purpose. The will contained nothing to suggest a different interpretation, and it was, therefore, void for uncertainty.

Per Lord Diplock:

'I turn to the context to see what justification it affords for reading the relevant words in any but their natural meaning. Reading and re-reading them ... I can find nothing which justifies such a departure. It is true that the word "other" introduces the phrase "charitable or benevolent object or objects" and to this the appellants attached some importance, suggesting that since "other" looked back to "charitable institution or institutions", so all that followed must be of the genus charitable. There can be no substance in this, for in the phrase so introduced the word "charitable" is itself repeated and is followed by the alternative "or benevolent". Apart from the slender point it seemed that the appellants relied on what is called a general, a dominant, an overriding charitable intention, giving charitable content to a word or phrase which might otherwise not have the quality. That such a result is possible there are cases in the books to show ... but here I look in vain for any such context. On the plain reading of this will I could only come to the conclusion that the testator intended exclusively to benefit objects if I excised the words "or benevolent" which he has used. That I cannot do.'

It is essential for the purposes of the 1954 Act that the invalid terms of the trust are such that they would have been considered valid had their objects been exclusively charitable: s 2(1). A trust which is, in essence, private and discretionary will not be validated under the Act. The following cases illustrate the nature of the Act.

- *Vernon v IRC* (1956)

  A scheme was sanctioned whereby property would be held as a clubhouse and recreational ground for a firm's employees and other persons authorised by the trustees. In order that the 1954 Act might apply, it had to be shown that the property could be used 'exclusively' for charitable purposes. It soon became apparent after the scheme had been sanctioned that the trust for the benefit of employees was not charitable, and it was suggested, therefore, that the trustees might consider using their powers so as to invite the inhabitants of a defined area to use the clubhouse and grounds. It was argued that in such a case there would be a charitable trust. This was not upheld: it was considered that the trustees' power to admit other persons to use the property did not impress the scheme with the nature of a public trust, so that it could not be held that the trust property would be used exclusively for charitable purposes.

- *Re Mead's Trust Deed* (1961)

  Under a trust deed of 1920 trustees of land were directed to hold it as a site for a memorial home in memory of trade unionists killed in the 1914-18 war. The home was to include: a sanatorium for consumptive members of trade unions; a convalescent home for members; a home for aged members who were unable to support themselves, and their wives. The first two objects were held not charitable (as lacking the necessary element of public benefit), the third was held charitable. Under the 1954 Act the trust was validated: the trust property was to be held by the trustees for the benefit of those members only who were poor persons, and, in the case of the home for aged members, for the aged, retired members of the union and their wives.

- *Re Wyke's WT* (1961)

  Under a testator's will, one-third of residue was given, subject to a life interest for the widow, to directors of a company, to be used 'at their discretion as a benevolent or welfare fund or for welfare purposes for the sole benefit of the past, present and future employees of the company'. The objects for which the one-third of residue were to be held were so described that the property could be used exclusively for charitable purposes, notwithstanding that it could be used, perhaps, for non-charitable purposes also. As a result, it was an 'imperfect trust provision' within the meaning of the 1954 Act, which could be validated.

* *Re Chitty's WT* (1970)

  Testator gave an interest in a trust fund to his wife for life, and subject thereto, one-sixth of the fund to 'the colonel and adjutants for the time being of the Suffolk Regiment on trust to use the income as to one half for benefit of the officers and as to one half for benefit of warrant officers, NCOs and men who belong, or have belonged, to the Regiment ...' Residue of the estate was given to his wife. Twenty-five years after testator's death, his widow died; within one year of her death, her executors commenced proceedings for a declaration as to whether the gift formed part of testator's estate and passed to the widow. The claim succeeded. It was held that the gift to the regiment was an imperfect trust provision within the terms of the 1954 Act. Until the widow's death it was 'subject to another disposition made by the same person', ie, the widow's life interest. Her right to challenge the gift's validity accrued on her death. The executors had commenced proceedings within one year from that date, and under the Act were in time. The Act was not effective to validate the gift in this case.

11.5 The classification of charitable trusts

There is no classification of trusts under statute. The most widely-known classification is to be found in *Pemsel's Case* (1891) in which charity, in its legal sense, was held to fall into four principal divisions. The classification itself is based closely upon arguments advanced by Sir Samuel Romilly in *Morice v Bishop of Durham* (1805).

Commissioners of Income Tax v Pemsel (1891) concerned the construction of the phrase 'charitable purposes' in the Income Tax Act 1842, s 61. *Per* Lord MacNaghten:

> 'How far, then, may it be asked, does the popular meaning of the word "charity" correspond with its legal meaning? *"Charity" in its legal sense comprises four principal divisions: trusts for the relief of poverty: trusts for the advancement of education; trusts for the advancement of religion; and trusts for other purposes beneficial to the community not falling under any of the preceding heads. The trusts last referred to are not the less* charitable in the eyes of the law because incidentally they benefit the rich as well as the poor, as indeed every charity that deserves the name must do either directly or indirectly.'

Note the following comment by Lord Wilberforce in *Scottish Burial Society v Glasgow CC* (1968):

> 'Lord MacNaghten's grouping of the heads of recognised charity in *Pemsel's Case* is one that has proved to be of value and there are many problems which it solves. But three things may be said about it, which its author would surely not have denied: *first*, that, since it is a classification of convenience, there may well be purposes which do not fit neatly into one or other of the headings; *secondly*, that the words used must not be given the force of a statute to be construed; and, *thirdly*, that the law of charity is a moving subject which may well have evolved even since 1891.'

11.6   The requirements for a charitable trust

The three requirements are: charitable nature of the trust; wholly and exclusively charitable nature of objects; promotion of a public benefit.

11.6.1   Charitable nature

In general, the charitable nature of a trust is considered as proved when its objects are held to be within the spirit and intendment of the Statute of Elizabeth, so that its purposes fall under one or more of the headings enumerated in Lord MacNaghten's classification. See, eg, *IRC v McMullen* (1981).

11.6.2   Wholly and exclusively charitable

The general rule that the objects of the trust must be charitable is qualified in certain ways.

- By ancillary objects

  A trust may be so designed that the ascertainment of its charitable objects also involves the promotion of some non-charitable object. If the non-charitable object is merely incidental, the charitable objects will not necessarily be invalidated. Per Greer LJ in *Geologists' Association v IRC* (1928):

  > 'If you come to the conclusion, as you may in many cases, that one of the ways in which the public objects of an association can be served is by giving special advantages to the members of the association, then the association does not cease to be an association with a charitable object because incidentally and in order to carry out the charitable object it is both necessary and desirable to confer special benefits on its members.'

  In *Re Coxen* (1948), a fund of £200,000 was held on trust for medical charities. It also provided in specific terms for the application of an annual sum not exceeding £100 for a dinner for alderman who were to meet to discuss the trust, and for a token payment of one guinea to each alderman who attended a committee meeting relating to the trust. The trust was upheld: such payments were to be construed as being made for the better administration of the trust, or as being ancillary to it. The payments were not for the personal benefit of the aldermen.

In *Incorporated Council of Law Reporting v A-G* (1971), the Council was incorporated in 1870 with its main object 'the preparation and publication in a convenient form, at a moderate price, and under gratuitous professional control, of reports of judicial decisions of the superior and appellate courts in England'. No part of its income could be paid as profit to members, and remuneration was authorised only for editors, reporters, etc. 'The subsidiary objects, such as printing and publishing statutes ... are ancillary to this primary object and do not detract from its exclusively charitable character': *per* Buckley LJ.

In *Royal College of Surgeons of England v National Provincial Bank* (1952), it was held by the House of Lords that the Royal College was a charity, its object being the promotion and encouragement of the study of surgery. Its other activities, such as protection of its members, were ancillary only.

In *Re Bernstein's WT* (1971), the testator left a part of his residuary estate in trust for the infirmary in which he had worked as a surgeon 'for the purpose of providing extra comforts at Christmas time for the nursing staff'. The gift contrasted with other gifts in the will to individual nurses; the trust for the nursing staff was subservient to the gift to the infirmary, which was an endowment in perpetuity, and contributed to the service of nurses to the infirmary. The gift was, therefore, charitable.

In *A-G v Ross* (1986), a students' union was held to be a charitable trust although one of its objects was affiliation to a non-charitable organisation (the National Union of Students). Per Scott J:

'The union was formed and exists for the charitable purpose of furthering the educational function of the North London Polytechnic. The non-charitable activities which the union is, under its constitution, organised to carry on and has carried on, are, in my judgment, as a matter of degree no more than ancillary means by which the charitable purpose may be pursued.'

See also *Webb v O'Doherty* (1991).

- By apportionment

  Where an executor or trustee is directed to apportion the trust property between charitable and non-charitable purposes, the gift will not wholly fail. In default of apportionment, the court will apportion the property equally between the classes of objects. The trust will fail only if the non-charitable purposes are void.

In *Salusbury v Denton* (1857), a fund was bequeathed by the testator to his widow. A direction was given that it be applied by the widow in her will 'part to the foundation of a charity school or such other charitable endowment for the benefit of the poor at Offley as she may prefer, and the remainder to be at her disposal among my relatives, in such proportions as she may be pleased to direct'. In the event, no will or apportionment was made. It was held that the fund should be divided into two equal parts, one for charitable purposes, and the other for plaintiff.

Per Wood VC:

'Here there is a plain direction to the widow to give a part to the charitable purposes referred to in the will, as she may think fit ... remainder among the testator's relatives as she may direct. The widow having died without exercising that discretion, the moiety in question must be divided equally.'

- By statutory validation and implication of charitable purposes

  For statutory validation, see Charitable Trusts (Validation) Act 1954 (para 11.4.2). The courts may imply charitable purposes to gifts of an indefinite nature in the following cases

  (i) Gifts *virtute officii* ('by virtue of the office held'). A gift to 'the vicar of the parish' would probably be held charitable since it is assumed that it will be used for his official (and, therefore, religious) duties. Difficulties of construction, resulting in the qualification of the phrase, may arise. A gift to the vicar and churchwardens 'for parochial work' may be held not charitable since the gift might be used for activities not charitable in the legal sense of the term (*Farley v Westminster Bank* (1939)); a gift 'for such objects connected with the Church as he [the vicar] shall think fit' would probably be held charitable (*Re Bain* (1930)).

  (ii) Gifts for the benefit of a locality. A gift for the benefit of a particular locality may, in itself, constitute a valid charitable gift although no charitable purpose is specified. See *Goodman v Mayor of Saltash* (1882); *Re Smith* (1932) (a trust in which a residuary estate was given 'unto my country England for its own use and benefit absolutely', was held charitable); *Re Strakosch* (1949) (a specific purpose not confined to charity was stated, so that no implication of charitable purposes was possible). Note that a trust which is not charitable cannot be changed into a charitable one by limiting the area in which it is to operate: *Re Gwyon* (1930).

The general rule requires that a valid charitable trust shall promote a public benefit, ie, that it is 'for the benefit of the community or of an appreciably important class of the community': *per* Lord Westbury in *Verge v Somerville* (1924). Note, however, that not every purpose that is beneficial to the public is charitable; it must be within the letter or spirit of the preamble to the Statute of Elizabeth.

11.6.3   Promotion of a public benefit

A trust may by its nature confer a public benefit even though a limited number of people only are capable of availing themselves of its benefits: *Neville Estates v Madden* (1962).

In *Re Compton* (1945) a trust for the education of the descendants of three particular persons was held not to be charitable since the *cestuis que trust* were defined in terms of a relationship to persons, and, therefore, the quality of a public trust was lacking.

In *Hobourn Air Raid Distress Fund* (1946), money was given voluntarily by employees of a munitions firm to be used to relieve distress suffered by employees as the result of air raids. It was held that this was not charitable. *Per* Greene MR:

> 'The point to my mind, which really puts this case beyond reasonable doubt, is the fact that a number of employees of this company, actuated by motives of self-help, agreed to a deduction from their wages to constitute a fund to be applied for their own benefit without any question of poverty coming into it. Such an arrangement seems to me to stamp the whole transaction as one having a personal character, money put up by a number of people, not for the general benefit, but for their own individual benefit.'

The donor's opinions concerning the likely public benefit of his gift are not material. The question is to be decided by the court on the evidence: *Re Hummeltenberg* (1923). A testator had bequeathed funds to the London Spiritualistic Alliance so as to establish a college at which persons could be trained as spiritualist mediums. The court held the gift invalid.

Per Russell J:

> 'It was contended that the court was not the tribunal to determine whether a gift or trust was or was not a gift or trust for the benefit of the public. It was held that the only judge of this was the donor of the gift or the creator of the trust. For this view reliance was placed on *Re Cranston* ... and on a sentence in the judgment of Chitty J in *Re Foveaux*. So far as the views so expressed declare that the personal or private opinion of the judge is immaterial, I agree; but so far as they lay down or suggest that the donor of the gift or

the creator of the trust is to determine whether the purpose is beneficial to the public, I respectfully disagree. If a testator by stating or indicating his view that a trust is beneficial to the public can establish that fact beyond question, trusts might be established in perpetuity for the promotion of all kinds of fantastic (though not unlawful) objects, of which the training of poodles to dance might be a mild example. In my opinion the question whether a gift is or may be operative for the public benefit is a question to be answered by the court by forming an opinion upon the evidence before it.'

An exception to the principle that a charitable trust must be for the public benefit is that a trust for the relief of poverty (see Chapter 12) may be charitable even though it is not for the benefit of the public or even a section of it.

In *Re Coulthurst* (1951) (see 12.2.3), the testator provided a fund to be applied 'to or for the benefit of such of the ... widows and orphaned children of deceased officers and deceased ex-officers of Coutts & Co ... as the bank shall in its absolute discretion consider by reason of his and her or their financial circumstances to be most deserving of such assistance'. It was held a valid charitable trust.

In *Re Scarisbrick's WT* (1951), the testatrix directed that, following the death of her children, her residuary estate should be held on trust 'for such relations of my said son and daughters as in the opinion of [their survivor] shall be in needy circumstances and for such charitable objects either in Germany or Great Britain ... for such interests and in such proportions as the survivor shall by deed or will appoint'. The gift was upheld. *Per* Jenkins LJ:

'It is a general rule that a trust or gift in order to be charitable in the true legal sense must be for the benefit of the public or some section of the public ... There is, however, an exception to the general rule, in that trusts or gifts for the relief of poverty have been held to be charitable even though they are limited in their application to some aggregate of individuals ascertained [by reference to some personal tie] and are therefore not trusts or gifts for the benefit of the public or a section thereof. This exception operates whether the personal tie is one of blood (as in the numerous so-called 'poor relations' cases) or of contract (eg, relief of poverty among the members of a particular society ... or amongst employees of a particular company or their dependants). This exception cannot be accounted for by references to any principle, but is established by a series of authorities of long standing.'

See also *Dingle v Turner* (1972). In this case the testator directed trustees to pay income from the residuary estate to his wife for life and, on her death, to pay £10,000 to trustees upon trust 'to apply the income thereof in paying pensions to poor employees of Dingle & Co'. At the date of the testator's death there were some 600 employees of the firm and a large number of former employees, who, it was held, constituted a 'section of the public', so that the will created a valid charitable trust.

Per Lord Cross:

'In truth the question whether or not the potential beneficiaries of a trust can fairly be said to constitute a section of the public is a question of degree and cannot be by itself decisive of the question whether the trust is a charity. Much must depend on the purpose of the trust. It may well be that, on the one hand, a trust to promote some purpose *prima facie* charitable will constitute a charity even though the class of potential beneficiaries might fairly be called a private class and that, on the other hand, a trust to promote another purpose, also *prima facie* charitable, will not constitute a charity even though the class of potential beneficiaries might seem to some people fairly describable as a section of the public.'

Summary of Chapter 11

Charitable Trusts (1)

A charitable trust is one by the terms of which the income is to be applied exclusively for purposes of a charitable nature. (There is no statutory definition.) In general the purposes of the trust must reflect the spirit and intendment of the (repealed) Statute of Elizabeth 1601.

Essence of the charitable trust

The courts will decide whether or not a trust is charitable; the intentions of the testator are not decisive. See *Royal Choral Society v IRC* (1943).

The charitable trust enjoys some taxation privileges, and is exempt from aspects of the rules against perpetuities and perpetual trusts.

A charitable trust will not fail provided there is certainty of intention to give the property to charity *and* that such intention is exclusively charitable.

Under the Charitable Trusts (Validation) Act 1954, retrospective validation may be possible where an imperfect trust is couched in terms such that the property which is the subject of the trust could be used either exclusively for charitable or non-charitable purposes. See *Re Mead's Trust Deed* (1961).

There is no statutory classification of charitable trusts. The most widely-used classification results from *Commissioners of Income Tax v Pemsel* (1891), based on an interpretation of the preamble to the Statute of 1601.

Classification

Charity was held, by Lord MacNaghten, in *Pemsel's Case*, to comprise four principal divisions: trusts for the relief of poverty, for the advancement of education, for the advancement of religion, and for other purposes beneficial to the community not falling under any of the preceding heads.

This classification is one of convenience, its words do not have the force of statute.

There are three requirements for a charitable trust:

The requirements for a charitable trust

- Charitable nature

    This is proved when the objects of the trust are held to be within the preamble to the 1601 Statute, so that its purposes fall under one or more of the headings enumerated by Lord MacNaghten.

- Wholly and exclusively charitable

  This general rule may be qualified where the trust is designed so that the ascertainment of its charitable objects also involves the promotion of some non-charitable (but not merely incidental) objects. See *Incorporated Council of Law Reporting v A-G* (1971); *A-G v Ross* (1986). It is also qualified where an executor or trustee is directed to apportion trust property between charitable and non-charitable purposes (which must not be void). Statutory validation is possible under the Charitable Trusts (Validation) Act 1954. The court may imply charitable purposes to gifts of an indefinite nature, eg, gifts for the benefit of a locality (see *Re Strakosch* (1949)).

- Promotion of a public benefit

  A valid charitable trust must promote a public benefit, ie, it must be for the benefit of the community or of an appreciably important class of the community. It must be within the spirit of the preamble to the 1601 Statute. (The donor's opinions as to the likely public benefit of his gift are not material.) Note that a trust for the relief of poverty may be held charitable even though it is limited in its application to an aggregate of individuals ascertained by reference to a personal tie: see *Re Scarisbrick's WT* (1951).

Chapter 12

Charitable Trusts (2)

In this chapter we consider the classification of charitable trusts based on the classification in *Pemsel's Case* (see Chapter 11). It is necessary to recall the significance of the preamble to the Statute of Elizabeth. The following observations should be kept in mind.

12.1 The Statute of Elizabeth - a reminder

Per Lord Simonds in *Gilmour v Coats* (1949):

> 'From the beginning it was the practice of the court to refer to the preamble of the Statute in order to determine whether or not a purpose was charitable. The objects there enumerated and all other objects which by analogy are decreed within its 'spirit and intendment' and no other objects are in law charitable.'

12.1.1 Spirit and intendment

Per Lord Russell in *Incorporated Council of Law Reporting v A-G* (1971):

> 'On this point [charitable purposes] the law is rooted in the Statute of Elizabeth, a statute the object of which was the oversight and reform of abuses ... The preamble to the Statute listed certain examples of purposes worthy of such protection. These were from an early stage regarded merely as examples, and have through the centuries been regarded as examples or signposts for the courts in the differing circumstances of a developing civilisation and economy. Sometimes recourse has been had by the courts to the instances given in the preamble in order to see whether in a given case sufficient analogy may be found with something specifically stated in the preamble, or sufficient analogy with some decided case in which already a previous analogy has been found ... For myself I believe that this rather vague and undefined approach is the correct one, with analogy its handmaid.'

12.1.2 Analogies

The preamble refers to 'the relief of aged, impotent and poor people'. It has been held that these words are to be read *disjunctively*. A trust is charitable, therefore, in general, where the beneficiaries are aged *or* impotent *or* poor: see *Re Glyn's WT* (1950).

12.2 Trusts for the relief of poverty

The term 'aged' has not been defined with precision in this context. The following cases are of relevance:

12.2.1 Relief of the aged

* *Re Glyn's WT* (1950). A residuary gift establishing a trust to build and endow free cottages for old persons of the

working class, aged sixty and above, was upheld. 'Aged persons' had not necessarily to be poor also to come within the spirit of the preamble.

- *Re Bradbury* (1950). A gift to pay money from a fund for the maintenance of 'an aged person or persons in a nursing home approved by my trustees' was upheld as charitable.

- *Re Robinson* (1951). A residuary estate was given by the testator to 'the old people over sixty-five years of age of Hazel Slade to be given as my trustees think best'. The gift was upheld. *Per* Vaisey J:

  'Here I think that 'the old people over sixty-five years' in a particular parish are a class of persons just as much objects of charity, having regard to the preamble of the Statute, as the poor of the parish or the sick of the parish. They are, I think, proper objects of the testator's charitable purposes.'

12.2.2   Impotent

The word 'impotent' has not been defined within the context of the Statute; several cases suggest that it is to be construed as meaning 'helpless' or 'lacking physical or mental powers'. It was used in *Re Hillier* (1944) to refer to trusts for the seriously ill, and in *Re Lewis* (1955) in relation to a bequest to blind children.

12.2.3   Poverty

In the sense applicable to this kind of trust, 'poverty' is a relative term which has not been defined precisely by the courts. *Per* Evershed MR in *Re Coulthurst* (1951):

'Poverty does not mean destitution; it is a word of wide and somewhat indefinite import; it may not unfairly be paraphrased for present purposes as meaning persons who have to 'go short' in the ordinary acceptation of that term, due regard being had to their status in life and so forth.'

Examples of *valid gifts* for the relief of poverty include:

- *Biscoe v Jackson* (1887) - a testator gave money out of a residuary estate to be applied so as to establish a soup kitchen and a cottage hospital adjoining.

- *Re Cottam* (1955) - a trust to apply money to build flats for persons over 65, living in a certain area, the flats to be let to them at economic rents.

- *Re Young* (1951) - a gift to persons 'of moderate means'.

Examples of *invalid gifts* for the relief of poverty include:

- *Re Drummond* (1914) - a gift to provide a contribution to the holiday expenses incurred by workpeople, who could not be described as 'poor people' within the meaning of the Statute.

- *Re Gwyon* (1930) - a testator established a fund to provide trousers for boys in Farnham, but there was no preference expressed in favour of the children of poor families. Qualifications included that a recipient should not belong to nor be supported by a charitable institution.

  Per Eve J:

  'None of the conditions necessarily imports poverty nor could the recipients be accurately described as a class of aged, impotent or poor people. The references to the receipt of parochial relief ... show, no doubt, that the testator contemplated that candidates might be forthcoming from a class of society where incidents of this nature might occur, but although a gift to or for the poor other than those who were in receipt of parochial relief - that is, paupers - would be a good charitable gift, it does not follow that a gift to all and sundry in a particular locality and not expressed for the poor ought to be construed as evidencing an intention to relieve poverty merely because the testator is minded to exclude paupers. I think that according to the true construction of these testamentary documents the benevolence of the testator was intended for all eligible boys other than paupers, and I cannot spell out of them any indication which would justify the Boys' Clothing Fundation Trustees refusing an applicant otherwise eligible on the ground that his material circumstances were of too affluent a character. In these circumstances I cannot hold this trust to be within the description of a legal charitable trust.'

- *Re Sanders' WT* (1954) - a gift to provide or assist in providing dwellings for the working classes and their families resident in a named area; it was held that the expression 'working classes' did not necessarily indicate poor people.

12.3   Trusts for the advancement of education

Trusts for the advancement of education derive their validity from the following words in the preamble: 'The maintenance of schools of learning, free schools and scholars in universities ... the education and preferment of orphans.' The meaning attached to the words has been extended so that they now embrace, eg, 'the improvement of a useful branch of human knowledge and its public dissemination': *per* Buckley LJ in *Incorporated Council of Law Reporting v A-G* (1971). 'Education' is not considered as confined to formal, classroom teaching.

12.3.1   Valid educational trusts

Examples of gifts upheld as valid educational charitable trusts include:

- *Royal Choral Society v IRC* (1943). The society's objectives were the formation and maintenance of a choir in order to promote the practice and performance of choral works. It was held that the society was charitable.

Per Lord Greene:

'Dealing with the educational aspect from the point of view of the public who hear music, the Solicitor-General argued that nothing could be educational which did not involve teaching - as I understood him, teaching in the sense of a master teaching a class. He said that in the domain of art the only thing that could be educational in a charitable sense would be the education of the executants: the teaching of the painter, the training of the musician, and so forth. I protest against that narrow conception of education when one is dealing with aesthetic education. Very few people can become executants, or at any rate executants who can give pleasure either to themselves or to others; but a very large number of people can become instructed listeners with a trained and cultivated taste. In my opinion, a body of persons established for the purpose of raising the artistic taste of the country and established by an appropriate document which confines them to that purpose, is established for educational purposes, because the education of artistic taste is one of the most important things in the development of a civilised human being.'

- *Re Shaw's WT* (1952). The widow of George Bernard Shaw bequeathed residue upon trusts for 'the teaching, promotion and encouragement in Ireland of self-control, elocution, oratory ... of social intercourse, and the other arts of public, private, professional and business life'. This was upheld as a valid, educational charitable trust. *Per* Vaisey J:

'I think that "education" includes ... not only teaching, but the promotion or encouragement of those arts and graces of life which are, after all, perhaps the finest and best part of the human character.'

12.3.2 Invalid educational trusts

Examples of gifts *not* upheld as valid educational trusts include:

- *Re Shaw's WT* (1957). George Bernard Shaw's gift of residuary property was to be applied through trusts to the creation of a new English alphabet. It was held that the trusts were not charitable because, *inter alia*, they were not for the advancement of education.

- *Re Pinion* (1965). A testator gave his studio, paintings and objets d'art to be offered to the National Trust to be kept intact and displayed to the public. It was held that the trust was for purposes which had neither public utility nor educative value; it was therefore, void.

Per Harman LJ:

'A reading of the will leads me rather to the view that the testator's object was not to educate anyone, but to

perpetuate his own name and the repute of his family ...
there is a strong body of evidence here that as a means of
education this collection is worthless ... I can conceive of
no useful object to be served in foisting upon the public
this mass of junk ... I would hold that the testator's project
ought not to be carried into effect and that his next-of-kin
is entitled to the residue of the estate.'

In general, a trust for party political education is *not* charitable.
Examples include

- *Re Hopkinson* (1949). A residuary estate was given to
  establish an educational fund for the advancement of adult
  education 'with particular reference to the education of men
  and women of all classes on the lines of [a Labour Party
  memorandum] to a higher conception of social, political
  and economic ideas and values ...'. It was held that the trust
  was not charitable. 'Political propaganda masquerading - I
  do not use the word in any sinister sense - as education is
  not education within the Statute of Elizabeth. In other
  words it is not charitable': *per* Vaisey J.

- *Re Bushnell* (1975). A gift providing for funds to be used in
  the propagation of the teaching of 'socialised medicine' by
  engaging lecturers to show that 'the full advantage of
  socialised medicine can only be enjoyed within a socialist
  state' was held invalid. The dominant and essential object
  of the trust was a political one.

- *Re Koeppler's WT* (1986). A residuary estate was left for the
  benefit of Wilton Park 'to the formation of an informed
  international public opinion and to the promotion of
  greater co-operation in Europe and the West in general'. It
  was held that the gift was valid.

  Per Slade LJ:

  '... In the present case ... the activities of Wilton Park are not
  of a party political nature. Nor, so far as evidence shows,
  are they designed to procure changes in the laws or
  governmental policy of this or any other country: even
  when they touch on political matters, they constitute, so far
  as I can see, no more than genuine attempts in an objective
  manner to ascertain and disseminate the truth. In these
  circumstances I think that no objections to the trust arise on
  a political score ... The trust is, in my opinion, entitled to
  what is sometimes called "benignant construction", in the
  sense that the court is entitled to presume that the trustees
  will only act in a lawful and proper manner appropriate to
  the trustees of a charity, and not, for example, by the
  propagation of tendentious political opinions, anymore
  than those running the Wilton Park project so acted in the
  13 years preceding the testator's death.'

12.3.3   Political education

12.3.4	For the public benefit	A trust for the advancement of education must involve some element of public benefit if it is to be held valid. Thus, in *Davies v Perpetual Trustee Co* (1959), land in Australia was given by will to 'Presbyterians ... to be held in trust for the purpose of establishing a college for the education and tuition of their youth in the standards of the Westminster Divines as taught in the Holy Scriptures'. The Privy Council held the trust to be void since it lacked the necessary element of public benefit. See also *Oppenheim v Tobacco Securities Trust Co* (1951); *IRC v Educational Grants Association* (1967) ('... the objects of the corporation, in order that they may be exclusively charitable, must be confined to objects for the public benefit': *per* Pennycuick J).

12.4 Trusts for the advancement of religion

The charitable nature of trusts for the advancement of religion is apparently derived from the following words in the preamble to the Statute: 'The repair of ... churches'. A trust of this nature generally qualifies today as a valid charity *if* it is intended strictly for a religious purpose *and* for the benefit of the public *or* some section of it.

> *Per* Donovan J in *United Grand Lodge v Holborn BC* (1957):
>
> 'To advance religion means to promote it, to spread its message ever wider among mankind; to take some positive steps to sustain and increase religious belief; and these things are done in a variety of ways which may be comprehensively described as pastoral and missionary.'
>
> *Per* Lord Harmsworth in *Keren Kayemeth v IRC* (1931):
>
> 'The "advancement of religion" has been interpreted as being synonymous with its "promotion". The promotion of religion has been said to involve "the promotion of spiritual teaching' in a wide sense, and the maintenance of the doctrines on which it rests, and the observances that serve to promote and manifest it.'

12.4.1   The meaning of religion

'The Court of Chancery makes no distinction between one religion and another, unless the tenets of a particular sect inculcate doctrines adverse to the very foundations of all religions': *per* Romilly MR in *Thornton v Howe* (1862). 'It seems to me that two of the essential attributes of religion are faith and worship; faith in a god and worship of that god': *per* Dillon J in *Re South Place Ethical Society* (1980) (in which it was held that the objects of a society which were 'the study and dissemination of ethical principles and the cultivation of a rational religious sentiment' were not 'for the advancement of religion').

> *Per* Dillon J:
>
> 'The first part of [the Society's] objects is the study and dissemination of ethical principles. Dissemination, I think, includes dissemination of the fruits of the study, and I have

no doubt that that part of the objects satisfies the criterion of charity as being for the advancement of education. The second part, the cultivation of a rational religious sentiment, is considerably more difficult. As I have already said I do not think that the cultivation is limited to cultivation of the requisite sentiment in the members of the Society and in no one else. In the context the Society is outward looking, and the cultivation would extend to all members of the public whom the Society's teachings may reach. The sentiment or state of mind is to be rational, that is to say founded in reason. As I see it, a sentiment or attitude of mind founded in reason can only be cultivated or encouraged to grow by educational methods ... The difficulty in this part of the Society's objects lies in expressing a very lofty and possibly unattainable ideal in a very few words, and the difficulty is compounded by the choice of the word "religious", which, while giving the flavour of what is in mind, is not in my view used in its correct sense.'

'As between different religions the law stands neutral, but it seems that any religion is at least likely to be better than none': *per* Cross J in *Neville Estates v Madden* (1962).

	12.4.2 The neutrality of the law

Trusts have been upheld in favour, not only of the established church, but of: the Church Army, the Salvation Army, the Jewish religion, Roman Catholics, Unitarians, the 'Moonies' (Unification Church).

Trusts have *not* been upheld in the case of: the Oxford Movement, the Theosophical Society, a trust requiring ancestor worship (see *Yeap Cheah Neo v Ong Cheng Neo* (1875)), Freemasonry (see *United Grand Lodge v Holborn BC* (1957)). *Per* Donovan J:

'Masonry ... says to a man "Whatever your religion or your mode of worship, believe in a Supreme Creator and lead a good moral life"; laudable as this precept is, it does not appear to us to be the same thing as the advancement of religion. There is no religious instruction, no programme for the persuasion of unbelievers, no religious supervision to see that its members remain active and constant in the various religions they may profess, no holding of religious services, no pastoral or missionary work of any kind.'

In relation to gifts for related purposes, see *Re Forster* (1938) - a gift for the relief of sick and aged Roman Catholic priests was upheld; *Re Royce* (1940) - a gift for the benefit of a church choir was held valid; *Re Moon's WT* (1948) - a bequest for 'mission work' was held to involve Christian mission work and, to be, therefore, valid. (The context of a gift of this nature ought to indicate that religious purposes were in the donor's mind.) For gifts to the clergy *virtute officii*, see para 11.6.2.

	12.4.3 Gifts for related purposes

12.4.4   For the public benefit

The general rule is that a trust for the advancement of religion must be beneficial to the public or a section of it.

- *Bourne v Keane* (1919). The House of Lords considered a gift of residuary personal estate to 'the Jesuit Fathers at Farm Street' for masses to be said for the testator. The trust was held to be not void (as superstitious).

- *Re Caus* (1934). A gift for the saying of masses was held charitable because it enabled the performance of an important ritual act and assisted in the endowment of the participating priests.

- *Gilmour v Coats* (1949). A trust fund was to be applied to the purposes of a Carmelite convent of strictly cloistered nuns. It was argued that their prayers and meditations were for the benefit of persons outside the convent. The House of Lords held that the purposes of the convent lacked the element of public benefit necessary to render the trust fund charitable. *Per* Lord Simonds:

  '[In *Cocks v Manners* (1871)] the learned judge ... said: "A voluntary association of women for the purpose of working out their own salvation by religious exercises and self-denial seems to me to have none of the requisites of a charitable institution, whether the word 'charitable' is used in its popular sense or legal sense." Whether I affirm or deny, whether I believe or disbelieve, what has that got to do with the proof which the court demands that a particular purpose satisfies the test of benefit to the community? Here is something which is manifestly not susceptible of proof.'

- In *Neville Estates v Madden* (1962) there was argument as to whether trustees holding land on trust for the advancement of the Jewish religion among a private group of people were holding for charitable purposes. *Per* Cross J:

  'The court is, I think, entitled to assume that some benefit accrues to the public from the attendance at places of worship of persons who live in this world and mix with their fellow citizens ... Generally speaking, no doubt, an association which is supported by its members for the purposes of providing benefits for themselves will not be a charity. But I do not think this principle can apply with full force in the case of trusts for religious purposes ... In my judgment, this trust ... is a charitable trust.'

- *Re Hetherington* (1990). The testatrix left funds to the Bishop of Westminster 'for the repose of the souls of my husband and my parents and sisters and also myself when I die', and residuary estate to a named church 'for masses for my soul'. Browne-Wilkinson VC stated that the cases established certain propositions. *First*, a trust for the advancement of religion is *prima facie* charitable and assumed to be for the public benefit; this can be rebutted by showing that the trust cannot operate so as to confer a legally recognised benefit on the public. *Second*, the celebration of a religious rite in public does confer a sufficient public benefit. *Third*, the celebration of a religious rite in private does not contain the necessary element of public benefit.

It was held that, applying these principles to the present case, the gift for the saying of masses to be celebrated in public provided a sufficient element of public benefit.

The provision of stipends for the priests saying the masses was a further benefit because it relieved the church *pro tanto* of the liability to provide stipends.

Per Viscount Cave in *A-G v National Provincial Bank* (1924):

'Lord MacNaghten did not mean that all trusts for purposes beneficial to the community are charitable, but that there were certain charitable trusts which fell within the category; and accordingly to argue that because a trust is for a purpose beneficial to the community it is therefore a charitable trust is to turn round his sentence and to give it a different meaning. So here it is not enough to say that the trust in question is for public purposes beneficial to the community or for the public welfare; you must also show it to be a charitable trust.'

The benefit to the public must be within the spirit and intendment of the Statute of Elizabeth.

12.5 Trusts for other purposes beneficial to the community

Trusts for the protection of animals will generally be held valid charitable trusts, since they are considered to benefit humanity by protecting morality through 'the checking of an innate tendency to cruelty': see *Re Wedgwood* (1915). Testatrix gave residuary estate upon trust for the protection and benefit of animals. She appeared to have agreed with the trustee's argument that her wishes might be met by providing municipal abbatoirs which would make the slaughtering of animals more humane, but she had allowed the trustee freedom as to the exact way in which her general object was to be effected. The court held the gift charitable.

12.5.1 Animals

Per Swinfen-Eady LJ:

'A gift for the benefit and protection of animals tends to promote and encourage kindness towards them, to discourage cruelty ... and by these means promote feelings of humanity and morality generally, repress brutality, and thus elevate the human race.'

- *University of London v Yarrow* (1857). A bequest to establish a hospital 'in which animals, which are useful to mankind, should be properly treated and cured and the nature of their disease investigated, with a view to public advantage', was held charitable.

- *Re Grove-Grady* (1929). A trust to found a society to acquire land 'for the purpose of providing a refuge or refuges for the preservation of all animals, birds or other creatures not human ... and so that they shall there be safe from molestation or destruction by man' was held not charitable since it did not contain any element of benefit to the community.

Per Russell LJ:

'It comes down to this, that the residuary estate may be applied in acquiring a tract of land, in turning it into an animal sanctuary, and keeping a staff of employees to ensure that no human being shall ever molest or destroy any of the animals there. Is that a good charitable trust within the authorities? In my opinion it is not ... It seems to me impossible to say that the carrying out of such a trust necessarily involves benefit to the public ... The authorities have, in my opinion, reached the furthest admissible point of benevolence in construing as charitable gifts in favour of animals, and for myself, I am not prepared to go any further.'

| 12.5.2 | Relief of the sick |

A gift for the relief of the sick or an allied purpose will generally be held to be charitable.

- *Re Chaplin* (1933). A gift 'to afford the means of physical and mental recuperation to persons in need of rest by reason of the stress and strain caused or partly caused by the conditions in which they ordinarily live or work', was held charitable.

- *Re Osmund* (1944). A gift for the furtherance of 'psychological healing in accordance with the teaching of Jesus Christ', was held charitable, as constituting a gift to further the art of healing the sick.

| 12.5.3 | Efficiency of the public services, etc |

Examples of gifts for the efficiency of the public services, etc are as follows:

- *Re Good* (1905). A testator gave residuary property on trust for his regimental officers' mess to be applied in maintaining a library for the mess, the surplus to be used for the purchase of plate for the mess. It was held that the gifts were charitable, as tending to increase the efficiency of the army.

- *Re Driffill* (1950). A trust was to be applied 'in whatever manner the trustees may consider desirable to promote the defence of the United Kingdom against the attack of hostile aircraft'. The gift was held charitable.

The following have been upheld: trust to preserve two ancient cottages; gift to the Royal National Lifeboat Institution; trust 'for showground park and recreational purposes' (*Brisbane CC v A-G for Queensland* (1979)).

The charitable status of some associations concerned with sporting activities was increasingly questioned, and the Recreational Charities Act 1958 attempted to remedy the situation.

Section 1(1): 'It shall be and be deemed always to have been charitable to provide, or assist in the provision of, facilities for recreation or other leisure-time occupation, if the facilities are provided in the interests of social welfare'.

The requirements of 'social welfare' are not to be treated as satisfied unless: the facilities are provided with the object of improving the conditions of life for the persons for whom the facilities are primarily intended; and, either, those persons have need of such facilities by reason of their youth, age, infirmity or disablement, poverty or social and economic circumstances, or the facilities are to be available to members of the public at large: s 1(2)(a), (b).

In *Guild v IRC* (1992), the House of Lords considered the 1958 Act, s 1. A testator left residuary estate to 'the town council of North Berwick for use in connection with the sports centre in North Berwick or some similar purpose in connection with sport'. The Inland Revenue argued that they did not consider the gift charitable for the purposes of exemption from capital transfer tax. The House of Lords rejected the argument that the requirement that the gift must be 'in the interests of social welfare' meant that the intended recipients should be in some form of need. This was not so: the conditions of life could be improved for the community by providing a recreational facility of suitable character. The argument that the phrase 'or some similar purpose in connection with sport' was so wide as to remove the gift from the scope of the 1958 Act was rejected. The testator's intention was limited to purposes closely similar to those of the original sports centre. This meant the provision of recreational facilities available to the public at large. The gift was, therefore, charitable; s 1 of the Act was satisfied. See also *Russell's Executor v IRC* (1992).

Charitable Trusts (2)

The preamble (to the 1601 Statute) refers to 'the relief of aged, impotent and poor people'.

Trusts for the relief of poverty

The words are now read disjunctively. See *Re Glyn's WT* (1950).

'Aged' has not been defined precisely. See *Re Bradbury* (1950).

'Impotent' has not been defined within the context of the preamble. It has been construed as meaning 'helpless' or 'lacking physical or mental powers': see *Re Lewis* (1955) (bequest to blind children).

'Poverty' is a relative term and has not been defined. It does not mean destitution. Thus, a gift to persons 'of moderate means' (*Re Coulthurst* (1951)) was upheld. Gift to provide dwellings for the working classes in a stated area (*Re Sanders' WT* (1954)) was not upheld.

The preamble refers to 'the maintenance of schools of learning, free schools and scholars in universities ... the education and preferment of orphans'.

Trusts for the advancement of education

'Education' is construed as ranging beyond formal classroom teaching.

Examples of gifts *upheld*: a gift to a society whose objectives related to the practice and performance of choral works (*Royal Choral Society* (1943)); a gift for the teaching and promotion of self-control, elocution, oratory (*Re Shaw's WT* (1952)). Examples of gifts *not upheld*: a gift for creation of new English alphabet (*Re Shaw* (1957)); a gift to display personal *objets d'art* to the public (*Re Pinion* (1965)).

In general, a trust for political education is not upheld. See *Re Bushnell* (1975); *Re Koeppler's WT* (1986).

A trust for the advancement of education must involve an element of public benefit if it is to be held valid. See *Davies v Perpetual Trustee Co* (1959).

The preamble refers to 'the repair of churches'. The essential attributes of religion were stated, in *Re South Place Ethical Society* (1980) as faith in a god and worship of that god.

Trusts for advancement of religion

Trusts have been upheld in favour of the established church, Salvation Army, Unitarians. Trusts have not been upheld in the case of the Oxford Movement, the Theosophical Society.

Trusts for related purposes, eg, relief of sick and aged priests, may be upheld.

A trust of this nature must be shown to be beneficial to the public or a section of it. See, eg, *Bourne v Keane* (1919); *Re Hetherington* (1990) - gifts for the saying of masses.

Trusts for other purposes beneficial to the community

The benefit to the public must be within the spirit and intendment of the 1601 Statute. Trusts for the protection of animals will generally be upheld, as will trusts for the relief of the sick (or an allied purpose), the promotion of efficiency of the public services, etc. See *Re Good* (1905); *Re Driffill* (1950).

Recreational charities

Under the Recreational Charities Act 1958, it is deemed charitable to provide - or assist in the provision of facilities - for recreation or other leisure-time occupation if those facilities are provided in the interests of social welfare: s l(l). 'Social welfare' must be related to the object of improving the conditions of life for those for whom the facilities are primarily intended. See *Guild v IRC* (1992).

Chapter 13

Charitable Trusts (3)

In general, a charitable trust which by its terms is impossible initially, or is impracticable, or becomes so subsequently, will not necessarily fail. The court may apply the trust property *cy-près* to some other charitable purpose which resembles the original purpose as nearly as possible. The settlor's intentions will be carried out in this way as nearly as is practicable. (*Cy-près* = *si pres*, so near, as near.) *Per* Kay J in *Re Taylor* (1888):

13.1   **Basis of the**
        ***cy-près* doctrine**

'If upon the whole scope and intent of the will you discover the paramount intention of the testator was to benefit not a particular institution, but to effect a particular form of charity independently of any special institution or mode, then, although he may have indicated the mode in which he desires that to be carried out, you are to regard the primary paramount intention chiefly, and if the particular mode for any reason fails, the court, if it sees a sufficient expression of a general intention of charity, will, to use the phrase familiar to us, execute that *cy-près*, that is, carry out the general paramount intention indicated without which his intention itself cannot be effectuated.'

Under the Charities Act 1993, two conditions are essential for the application of the *cy-près* doctrine: there must exist (in most cases) a general charitable intention; it must be 'impossible' (in the sense laid down by the Act) to carry out the trust. (The Commissioners now have concurrent jurisdiction with the High Court to direct an application *cy-près:* s 16(1).)

Prior to the Charities Act 1960 the *cy-près* doctrine was applicable only if the carrying out of the trust was impossible or impracticable. The terms were construed restrictively, so that the doctrine could not be applied where, eg, the objects of the trust had become less significant because of changed economic or social conditions. (It should be noted that the Charities Act 1993 consolidated the Charitable Trustees Incorporation Act 1872 and, save for certain spent or transitional provisions, the Charities Act 1960 and the Charities Act 1992, Part 1. It is *not* a consolidation of the law of charity in its entirety; thus the Recreational Charities Act remains apart from the 1993 Act.)

It is no longer necessary in considering a charitable trust to decide whether 'impossibility' in the old sense of that term exists or not. It now suffices that the case can be brought under any one of the heads stated in the 1993 Act, s 13,

13.2   **The Charities**
        Act 1993, s 13

so that the court may direct a *cy-près* application in any of these circumstances. See, eg, *Re JW Laing Trust* (1984); *Alton BC v A-G* (1993).

13.2.1   Section 13(1)(a)

Cy-près application is possible where 'the original purposes, in whole or part, have been as far as may be fulfilled, or cannot be carried out, or not according to the directions given and to the spirit of the gift': s 13(1)(a).

See *Re Lysaght* (1966), in which the testator gave funds for the foundation of medical scholarships with a qualifying condition which excluded persons of the Catholic or Jewish faiths. The Royal College of Surgeons refused the gift because the condition was so alien to its work 'as to make the gift inoperable in its present form'. It was prepared to accept the gift if the condition were deleted. The court ordered a scheme for the money to be paid to the Royal College with the condition omitted. *Per* Buckley, J:

> 'A general charitable intention may be said to be a paramount intention on the part of the donor to effect some charitable purpose which the court can find a method of putting into operation, notwithstanding that it is impracticable to give effect to some direction by the donor which is not an essential part of his true intention - not, that is to say, part of his paramount intention. In contrast, a particular charitable intention exists where the donor means his charitable disposition to take effect, but only if it can be carried into effect in a particular specified way, for example, in connection with a particular school to be established at a particular place ...'

13.2.2   Section 13(1)(b)

Cy-près application is possible where 'the original purposes provide a use for part only of the property available by virtue of the gift': s 13(1)(b).

13.2.3   Section 13(1)(c)

Cy-près application is possible where 'the property available by virtue of the gift and other property applicable for similar purposes can be more effectively used in conjunction, and to that end can suitably, regard being had to the spirit of the gift, be made applicable to common purposes': s 13(1)(c).

13.2.4   Section 13(1)(d)

Cy-près application is possible where 'the original purposes were laid down by reference to an area which was then, but has since ceased to be a unit for some other purpose, or by reference to a class of persons or to an area which has for any reason since ceased to be suitable, regard being had to the spirit of the gift, or to be practical in administering the gift': s 13(1)(d).

In *Peggs and Others v Lamb and Others* (1993), it was held that the 'freeman and the widows of freemen of the ancient borough of Huntingdon' were not entitled to any part of the property held by plaintiff trustees whether under a private trust or otherwise pursuant to the Municipal Corporations Act 1835 and its statutory successors.

Morritt, J stated that all such property was applicable to charitable purposes generally among the class of qualifying 'freemen' and their widows, but a scheme should be directed so as to widen the class by reference to which the charitable purposes were laid down to include the inhabitations of the ancient borough as a whole.

The effect of the 1835 Act had been to destroy the political importance of 'freemen', thus undermining their social and economic importance. The membership of the class was thereby restricted and the inevitable consequence was that over 150 years the class had dwindled very considerably. A time would come when the class of 'freemen' ceased to be a section of the public at all.

The original basic intention or spirit of the gift was the benefit of the borough of Huntingdon. It was entirely consistent with that that in 1993 the class of persons by reference to which the charitable purposes were laid down should be enlarged from the 'freemen' to the inhabitants as a whole. The trust property should be held for charitable purposes for all the borough.

Cy-près application is possible where 'the original purposes, in whole or part, have, since they were laid down, (i) been adequately provided for by other means; or (ii) ceased, as being useless or harmful to the community or other reasons, to be in law charitable; or (iii) ceased in any other way to provide a suitable and effective method of using the property available by virtue of the gift, regard being had to the spirit of the gift': s 13(1)(e).

13.2.5   Section 13(1)(e)

In *Re Lepton's Charity* (1971), L, under the will of 1715, devised land ('Dickroyd'), in Pudsey, on trust to pay £3 per annum to the 'Protestant Dissenting Minister' at Pudsey, surplus to go to the poor and aged people of Pudsey. L died in 1716, the total income was £5 pa; in 1971 the income was £791. There was, in 1970, a 'Protestant Dissenting Minister' at Pudsey. The question arose as to whether the court had jurisdiction to vary the will by ordering a scheme under the the Charities Act 1960, s 13 [re-enacted in the 1993 Act], so as to increase the annual payment to £100. The court ordered such a scheme. *Per* Pennycuick, VC:

'It is to my mind clear that in circumstances of the present case the original purposes of the gift of "Dickroyd" cannot be carried out according to the spirit of the gift ... The intention underlying the gift was to divide a sum which, according to the values of 1715, was modest but not negligible, in such a manner that the minister took what was then a clear three-fifths of it. The intention is plainly defeated when in the conditions of today the minister takes a derisory £3 out of a total of £791 ... I conclude that the new conditions for *cy-près* applications introduced by s 13 have been satisfied.'

13.2.6   **Section 13(2) -(3)**

The following subsections should be noted:

- Section 13(2)

  Subsection (1) [see above] shall not affect the conditions which must be satisfied in order that property given for charitable purposes, may be applied *cy-près*, except in so far as those conditions require a failure of the original purposes.

- Section 13(3)

  References in the foregoing subsections to the original purposes of a gift shall be construed, where the application of the property given has been altered or regulated by a scheme or otherwise, as referring to the purposes for which the property is for the time being applicable.

13.3   **Trustee's duty**

'A trust for charitable purposes places a trustee under a duty, where the case permits and requires the property or some part of it to be applied *cy-près*, to secure its effective use for charity by taking steps to enable it to be so applied': s 13(5). (Note the comments of Lord Simonds in *National Anti-Vivisection Society v IRC* (1948).)

The time for determining whether or not a charitable gift is 'impossible' is generally the date of the testator's death.

Should a trust, at that time, be impracticable, and should it seem that there is no prospect of its ever becoming practicable, the property should be distributed *cy-près*. See *Re Wright* (1954).

13.4   **General charitable intent**

If the *cy-près* doctrine is to be applied, the settlor must have shown, in most cases, a general charitable intention; but this applies only where the trust has failed *ab initio*. Absence of a general charitable intention will not necessarily be fatal to a trust which has taken effect, but which has failed at a later stage. In such a case funds may be applied *cy-près*.

Whether or not a general charitable intention exists is a matter of construction of the document purporting to create the trust. In *Re Finger's WT* (1972), the testatrix bequeathed residuary estate in 1939 in equal shares to charitable institutions including the National Radium Commission, and the National Council for Maternity and Child Welfare (NCMCW). The National Radium Commission and Trust was wound up in 1947 and its work was continued by the Ministry of Health. The

NCMCW was wound up in 1948, its work being carried on by the National Association for Maternity and Child Welfare. It was held that the gift to the National Radium Commission was *per se* a purpose trust for the work of the Commission; effect would be given to it by a *cy-près* scheme. In the case of the second gift: 'I do find a general charitable intention. Accordingly this share is applicable *cy-près* ... and I order ... that this share be paid to the proper officer of the association to be held on trust to apply the same for its general purposes': *per* Goff J. See also *Liverpool and District Hospital v A-G* (1981).

Where a gift is made to an institution which existed at the testator's death but ceased to exist before it received the legacy, the legacy passes with other property of that institution to the Crown and is applied *cy-près* irrespective of the question of general charitable intention. See *Re Slevin* (1891); *Re Hanbey's WT* (1956).

The intention to devote the gift to charity must be of 'an overriding nature': see *Re Sanders' WT* (1954). The assertion in express terms of a general charitable intention will not suffice if contradicted by its context.

A gift to a charitable institution which has never existed may indicate a general charitable intention if the name suggests a charitable object: see *Re Davis* (1902) ('Homes for the Homeless'). In *Re Satterthwaite's WT* (1966), a gift to 'London Animal Hospital' was applied *cy-près*; no hospital of that name existed but other gifts had been made by the testatrix to animal charities. *Per* Russell, LJ:

> 'I have indicated that [testatrix] is to be taken as intending to benefit a charitable activity. But the organisation picked by name was not such. *Prima facie*, therefore, the bequest would fail and there would be a lapse, with the result in this case in fact - owing to the incidence of liabilities and death duties - of mere relief of other residuary objects. But my assumption is that the testatrix was pointing to a particular charitable application of this one-ninth of residue. If a particular mode of charitable application is capable of being performed as such, but it can be discerned from his will that the testator has a charitable intention (commonly referred to as a general charitable intention) which transcends the particular mode of application indicated, the court has jurisdiction to direct application of the bequest to charitable purposes *cy-près*. Here I have no doubt from the nature of other dispositions by this testatrix of her residuary estate that a general intention can be discerned in favour of charity through the medium of kindness to animals. I am not in any way deterred from this conclusion by the fact that one-ninth of residue was given to an anti-vivisection society which in law - unknown to the average testator - is not charitable.'

No such intention can be easily implied where there is a gift to a precisely-described charity which has ceased to exist before the testator's death. In *Re Spence* (1979), a testatrix left a moiety (half) of her residue to 'the Old Folks Home at Hillworth Lodge, Keighley for the benefit of the patients'. It had been closed down one year before the death of the testatrix. *Per* Megarry VC:

'The moiety was given for a specific charitable purpose which, though possible when the will was made, became impossible before the testatrix died. The gift of the moiety fails, and it passes on intestacy'.

A particular charity may no longer exist in its original form, but the court may find that it is continuing elsewhere. See *Re Faraker* (1912).

The assertion in express terms of a general charitable intention will not suffice if contradicted by its context: see *Re Sanders' WT* (1954).

See also *Shorthouse's Trustees v Aberdeen Medico-Chirurgical Society* (1977), in which the testator left property to the society for the benefit of disabled, aged or retired doctors, preferably Aberdeen graduates, living in certain areas, and their widows. Residue was left on a similar basis. The bequest was refused. It was held that the testator had evinced a general charitable purpose, so that the property and residue would be applied *cy-près*.

13.5 Cy-près application of gifts of donors who are unknown or who disclaim

Assume that an appeal for a charitable purpose was followed by events which make achievement of the appeal's objectives impracticable or impossible. The disposal of surplus funds will present a problem. Prior to the 1960 Act, the decisions of the courts indicated that *cy-près* application was possible where the contributors had shown a general charitable intent. See *Re Ulverston and District New Hospital Building Fund* (1956). In any other case, however, any unclaimed surplus would have gone to the Crown as *bona vacantia*, or reverted to the donors on resulting trust, and this would have involved the identification of many donors who might have been anonymous. Basic reforms were introduced by the Charities Act 1960, s 14, and the Charities Act 1992.

13.5.1 Charities Act 1993, s 14

Charities Act 1993, s 14:

'(1) Property given for specific charitable purposes which fail shall be applicable *cy-près* as if given for charitable purposes generally, where it belongs-

(a) to a donor who after such advertisements and inquiries have been published and made, and the prescribed period beginning with the publication of those advertisements has expired, cannot be identified or cannot be found; or

(b) to a donor who has executed a disclaimer in the prescribed form to have the property returned

(2) Where the prescribed advertisements and inquiries have been published and made by or on behalf of trustees with respect to any such property, the trustees shall not be liable to any person in respect of the property if no claim by him to be interested in it is received by them before the expiry of the period mentioned in sub-section (l)(a).'

Property is conclusively presumed (without advertisement or inquiry) to belong to donors who cannot be identified in so far as it consists of cash collections made by collecting boxes, proceeds of lotteries, competitions, etc: s 14(3).

The court may order that property not falling within s 14(2) shall be treated as belonging to donors who cannot be identified, where it appears to the court that it would be unreasonable to incur expense with a view to returning the property: s l4(4).

Sections 74-75 of the 1993 Act allow, in the case of small charities, the transfer of assets to another charity, the alteration of objects, procedures and power to spend capital, all of which may be considered as an alternative to the creation of a *cy-près* scheme.	**13.6 Modification of small charities under the Charities Act 1993**

Section 74 applies to a charity if its gross income in its last financial year did not exceed (currently) £5,000, and it does not hold land on any trusts which stipulate that the land is to be used for the purposes, or any particular purposes, of the charity, and it is neither an exempt charity nor a charitable company.

13.6.1   Section 74

Where the trustees are satisfied that the existing purposes of the transferor charity have ceased to be conducive to 'a suitable and effective application of the charity's resources' and that the purposes of the charity specified in the resolution passed by the charity trustees (stating the the property of the charity is to be transferred), the trustees should give public notice of that resolution and send a copy to the Commissioners: s 74(6).

Where the Commissioners concur with the resolution, the trustees must arrange for a transfer of the property by a date specified in the resolution: s 74(9).

The trusts of the transferor charity may be modified by replacing all or any of the purposes of the charity with such other purposes, being in law charitable, as are specified in the resolution (of the charity trustees): s 74(9).

Section 75 applies to a charity which has a permanent endowment which does not consist of or comprise any land, and its gross income in its last financial year did not exceed

13.6.2   Section 75: power to spend capital

(currently) £1,000, and it is neither an exempt charity nor a charitable company. Where the trustees are of the opinion that the charity is too small, in relation to its purposes, for any useful purpose to be achieved by the expenditure of income alone, they may resolve that the charity ought to be freed from restrictions with respect to capital expenditure to which its permanent endowment is subject: s 75(2). The Commissioners must notify the trustees that they concur or do not concur with the resolution: s 75(7). In this section 'charitable company' means a charity which is a company or other body corporate: s 75 (10).

13.7   The Charity Commissioners

The Commissioners (first appointed under the Charitable Trusts Act 1853) consist of a Chief Commissioner and others appointed by the Secretary of State. Their general function is to promote 'the effective use of charitable resources by encouraging the development of better methods of administration, by giving charity trustees information or advice on any matter affecting the charity, and by investigating and checking abuses': Charities Act 1993, s 1(3). Their object is 'so to act in the case of any charity (unless it is a matter of altering its purposes) as best to promote and make effective the work of the charity in meeting the needs designated by its trusts': s 1(4). (The trustees of a charity remain responsible for its administration.)

13.7.1   Powers

They have no power, in general, to act in the administration of a trust: s l(4), and they must report annually to the Secretary of State on their operations: s l(5). The following are examples of the powers of the Charity Commissioners.

- The Commissioners keep a register of charities in such manner as they think fit (eg on computer) and every charity, save those exempted, shall be entered on the register: s 3(1)(2). An excepted charity may apply for registration.

  Exempt charities (see the Second Schedule to the 1993 Act) include: the Universities of Oxford and Cambridge, certain other universities, Eton and Winchester colleges, the British Museum, Friendly Societies registered under the Friendly Societies Acts 1896-1992.

  A charity which has neither any permanent endowment nor the use or occupation of any land and whose income from all sources does not in aggregate amount (currently) to more than £1,000 a year, need not be registered.

  Registered places of worship (under the Places of Worship Registration Act 1855) are exempt.

- They may give a direction requiring the name of a charity to be changed, within the period specified in the direction, to such other name as the charity trustees may determine with the approval of the Commissioners: 1993 Act, s 6(1).

  Section 6(1) applies to a registered charity only if its registered name is the same as, or is in the opinion of the Commissioners, too like the name, at the time when the registered name was entered in the register in respect of the charity, of any other charity (registered or not): s 6(2). It applies also to a charity if the name of the charity is, in the Commissioners' opinion, likely to mislead the public as to the true nature of the purposes of the charity as set out in its trusts, or of the activities which the charity carries on under its trusts in pursuit of those purposes: s 6(2)(b). The Commissioners will require a change in name also: where the name of the charity includes any word or expression for the time being specified in regulations and the inclusion in its name of that word or expression is in the opinion of the Commissioners likely to mislead the public in any respect as to the status of the charity; where the name of the charity is, in the opinion of the Commissioners likely to give the impression that the charity is connected in some way with the Government, or any local authority, or with any other body of persons or any individual, when it is not so connected; where the Commissioners consider the name of the charity to be offensive: s 6(2).

  See SI 1992/1901 (Charities (Misleading Names) Regulations) for proscribed words.

- They may institute inquiries and may order the investigation and auditing of accounts: s 8.

  Where the Commissioners have instituted an inquiry with respect to a charity and are satisfied that there has been misconduct or mismanagement in the administration of the charity or are satisfied that it is necessary to act so as to protect charity property, they may suspend any trustee or officer of the charity, appoint additional charity trustees, vest property in the official custodian for charities, appoint a receiver and manager in respect of the charity's property and affairs: ss 18,19.

- The supplier of false or misleading information to the Commissioners is guilty of an offence: s 11. The consent of the DPP is required for the institution of proceedings under s 11: s 94.

- Failure to comply with an order of the Commissioners is capable of being considered a contempt of court: s 88.

- Where the Commissioners are informed by 'a relevant institution' (eg, Bank of England, an institution authorised to operate a deposit taking business, a building society) that it holds accounts in the name of a charity and that they are 'dormant', ie, unused for five years, they may require the institution concerned to transfer the aggregate amount standing to the credit of the charity to some other charity specified in the Commissioners' directions: s 28.

13.8 Restrictions on dispositions of charity land

In general, no land held by or in trust for a charity shall be sold, leased or otherwise disposed of without an order of the court or of the Commissioners: s 36(1). This sub-section does not apply where the disposition is made to a person who is not a connected person, or a trustee for, or nominee of, a connected person: s 36(2). 'Connected person' is defined in the 1993 Act, Sch 5, as including a trustee for the charity; a person who is the donor of any land to the charity; child, parent, grandparent, brother or sister of any such trustee or donor; officer, agent or employee of the charity.

Except where the proposed disposition is the granting of a lease for not more than a seven-year term, the charity trustees must, before entering into an agreement for sale, or other disposition, obtain and consider a written report from a surveyor; advertise the proposed disposition; and decide that they are satisfied, having considered the surveyor's report, that the terms on which the disposition is proposed to be made are the best that can reasonably be obtained for the charity: s 32.

No mortgage of land held by or in trust for a charity shall be granted without an order of the Court or of the commissioners. This shall not apply, however, to a mortgage of charity land by way of a security for the repayment of a loan where the charity trustees have, before executing the mortgage, obtained and considered proper advice (given by a person who is reasonably believed by the trustees to be qualified and who has no financial interest in the making of the loan in question): s 38.

13.9 Official Custodian for Charities

Under s 2(1) there shall continue to be an officer, having corporate status, known as the official custodian for charities. His function is to act as trustee for charities in cases provided for by the 1993 Act. The Commissioners shall designate the official custodian. He is not liable as trustee for any charity in respect of any loss or of the mis-application of any property unless it is occasioned by or through the wilful neglect or default of the custodian or any person acting for him; but the

Consolidated Fund shall be liable to make good to a charity any sums for which the custodian may be liable by reason of any such neglect or default: s 2(5).

The custodian is expected to keep such books of account and such records as may be directed by the Treasury. The accounts will be examined and certified by the Comptroller and Auditor General: s 2(6)(7).

Charitable Trusts (3)

(*Cy-près* = so near.) In general, a charitable trust which cannot be carried out because it is impossible or impracticable to do so will not necessarily fail; the court may apply the trust property *cy-près* to some other similar charitable purpose.

Cy-près doctrine

Prior to the Charities Act 1960, the *cy-près* doctrine was applicable only where it was impossible or impracticable to carry out the trust. Under the Charities Act 1993, s 13, the doctrine may be applied: where there is a charitable intention; *and* the original purposes, in whole or part, have been as far as may be fulfilled or cannot be carried out according to the directions; where the original purposes provide a use for only part of the gift; where the gift may be more effectively used in conjunction with other property; where the original purposes referred to have ceased to be suitable in relation to the spirit of the gift; where the original purposes are adequately provided for by other means, or have ceased in law to be charitable.

See *Re Finger's WT* (1972); *Re Spence* (1979).

Whether or not a general charitable intention exists is a matter of construction of the document purporting to create the trust.

Cy-près application arises, eg, in the case of appeals to the public for gifts, followed by events which make the attainment of the appeal's objectives impossible or impracticable.

Cy-près application where donors are unknown or disclaim

Under the Charities Act 1993, s 14, property given for specific charitable purposes which fail may be applicable *cy-près* where it belongs to donors who cannot be found or identified after appropriate advertisement, or where it belongs to a donor who has executed a disclaimer in the prescribed form to have the property returned.

The court may order that property not falling within s 14(3) shall be treated as belonging to donors who cannot be identified, where it appears to the court that it would be unreasonable to incur expense with a view to returning the property: s 14(4).

The 1993 Act allows, in the case of small charities, for the transfer of assets from one charity to another, the alteration of objects and procedures (as an alternative to the creation of a *cy-près* scheme).

The modification of 'small charities' by the Charities Act 1993

Trustees of the small charity must pass an appropriate resolution, and the Charity Commissioners must concur with it.

The trusts of the transferor charity may be modified by replacing all or any of the purposes of the charity with such other purposes, being in law charitable, as are specified in the resolution of the charity trustees.

The Charity Commissioners

The function of the Charity Commissioners is to promote the effective use of charitable resources. They keep a register of charities and every charity, except those exempted, must be entered on it. Exempted charities include, eg, certain universities, registered places of worship. The Commissioners may institute inquiries with respect to a charity; they may suspend or appoint additional trustees. Failure to comply with their orders is a contempt of court: s 88.

In general, no land held by or in trust for a charity shall be sold, leased or otherwise disposed of without an order of the court or of the Commissioners: 1993 Act, s 36(1).

This sub-section does not apply where the disposition is made to a person who is not a 'connected person', or a trustee for or nominee of such person. 'Connected person' is defined in the 1993 Act as including a charity trustee, donor of land to the charity, child, parent, etc, of trustee or donor.

Chapter 14

Appointment of Trustees and Termination of Appointment

In general, the capacity to be a trustee rests on the capacity to take or hold property. The following categories should be noted.

An infant may not be expressly appointed as a trustee. Such an appointment is void 'but without prejudice to appoint a new trustee to fill the vacancy': Law of Property Act 1925, s 20. An implied, constructive or resulting trust may have a trustee who is an infant: see *Re Vinogradoff* (1935).

Few restrictions now apply. It should be noted that an alien may not own a British ship: see Status of Aliens Act 1914, s 17, as amended by the British Nationality Act 1948.

Under the Charities Act 1993, s 72, certain persons are disqualified from acting as charity trustees: eg, persons convicted of any offence involving dishonesty or deception, those adjudged bankrupt, those who have been removed from the office of charity trustee by an order made by the Commissioners, or by the High Court on grounds of misconduct or management. Under s 73, a person who acts as a charity trustee while disqualified by virtue of s 72 is guilty of an offence. Any acts done as a charity trustee by a disqualified person shall not be invalid by reason only of that disqualification: s 73(1). Where the Commissioners are satisfied that a disqualified person has acted as charity trustee, and while so acting he has received from the charity any sums by way of remuneration or expenses, or any benefit in kind, in connection with his acting as charity trustee, they may direct him to repay to the charity the whole or part of the monetary value of any such benefit or sums: s 73(4).

The general principle is that any number of trustees may be appointed. There are restrictions, however, as follows:

* In the case of a settlement of land held on *trust for sale*, the maximum number of trustees is *four*; where more than four are appointed, the four first named shall alone be the trustees, and the other persons named shall not be trustees unless appointed on the occurrence of a vacancy: Trustee Act 1925, s 34(1), (2). Section 34 has no application, however, to land held on trust for charitable, ecclesiastical or public purposes: s 34(3).

14.1   Capacity

14.1.1   Infants

14.1.2   Aliens

14.1.3   Charitable trustees

14.2   Number of trustees

- There need be *one* trustee only to hold land, but, except where the trustee is a trust corporation, a sole trustee cannot give a valid receipt for the proceeds of sale or other capital money arising under a disposition on trust for sale of land, or for capital money arising under the Settled Land Act 1925: Trustee Act 1925, s 14, as amended by Law of Property (Amendment) Act 1926.

- Where a trustee wishes to retire but there is no proposal to replace him by the appointment of a new trustee, he may retire only if at least *two* trustees remain: Trustee Act 1925, s 39.

- The personal representative of a testator may appoint *two or more trustees* (and vest the property in them) where the testator leaves property to an infant absolutely: see Administration of Estates Act 1925, s 42.

14.3	**Disclaimer and acceptance**	No person is bound to accept the office of trustee: see *Robinson v Pett* (1734). Acceptance of the office of trustee may be express or presumed. In general, in the absence of any evidence to the contrary, acceptance is presumed: *Re Sharman's WT* (1942).
14.3.1	Disclaimer	A disclaimer should be made within a reasonable period: see *James v Frearson* (1842). It may be made by deed; but conduct inconsistent with acceptance may suffice: *Stacey v Elph* (1833). A part of the trust cannot be disclaimed if other parts have been accepted: *Re Lord and Fullerton's Contract* (1896). A disclaimer by a trustee effectively avoids the grant, bequest or devise *ab initio*.
14.3.2	Acceptance	An express acceptance will usually involve an express declaration (or the execution of a settlement): *Jones v Higgins* (1866). To exercise any act of ownership, or to allow the trust property to be dealt with in one's name, constitutes acceptance: *Bence v Gilpin* (1868).

- Conduct may operate as acceptance. See *Conyngham v Conyngham* (1750) in which X was appointed trustee, but did not accept expressly. One of the trusts involved rents of land leased to Y, the testator's son. X acted as Y's agent and he received the rents from him. It was held that X could not repudiate the trust.

- Parol evidence of acceptance or non-acceptance is admissible: *James v Frearson* (1842).

- There can be no renunciation following an acceptance.

Initial trustees are usually appointed by the will or settlement creating the trust.

Generally, where a trust is declared, but there is no trustee as such, the person in whom the trust property has been vested is considered to be the trustee.

Where a trust is declared by a testator who fails to appoint a trustee, the testator's personal representatives are deemed trustees.

Where a trust is declared by a settlor who fails to make a conveyance of the trust property, the settlor holds as trustee.

Where a trust is created and the settlor appoints as trustee a person who later disclaims, the trust property reverts to the settlor or his personal representatives.

Where a trust is created and the last surviving (or sole) trustee dies, the trust property passes to that trustee's personal representatives, who may appoint new trustees: see Administration of Estates Act 1925, ss 1, 3. Until the appointment of the new trustees, the personal representatives may exercise or perform any power or trust capable of being exercised by the sole or last surviving trustee: Trustee Act, s 8(2).

A trust will not necessarily fail if trustees have not been appointed or are unable to act. Where the settlor has manifested an unambiguous intention to create a trust, that trust 'follows the legal estate wherever it goes': *per* Lord Wilmot in *A-G v Lady Downing* (1767). There is an exception to this rule: if 'it is of the essence of the trust that the trustees selected *and no other person* shall act as the trustees of it, and those trustees cannot or will not undertake the office, the trust must fail': *per* Buckley J in *Re Lysaght* (1966). (Should the trust be charitable, however, the *cy-près* doctrine (see Chapter 13) may be applied.)

Under the Trustee Act 1925, s 36(1) new trustees may be appointed (in writing) by the person(s) nominated in the trust instrument, existing trustees, personal representatives of the last surviving trustees, in the following cases:

- Where a trustee is dead. This includes the case of a person who has been nominated as trustee in a will, but who predeceases the testator: s 36(8).

- Where a trustee remains out of the UK for more than 12 months. This involves a continuous period; even a short break suffices: *Re Walker* (1901) (break of one week only).

- Where a trustee wishes to be discharged from all or any of the trusts: see *Re Cockburn's WT* (1957).

14.4   Appointment of trustees by the settlor or nominated persons

14.4.1   Equity does not want for a trustee

14.4.2   Trustee Act 1925, s 36

- Where a trustee refuses to act. This will include the act of disclaiming.

- Where a trustee is unfit or incapable of acting. 'Unfit' refers not to a physical defect, but, rather, a defect of character: see *Re Barker's Trusts* (1875) (bankrupt trustee removed). 'Incapable of acting' refers to some physical or mental capacity: see Mental Health Act 1983.

- Where the trustee is a minor.

Under s 36(6) existing trustees have the power to appoint an additional trustee or trustees, always provided that this does *not* lead to an increase in the number of trustees *beyond four*.

The powers under s 36 may be excluded by the settlor: Trustee Act 1925, s 69(2).

14.5 Appointment by the court

Trustees may be appointed by the court by virtue of its inherent jurisdiction which will become available whenever the interests of the beneficiaries require its exercise (see *Re Wrightson* (1908)), under the Judicial Trustees Act 1896, the Public Trustee Act 1906 (which are discussed later)).

Under the Trustee Act 1925, s 41(1), as amended, the court may 'whenever it is expedient to appoint a new trustee or trustees, and it is found inexpedient, difficult or impracticable to do so without the assistance of the court, make an order appointing a new trustee or trustees either in substitution for or in addition to any existing trustee or trustees'.

Application for an appointment by the court may be made by a trustee or beneficiary: s 58(1).

Examples of appointment under s 41 include: *Re Henderson* (1940) - continuous argument among trustees; *Re May's WT* (1941) - trustee detained in enemy-occupied territory.

'Every trustee appointed by a court of competent jurisdiction shall ... have the same powers, authorities, and discretions, and may in all respects act as if he had been originally appointed a trustee by the instrument, if any, creating the trust': s 43.

14.5.1   Exercise of discretion

The court may exercise its *discretion* in the appointment of trustees. The basis for the exercise of this discretion was considered in *Re Tempest* (1866). Under the will of Sir Charles Tempest, a family settlement was created. X and Y were appointed as trustees, but X predeceased Sir Charles. Those to whom the power of appointing new trustees was given failed to agree upon a selection. The court was asked to appoint Z, but the petition was opposed by a beneficiary on the ground that Z was proposed by a branch of the family towards which

Sir Charles had displayed unfriendliness (and which had been excluded by him from management of his property). The Master of the Rolls appointed Z and Lord Camoys, in the hope that both parties would be satisfied. The Court of Appeal held that Z was not a person whom the court would appoint. The following principles emerged from the decision:

- The court will have regard to the settlor's wishes where these have been made known expressly or by implication.

- It is unlikely that an appointment will be made if the person so appointed would have interests likely to conflict with those of beneficiaries.

- The court will take into account whether the proposed appointment will result in the promotion of the execution of the trust, or whether it will impede it.

Other matters to be kept in mind by the court in making an appointment include the following: appointment of near relations (generally acceptable); appointment of persons out of the jurisdiction (not generally acceptable save in very exceptional circumstances: *Re Curtis' Trusts* (1871)); appointment of an alien (not generally acceptable unless he is permanently domiciled in the United Kingdom); appointment of a corporation sole (acceptable); appointment of solicitors and bankers (the appointment of the solicitor to the trust as a new trustee is acceptable in exceptional circumstances: see *Re Norris* (1884), and a beneficiary's banker may be appointed).

It is necessary on the appointment of new trustees that the trust property be vested in them jointly with any continuing trustees.

14.6 The vesting of trust property in new trustees

Where by deed a new trustee is appointed to perform any trust, then if the deed contains a declaration by the appointor that any estate or interest in land subject to the trust shall vest in the persons who by virtue of the deed become or are the trustees for performing the trust, the deed shall operate, without any conveyance or assignment, to vest in those persons as joint tenants, and for the purposes of the trust, the estate, interest or right to which the declaration relates: Trustee Act 1925, s 40(1)(a).

If the deed does not contain such a declaration, the deed shall, subject to any express contrary provision contained therein, operate as if it had contained such a declaration by the appointor extending to all the estates, interests and rights with respect to which a declaration could have been made: s 40(1)(b).

14.6.1	Exclusions	There are *exclusions* from the operation of s 40:

- Land conveyed by way of mortgage for securing money subject to the trust, except land conveyed on trust for securing debentures or debenture stock is excluded.
- Land held under a lease which contains a covenant, condition or agreement against assignment or disposing of the land without licence or consent (unless licence or consent has been obtained) is excluded.
- Shares, stocks, annuities or property only transferable in the books by a company or other body, or in a manner directed by or under statute, are excluded.

In such cases transfer and vesting must be carried out in the appropriate modes, eg, freehold land by conveyance, or registration at the Land Registry, leaseholds by assignment and registration, shares by transfer and registration. Where transfer proves difficult to effect, the court may make a vesting order, vesting the land or interest therein in any such person in any such manner and for any such estate or interest as the court may direct, or releasing or disposing of the contingent right to such person as the court may direct: see s 44.

14.7   Special trustees

Special trustees may be appointed under statute, eg, Judicial Trustees Act 1896, Public Trustee Act 1906.

14.7.1   Judicial trustees

Under the Judicial Trustees Act 1896, s 1, the court may appoint at its discretion, on application by the settlor, trustee or beneficiary, a judicial trustee.

Any 'fit and proper person' nominated in the application may be appointed; but in the absence of a nomination, or if the court is not satisfied of the fitness of the person nominated, the court may appoint an official of the court: s 1(3). On appointment he will exercise all the powers of any other trustee and is under the control of the court.

He may be given special directions by the court and may be suspended or removed by order of the court. See *Re Ridsdel* (1947), in which it was held that a judicial trustee has power to compromise with a debtor.

He must audit accounts annually on the request of a beneficiary or trustee.

A judicial trustee who is a practising solicitor may be allowed to claim costs for work done: see the Judicial Trustee Rules 1983.

Under the Public Trustee Act 1906, the Public Trustee may be appointed as a judicial trustee.

Under the Public Trustee Act 1906, as amended, the court may appoint the Public Trustee as a new or additional trustee. He is allowed to charge for his services: s 9.

14.7.2   The public trustee

The principal functions of the Public Trust Office include: the administration of estates and trusts under the 1906 Act, with the aim of providing the services of an experienced executor or trustee, particularly where a commercial or private trustee cannot be found to act; protection of the affairs of mentally incapable persons.

He may act alone or with others, as a custodian trustee, or administrator of an estate.

He may decline to accept a trust but not on the ground only of the small value of the trust property.

He may not accept a religious or charitable trust or one under a deed of arrangement for the benefit of creditors.

He may manage a business (but only with Treasury consent) and for a limited period only, with a view to its sale.

He is appointed by the Lord Chancellor: Public Trustee and Administration of Funds Act 1986, Sch 1, substituted for the Public Trustee Act 1906, s 8(1).

Property may be vested in a custodian trustee for greater security while the trust is managed by the remaining, or 'managing', trustees. The custodian trusteeship may be ended by order of the court on application of the custodian trustee, or the managing trustees, or any of the beneficiaries.

14.7.3   Custodian trustee

The trust property must be transferred to the custodian trustee as if he were sole trustee, and for that purpose vesting orders may, where necessary, be made: Public Trustee Act 1906, s 4(2)(a).

Included in the Trustee (Custodian Trustee) Rules 1975, as amended, are the following who may act:

- The Treasury Solicitor.
- Any trust corporation which is constituted under the law of the United Kingdom or of any other Member State of the EEC, and is empowered to undertake trust business, has a place of business in the United Kingdom and is incorporated, or registered under the Companies Act 1985, having a capital of not less than [currently] £250,000, of which not less than £100,000 has been paid up, or a company registered without limited liability in the United Kingdom, or a corporation incorporated and empowered to act as trustee for charitable purposes. (Local authorities may act in some cases as custodian trustees, but only in relation to charitable trusts and public trusts for the benefit of inhabitants of the area administered by the local authority.)

14.8   Termination of trusteeship

Trusteeship ends on retirement or removal of a trustee from office, or on his death.

14.8.1   Retirement of trustee

A trustee may retire only in the following circumstances:

- Under an express power of appointing new trustees in the trust instrument.

- Under the Trustee Act 1925, s 39:

  'Where a trustee is desirous of being discharged, and after his discharge there will be either a trust corporation or at least two individuals to act as trustees to perform the trust, then, if such trustee as aforesaid by deed declares that he is desirous of being discharged from the trust, and co-trustees and such other person, if any, as is empowered to appoint trustees, by deed consent to the discharge of the trustee, and to the vesting in the co-trustees alone of the trust property ... [he] shall be deemed to have retired from the trust ...'.

  See also s 36.

- Where all the *cestuis que trust* are of full age and *sui juris*, they may collectively consent to the retirement of a trustee.

- Discharge may usually be obtained by order of the court if there is at least one other continuing trustee, or some new trustee can be found. See *Courtenay v Courtenay* (1846).

14.8.2   Removal of trustees

A trustee may be removed from office in certain circumstances:

- Under an express power.

- Under the statutory power: see Trustee Act, ss 36, 41.

- By order of the court, eg, where the trustee has been convicted of an offence involving dishonesty, or has otherwise behaved improperly: see *Jones v A-G* (1974). (See also *Clarke v Heathfield (No 2)* (1985), in which trustees of the funds of the National Union of Mineworkers who had complied with the unlawful instructions of the union's national executive (which involved frustrating a sequestration order) were removed as trustees, and a receiver appointed.)

  In *Letterstedt v Broers* (1884), the Privy Council examined its power to remove the Board of Executors of Cape Town, who were the sole surviving trustees and executors of the will of Letterstedt, against whom accusations of misconduct in the administration of the trust had been made by the appellant, who was a beneficiary. *Per* Lord Blackburn:

  'Story says [in *Equity Jurisprudence*, s 1289], "In cases of positive misconduct, Courts of Equity have no difficulty in interposing to remove trustees who have abused their trust; it is not indeed every mistake or neglect of duty, or inaccuracy of conduct of trustees, which will induce Courts of Equity to adopt such a course. But the acts or omissions must be such as to endanger the trust property or to show a want of honesty, or a want of proper capacity to execute the duties, or a want of reasonable fidelity" ...

... It seems to their Lordships that the jurisdiction which a Court of Equity has no difficulty in exercising under the circumstances indicated by Story is merely ancillary to its principal duty, to see that the trusts are properly executed. This duty is constantly being performed by the substitution of new trustees in the place of original trustees for a variety of reasons in non-contentious cases. And, therefore, though it should appear that the charges of misconduct were either not made out, or were greatly exaggerated, so that the trustee was justified in resisting them, and the court might consider that in awarding costs, yet if satisfied that the continuance of the trustee would prevent the trusts being properly executed, the trustee might be removed. It must be borne in mind that trustees exist for the benefit of those to whom the creator of the trust has given the trust estate ...

... In exercising so delicate a jurisdiction as that of removing trustees, their Lordships do not venture to lay down any general rule beyond the very broad principle enunciated above, that their main guide must be the welfare of the beneficiaries. Probably it is not possible to lay down any more definite rule in a matter so essentially dependent on details often of great nicety ...'

Where there are two or more trustees and one dies, the rule of survivorship applies and the office devolves on the surviving trustee(s). On the death of a sole surviving trustee, the estate devolves on his personal representatives. See the Trustee Act, s 18; Administration of Estates Act 1925, ss 1-3.

14.8.3   Death

Appointment of Trustees and Termination of Appointment

In general, capacity to be a trustee reflects capacity to hold property. An infant may not be expressly appointed as trustee (but this is not so in the case of implied, resulting or constructive trusts). Few restrictions apply in the case of aliens. Under the Charities Act 1993, s 72, certain persons are disqualified from acting as charity trustees.

Capacity

In general, any number may be appointed; there are, however, certain restrictions.

Number of trustees

- Land held on *trust for sale*: maximum of four (or the first four named). See Trustee Act 1925, s 34(1)(2).

- One trustee only is necessary to hold land, but (except where the trustee is a trust corporation) a sole trustee cannot give a valid receipt for proceeds of sale.

- A trustee may retire only if at least two trustees remain: Trustee Act 1925, s 39.

- Where a testator leaves property absolutely to an infant, the personal representatives may appoint two or more trustees.

Acceptance may be express or implied; conduct may operate as acceptance: *Conyngham v Conyngham* (1750). There can be no renunciation following acceptance. Disclaimer must be made within a reasonable period; it may be made by deed, but may be implied from inconsistent conduct.

Disclaimer and acceptance

Initial trustees are usually appointed by the will or settlement creating the trust. Where a trust is declared but there is no trustee as such, the person in whom the property is vested is considered to be the trustee. Where the testator fails to appoint a trustee, the personal representatives are considered to be trustees.

Appointment of trustees by settlor or nominated persons

Equity does not want for a trustee. See *A-G v Lady Downing* (1767). A trust will not necessarily fail where there is an unambiguous intention to create a trust and no trustee has been appointed.

Under Trustee Act 1925, s 36(1), new trustees may be appointed by nominated persons, personal representatives of last surviving trustee, where: a trustee is dead; where he remains out of UK for more than twelve months; where he wishes to be discharged; where he refuses to act; where he is unfit or incapable of acting, or is a minor.

Existing trustees may appoint additional trustees provided that this does not increase the number beyond four: s 36(6). This power may be excluded by the settlor: s 69(2).

Appointment by court

The court may appoint a trustee by virtue of its inherent jurisdiction, or under the Trustee Act 1925, s 41(1). An application may be made by a trustee or beneficiary. The court will exercise its discretion (see *Re Tempest* (1866)) and have regard to the wishes of the settlor.

Vesting of trust property in new trustees

When new trustees are appointed the trust property must be vested in them jointly with continuing trustees. See Trustee Act 1925, s 40. Transfer and vesting of property must be carried out in the appropriate mode. Where transfer proves difficult to effect, the court may make a vesting order: s 44.

Special trustees

Judicial trustees may be appointed by the court: see Judicial Trustees Act 1896. They may audit accounts and carry out directions of the court.

The court may appoint a public trustee as a new or additional trustee (Public Trustee Act, s 9). He may administer estates and trusts, but may manage a business for a limited period only.

Property may be vested in a custodian trustee, eg, for greater security. He may be the Treasury Solicitor or a corporation constituted according to the Trustee (Custodian Trustee) Rules 1975, as amended.

Termination of trusteeship

Trusteeship ends on the *retirement* of a trustee, under an express power in the trust instrument, under the Trustee Act 1925, s 39 (where he wishes to be discharged and at least two trustees remain), where all the *cestuis que trust* are of full age and *sui juris* and consent to his retirement, where the court orders his discharge; *removal*, under an express power, under the statutory power (see Trustee Act 1925, ss 36, 41), or by order of the court; *death*.

Chapter 15

Duties of Trustees (1)

The office of trustee 'is attended with no small degree of trouble and anxiety ... it is an act of great kindness in any one to accept it': *per* Lord Hardwicke in *Knight v Earl of Plymouth* (1747). The trustee must act with diligence, obey the trust instrument, not deviate from its terms, observe the rules concerning investment, keep accounts, act impartially, must not, unless otherwise expressly authorised, make any profit from his position as trustee.

15.1   **Essence of the trustee's duties**

Before accepting the trust, a person who has been nominated as trustee should disclose any circumstances which might result in a conflict between his interest and duty: *Peyton v Robinson* (1823). In that case, the settlor was not aware that a beneficiary, X, was personally indebted to Y, the trustee. Under the terms of the trust, Y had a discretion to make payments to X. The court held that Y could not accept any repayment of his debt from money paid to X.

On accepting the trust, four major duties fall to the trustee.

15.2   **Duties on acceptance of the trust**

A trustee must be certain of the validity of his appointment and must ensure that he understands the nature of the trust property and the terms on which it is to be held: see *Harvey v Olliver* (1887).

15.2.1   To become acquainted with the terms of the trust

Per Kekewich J in *Hallows v Lloyd* (1888):

'When persons are asked to become new trustees, they are bound to inquire of what the property consists that is proposed to be handed over to them, and what are the trusts. They ought also to look into the trust documents and papers to ascertain what notices appear among them of incumbrances and other matters affecting the trust.'

Previous trustees may be asked to produce relevant documents.

15.2.2   To inspect the documents

Property not covered by the Trustee Act 1925, s 40 (vesting of trust property in new or continuing trustees), must be placed in the trustee's name. The legal title must be properly transferred to the trustees. Steps must be taken to effect transfer to the trustees of outstanding trust property: see *Westmoreland v Holland* (1871).

15.2.3   To ensure that trust property is vested

| 15.2.4 | To investigate possible previous breaches of trust | In the absence of suspicious circumstances a new trustee is entitled to assume that there has been no breach of trust involving his predecessors: see *Re Strahan* (1856). Failure to investigate suspicious circumstances which later results in loss to the trust fund may constitute a breach of trust: *Harvey v Olliver* (1887). |

15.3 Standard of care

The trustee, in carrying out the purposes of the trust, must act *with diligence* in the discharge of his duties and the exercise of his discretion.

| 15.3.1 | The exercise of the trustee's duties | A high standard of diligence is demanded from the *paid trustee* in the exercise of his duties: see *Re Waterman's WT* (1952). In the case of the *unpaid trustee*, it is expected that he will use the diligence and care that a prudent man of business would show in the management of his own affairs. If he 'ventures to deviate from the letter of his trust, he does so under the obligation and at the peril of afterwards satisfying the court that the deviation was necessary or beneficial': *per* Turner VC in *Harrison v Randall* (1852). See *Bartlett v Barclays Trust Co* (1980); *per* Brightman, J: |

> 'I am of opinion that a higher duty of care is plainly due from someone like a trust corporation which carries on a specialised business of trust management. A trust corporation holds itself out in its advertising literature as being above ordinary mortals. With a specialist staff of trained trust officers and managers, with ready access to financial information and professional advice, dealing with and solving trust problems day after day, the trust corporation holds itself out, and rightly, as capable of providing an expertise which it would be unrealistic to expect and unjust to demand from the ordinary prudent man or woman who accepts, probably unpaid and sometimes reluctantly from a sense of family duty, the burdens of a trusteeship. Just as, under the law of contract, if he neglects to use the skill and experience which he professes, so I think that a professional corporate trustee is liable for breach of trust if loss is caused to the trust fund because it neglects to exercise the special care and skill which it professes to have.'

| 15.3.2 | The exercise of the trustee's discretion | This demands honesty and the standard of diligence which ought to be shown by a business man acting with prudence in the ordering of his own affairs. Where a trustee has acted *bona fide*, the court is unlikely to interfere with the results of an exercise of his discretion. See *Marley v Mutual Security Ltd* (1991) - in assisting trustees in the exercise of a discretion, the court should not be concerned with arguments that the trustees were |

incompetent or had not acted in good faith; the only question to be determined was what ought to be done in the interests of the estate.

Per Lord Truro in *Re Beloved Wilkes' Charity* (1851):

'It is to the discretion of the trustees that the execution of the trust is confided, that discretion being exercised with an entire absence of indirect motive, with honesty of intention, and with a fair consideration of the subject. The duty of supervision on the part of this court will thus be confined to the question of the honesty, integrity and fairness with which the deliberation has been conducted, and will not be extended to the accuracy of the conclusion arrived at, except in particular cases. If, however ... trustees think fit to state a reason, and the reason is one which does not justify their conclusion, then the court may say that they have acted by mistake and in error, and that it will correct their decision; but if, without entering into details, they simply state as in many cases it would be most prudent and judicious for them to do, that they have met and considered and come to a conclusion, the court has then no means of saying that they have failed in their duty, or to consider the accuracy of their conclusion.'

See Lord Herschell in *Bray v Ford* (1896) at para 9.2.

A trustee is not usually entitled to remuneration for his services. The rule is, *per* Lord Normand in *Dale v IRC* (1954):

'not that reward for services is repugnant to the fiduciary duty, but that he who has the duty shall not take any secret remuneration or any financial benefit not authorised by the law, or by his contract, or by the trust deed under which he acts, as the case may be.'

There are exceptions, as follows:

- *Authority under the trust instrument*. In such a case charges will be limited strictly to those stated by the settlor: *Re Sandys' WT* (1947).

- *Inherent jurisdiction of the court*. The court may allow remuneration in exceptional circumstances: see *Re Worthington* (1954); *Boardman v Phipps* (1966) (in which a trustee was allowed 'generous remuneration').

In *O'Sullivan v Management Agency* (1985), the court set aside, on grounds of undue influence, a contract between a composer and his manager. In holding that defendants ought to account for profits, the Court of Appeal stated that they were entitled to reasonable remuneration based upon their skill and labour in promoting the composer's reputation in the entertainment world. *Per* Fox, LJ:

15.4   Duty to act gratuitously

15.4.1   Exceptions

'Once it is accepted that the court can make an appropriate allowance to a fiduciary for his skill and labour I do not see why, in principle, it should not be able to give him some part of the profit of the venture if it was thought that justice as between the parties demanded that. To give the fiduciary any allowance for his skill and labour involves some reduction of the profits otherwise payable to the beneficiary ... It would be one thing to permit a substantial sharing of profits in a case such as *Boardman v Phipps* (1967) where the conduct of the fiduciaries could not be criticised and quite another to permit it in a case such as the present where although fraud was not alleged, there was an abuse of personal trust and confidence ... I would be prepared ... to authorise the payment (over and above out of pocket expenses) of an allowance for the skill and labour of [defendants] in promoting the compositions and performances and managing the business affairs of Mr O'Sullivan ...'

The court's inherent jurisdiction to allow remuneration over and above that permitted by the trust instrument will be exercised only sparingly: *Re Duke of Norfolk's Settlement* (1981).

In *Re Duke of Norfolk*, X had settled land in 1958 and had created discretionary trusts involving a distribution date which might not occur until 2038. Under the trust there was a provision for remuneration for trustees; they were to be paid the scale fees in force at the time the settlement was made. Further property was added to the settlement as a result of which the trustees were involved in unforeseen additional tasks. X died in 1975. Following the application by the trustees, the judge held that he possessed jurisdiction to authorise additional remuneration for work claimed in the past, but not to order any future general increases.

The Court of Appeal allowed the trustees' appeal. The court did possess an inherent jurisdiction to increase or vary trustees' remuneration in relation to future services on the ground that the exercise of its jurisdiction was intended to secure the competent administration of the trust. Lord Brightman stated that if the court has an inherent power to authorise a prospective trustee to take remuneration for future services, and has a similar power concerning an unpaid trustee who has accepted office and commenced his fiduciary duties on a voluntary basis, he would have some difficulty in accepting the logic of the principle that the court lacks the power to increase or otherwise vary the future remuneration of a trustee who has accepted office.

The jurisdiction will be exercised where the circumstances suggest an implied promise of the beneficiaries to pay.

In *Re Berkeley Applegate (No 3)* (1989), the court gave directions as to how remuneration, costs and expenses of a liquidator in a creditors' voluntary liquidation ought to be borne in his administration of what were, essentially, trust assets.

- *Under statute.* Under the Trustee Act 1925, s 42, where the court appoints a corporation other than the Public Trustee, to be a trustee, the court may authorise the corporation to charge remuneration. Under the Judicial Trustees Act 1896, s 1(5), a judicial trustee may be paid remuneration out of the trust property.

- *Agreement with beneficiaries.* Where the beneficiaries are *sui juris* and absolutely entitled between them to the entire beneficial interest they may contract with the trustees for remuneration: *Aycliffe v Murray* (1740). An individual beneficiary may make his own agreement with a trustee for remuneration, but that will bind only that beneficiary.

- *The rule in Cradock v Piper (1850).* A solicitor-trustee acting for himself and other trustees may charge profit costs, but not where those costs have been incurred as the result of his being a party. He may not charge where he is acting alone. The rule ('exceptional, anomalous and not to be extended') is limited to costs incurred in an action and has no application to business done out of court: *Re Corsellis* (1887).

A trustee is not expected, in general, to bear the expenses arising from his trusteeship. 'A trustee may reimburse himself or pay or discharge out of the trust all the expenses incurred in or about the execution of the trusts or powers': Trustee Act 1925, s 30(2).

15.4.2   Reimbursement of expenses

The trustee's right to indemnity against costs and expenses properly incurred by him in the execution of the trust is 'a first charge on all the trust property, both income and corpus': *per* Lord Selborne in *Stott v Milne* (1884).

In *Holding and Management v Property Holding and Investment Trust* (1989), the Court of Appeal held that where trustees of a maintenance fund brought an action to ratify expenditure to which the tenants and landlord of a block of flats were opposed, they had acted unreasonably and could not recover costs of litigation from the maintenance fund.

Where the court grants trustees leave to sue or defend in an action considered to be in the interests of the trust, the trustees will be reimbursed irrespective of the results of the action. Where the court has not granted leave, costs will be reimbursed only if the action was defended or brought in the interests of the trust.

15.5 Duty not to profit from the trust

'Equity prohibits a trustee from making any profit by his management, directly or indirectly': see *Regal (Hastings) Ltd v Gulliver* (1952) (at para 9.2.2).

15.5.1 Duty to account as constructive trustee for profits received

The general rule is that a trustee who acquires a benefit in his position as trustee must surrender that benefit for the beneficiary. In *Re Macadam* (1945), trustees, who were empowered to appoint two directors, appointed themselves and were held liable to account for remuneration received as directors, because their appointment had resulted from their use of trust powers. 'I think the root of the matter really is: Did the trustee acquire the position in respect of which he drew the remuneration by virtue of his position as trustee?': *per* Cohen J.

15.5.2 Purchase of trust property by the trustees

The general rule is that a trustee should not buy the trust property from himself *qua* trustee and his co-trustees, either directly or through a third party: *Campbell v Walker* (1800). 'The purchase is not permitted in any case, however honest the circumstances; the general interests of justice requiring it to be destroyed in every instance': *per* Lord Eldon in *Ex p James* (1803). A provision in the trust instrument authorising purchase by a trustee will be generally upheld.

A sale by a trustee to his wife will be viewed by the court 'with much suspicion': *Ferraby v Hobson* (1847).

The rule will apply to a recently-retired trustee, but not to one who completes the purchase after a relatively-lengthy period of retirement: *Re Boles* (1902) (interval of 12 years).

The rule may not apply to a 'bare trustee': *Parkes v White* (1805).

Where trustees lease the trust estate to one of their number, the lessee must account for profits: *Ex p Hughes* (1802).

15.5.3 Purchase from beneficiary

Per Lord Cairns in *Thomson v Eastwood* (1877):

> 'There is no rule of law which says that a trustee shall not buy property from a *cestui que trust*, but it is a well-known doctrine of equity that if a transaction of that kind is challenged in the proper time, a court of equity will examine into it, will ascertain the value that was paid by the trustee, and will throw upon the trustee the onus of proving that he gave full value, and that all information was laid before the *cestui que trust* when it was sold.'

See *Dougan v MacPherson* (1902), in which X and Y were brothers and beneficiaries. X, who was also a trustee, purchased Y's interest, but had failed to show him an important valuation. On Y's bankruptcy, the sale was set aside.

In general, an improper sale is voidable. The beneficiaries may apply to have the sale aside against any person who has the legal estate. If the trustee has sold at a profit the beneficiaries may claim it: *Baker v Carter* (1835). Beneficiaries may confirm a purchase by a trustee by express ratification: *Morse v Royal* (1806). A beneficiary who has delayed unreasonably before commencing proceedings, or who has apparently acquiesced in the sale, may not be able to rely on the equitable remedy: *Campbell v Walker* (1800).

15.5.4   Remedies of the beneficiary

See Chapter 9 for the doctrine in *Keech v Sandford* (1726).

15.5.5   The doctrine in *Keech v Sandford*

A trustee must not set up an adverse title of a third party against a beneficiary: *Devey v Thornton* (1851). Where a trustee has undertaken a trust he may not afterwards refuse to perform it because he believes that the property belongs rightfully to some third person: *Beddoes v Pugh* (1859). He must assume that the beneficiaries' title is valid until it is proved otherwise.

15.6   Duty not to set up *jus tertii*

In general, the act of a majority of trustees will not bind the minority or the trust estate. The trust estate is bound only when the trustees act in unanimity: *Swale v Swale* (1856). (This does not apply to charity trustees.)

15.7   Duty of the trustees to act unanimously

All trustees must join in the receipt of money unless the settlement authorises a single trustee to give receipts. See *Re Flower* (1884). *Per* Kay, J:

> 'The theory of every trust is that the trustees shall not allow the trust moneys to get into the hands of any one of them, but that all shall exercise control over them ... The reason why more than one trustee is appointed is that they shall take care that the moneys shall not get into the hands of one of them alone.'

The court will not generally interfere to compel a minority at the request of the majority of trustees. Note, however, under the Trustee Act 1925, s 63(3): 'Where money or securities are vested in any persons as trustees, and the majority are desirous of paying the same into court, but the concurrence of the other or others cannot be obtained, the court may order the payment into court to be made by the majority without the concurrence of the other or others.'

The general principle is *delegatus non potest delegare* - a trustee cannot delegate his duty. 'Trustees who take on themselves the management of property for the benefit of others have no right to shift their duty on other persons': *per* Langdale MR in

15.8   Duty not to delegate

Turner v Corney (1841). 'The law is not that trustees cannot delegate: it is that trustees cannot delegate unless they have authority to do so': *per* Lord Radcliffe in *Pilkington v IRC* (1964). This strict rule has been modified in the following ways:

15.8.1 Trustee Act 1925, s 23(1)	Trustees may, instead of acting personally, employ and pay an agent, eg, a solicitor, banker, stockbroker, to transact business necessary in the execution of the trust, and may be allowed and paid all charges and expenses incurred, and shall not be responsible for the default of any agent if employed in good faith.
15.8.2 Trustee Act 1925, s 34(3)	A trustee may appoint a solicitor to be his agent to receive and give a discharge for any money or valuable consideration or property receivable by the trustee under a trust.
15.8.3 Law of Property Act 1925, ss 29, 30	A trustee for the sale of land may delegate powers of leasing, accepting surrenders of leases and management to a person of full age, beneficially entitled in possession to the net rents and profits of the land during his life or for any lesser period. If the trustees for sale refuse to exercise this power, any person interested may apply to the court for an order directing the trustees for sale to give effect thereto. See *Norman v Norman* (1983); *Huntingford v Hobbs* (1992).
15.8.4 Trustee Act 1925, s 25, as amended by the Powers of Attorney Act 1971, s 9	The Powers of Attorney Act 1971 deals with the trustees' powers to delegate the exercise of trusts, powers and discretions to an attorney under the Trustee Act 1925, s 25. See also the Enduring Powers of Attorney Act 1985.

A trustee may, by power of attorney, delegate for a period not exceeding 12 months, the execution or exercise of all or any of the trusts, powers and discretions vested in him as trustee either alone or jointly with others.

The donees of a power of attorney include a trust corporation, but not (unless a trust corporation) the only other co-trustee of the donor of the power.

A trustee who gives the power under the 1925 Act, s 25, must give written notice to others who have the power to appoint new trustees and to each of the other trustees: 1971 Act, s 9.

The donor of a power of attorney is liable for the acts or defaults of the donee in the same manner as if they were the acts or defaults of the donor.

15.8.5 Further aspects of delegation	The following points are of importance: • A trustee may leave, for a reasonable time, deposit and purchase money in the hands of an auctioneer who is auctioning the trust property: *Edmonds v Peake* (1843).

- Under Trustee Act 1925, s 21: 'Trustees may deposit any documents held by them relating to the trust, or to the trust property, with any banker or banking company or any other company whose business includes the undertaking of the safe custody of documents ...'

- The court may exercise its inherent jurisdiction so as to authorise trustees to delegate: *Steel v Wellcome Custodian Trustees* (1988) (delegation of the power of investment).

Trustees have a general duty to keep proper accounts and to make them available for inspection and examination: *Pearse v Green* (1819). Beneficiaries have a general right to investigate trustees' accounts: *Re Fish* (1893).

15.9   Duties concerning information

A solicitor-trustee must preserve for at least six years from the date of the last entry all accounts he has kept relating to the trust. A trustee who fails to keep accurate accounts is generally responsible for costs arising. See *Smith v Cremer* (1875).

Under the Trustee Act 1925, s 22(4), trustees may, in their discretion, from time to time, but not more than once in every three years (unless the trust is such that a more frequent exercise of the right is reasonable), have the accounts examined by an independent auditor, the costs to be paid out of the capital or income of the trust property.

Under the Public Trustee Act 1906, s 13, a trustee or beneficiary may apply for an audit of trust accounts, but this may not be made within one year of the previous audit.

'The beneficiary is entitled to see all the trust documents because they are trust documents and because he is a beneficiary. They are in a sense his own': *per* Lord Wrenbury in *O'Rourke v Darbishire* (1920).

In *Re Londonderry's Settlement* (1965) trustees of a family settlement took a decision, in accordance with the terms of the settlement, to distribute capital among beneficiaries and to bring the settlement to an end. They called for a perusal of minutes of the trustees' meetings, agendas, documents and correspondence. The trustees argued that it was not in the interests of the family as a whole to disclose all the documents; they supplied the family only with copies of trust accounts. It was held that the trustees were not under a duty to supply other documents or to give the reasons for their decisions.

Per Harman LJ:

'I cannot think that communications passing between individual trustees and appointors are documents in which beneficiaries have a proprietary right ... I do not think letters to or from an individual beneficiary ought to be open to inspection by another beneficiary ...'

Per Salmon LJ:

'Trust documents do have these characteristics in common:
(1) they are documents in the possession of the trustees as
trustees; (2) they contain information about the trust which
the beneficiaries are entitled to know; (3) the beneficiaries
have a proprietary interest in the documents and, accordingly,
are entitled to see them. If any parts of a document contain
any information which the beneficiaries are not entitled to
know, I doubt whether such parts can truly be said to be
integral parts of a trust document. Accordingly, any part of a
document that lacked the second characteristic to which I
have referred would automatically be excluded from the
document in its character as a trust document.'

Duties of Trustees (1)

Four major duties arise: to become acquainted with the terms of the trust; to inspect appropriate documents, see *Hallows v Lloyd* (1888); to ensure that trust property is vested; to investigate possible breaches of trust.

Duties on acceptance of the trust

Trustees must act with diligence. A high standard of diligence is expected from the *paid trustee* in the exercise of his duties; the *unpaid trustee* is expected to use the diligence and care that a prudent man would use in the exercise of his business. The exercise of the trustee's discretion demands honesty and the standard of diligence is that expected of a business man acting prudently. Where a trustee has acted *bona fide*, the court is unlikely to interfere with the results of an exercise of his discretion.

Standard of care

A trustee is not usually entitled to remuneration for his services. There are exceptions: authority under the trust instrument; inherent jurisdiction of the court (*Boardman v Phipps* (1966)); under Trustee Act 1925, s 42; agreement with beneficiaries; rule in *Cradock v Piper* (1850) (referring to solicitor-trustee who acts for himself and co-trustees). He may reimburse himself out of the trust in relation to expenses arising from administration.

Duty to act gratuitously

'Equity prohibits a trustee from making any profit by his management, directly or indirectly.'

He must account as constructive trustee for profits received. See *Re Macadam* (1945).

Note the doctrine in *Keech v Sandford* (1726).

He may not, in general, buy trust property from himself, *qua trustee*, and co-trustees.

If he purchases from a beneficiary he may be required to show that he gave full value. See *Thomson v Eastwood* (1877). An improper sale may be set aside.

Duty not to profit from the trust

A trustee must not set up an adverse title of a third party against a beneficiary: *Devey v Thornton* (1851).

Duty not to set up *jus tertii*

Duty of trustees to act unanimously

In general, the trust estate is bound only when trustees act unanimously: *Swale v Swale* (1856). (There are different rules relating to charity trustees.) Note Trustee Act 1925, s 63(3).

Duty not to delegate

Delegatus non potest delegare. The strict rule has been modified:

- Trustee Act 1925, s 23(1), allowing a trustee to employ an agent such as a banker, stockbroker.

- Law of Property Act 1925, ss 29,30, allowing, in the case of a trust for the sale of land, the delegation of powers of leasing, management to a person of full age, beneficially entitled in possession to rents, etc. See *Norman v Norman* (1983).

- Trustee Act 1925, s 25, as amended. A trustee may, by power of attorney, delegate the exercise of trusts, powers and discretions to an attorney.

Duties concerning information

See *Re Londonderry's Settlement* (1965). Trustees have the duty to keep accounts and make them available for inspection. Beneficiaries have the right to investigate trustees' accounts and call for a perusal of certain documents relating to the trust.

Chapter 16

Duties of Trustees (2)

Per Lord Watson in *Learoyd v Whiteley* (1887):

> 'As a general rule, the law requires of a trustee no higher degree of diligence in the execution of his office than a man of ordinary prudence would exercise in the management of his own private affairs. Yet he is not allowed the same discretion in investing the moneys of the trust as if he were a person *sui juris* dealing with his own estate. Business men of prudence may, and frequently do, select investments which are more or less of a speculative character but it is the duty of a trustee to confine himself to the class of investments which are permitted by the trust and likewise to avoid all investments of that class which are attended with hazard. So long as he acts in the honest observance of those limitations the general rule already stated will apply.'

16.1 Duties relating to investment: the standard of care

'Invest' as used in an investment clause is usually interpreted to include as one of its meanings 'to apply money in the purchase of some property from which interest or profit is expected and which property is purchased in order to be held for the sake of the income which it will yield': *Re Wragg* (1919).

16.1.1 Meaning of 'invest'

Under the Trustee Investments Act 1961, s 6(1), a trustee must have regard to 'the *suitability* to the trust of investments of the description proposed and of the investment proposed as an investment of that description'. He must also have regard to the need for *diversification* of investments of the trust, 'in so far as is appropriate to the circumstances of the trust'.

    In *Re Harari's ST* (1949), a settlement empowered trustees to retain or sell (with the consent of the settlor's daughter) and invest proceeds and other capital moneys subject to the trust 'in or upon such investments as to them may seem fit'. The investments were, in fact, Egyptian securities and bonds, but none was classed as a trustee investment. The court was asked to decide whether the provisions allowed the trustees the power to invest outside the usual range of trustee investments, or whether the trustees were empowered to exercise their discretion only within the authorised range. The court held that the trustees were authorised to invest in any investment which they honestly considered to be desirable. *Per* Jenkins, J:

16.1.2 Suitability of investments

> 'There is a good deal of authority to the effect that investment clauses should be strictly construed and should not be construed as authorising investments outside the trustee range unless they clearly and unambiguously

indicate an intention to that effect ... It seems to me that I am left free to construe this settlement according to what I consider to be the natural and proper meaning of the words used in their context, and, so construing the words "in or upon such investments as to them may seem fit", I see no justification for implying any restriction ...

... I think the trustees have power, under the plain meaning of those words, to invest in any investments which ... they honestly think are desirable investments for the investment of moneys subject to the trusts of the settlement. To hold otherwise would really be to read words into the settlement which are not there ... The real ground, however, for my decision is the plain and ordinary meaning of the words "in or upon such investments as to them may seem fit". Having found nothing in the authorities to constrain me to construe those words otherwise than in accordance with their plain meaning, that is the meaning I propose to place on them.'

16.2 Statutory powers under the 1961 Act

The powers given to the trustees under the Trustee Investments Act 1961 allow them to invest more widely. Trustees may now invest trust funds in investments authorised by the terms of the trust instrument *and* the provisions of the 1961 Act.

Subject to the provisions of the Act relating to the division of the trust fund, trustees may invest in the shares of a company which has its shares quoted on the London Stock Exchange (or any other recognised stock exchange), is incorporated in the United Kingdom, has a total share capital of not less than £1m, has paid a dividend on its shares in each of the five years preceding the year of the proposed investment, and has fully-paid shares (or shares which must be fully-paid within nine months of the date of issue).

The Act allows three categories of investment, which may be added to by Orders in Council:

- *Part I investments*. The safer type, eg, deposits in National Savings Bank.

- *Part II investments*. Other investments authorised by the Trustee Act 1925.

- *Part III investments*. Largely comprising shares in commercial concerns satisfying the conditions mentioned above.

The 'narrower-range' part of the fund may be invested in Part I and Part II investments. The 'wider-range' part of the fund may be invested in Part III investments.

16.3 Narrower-range investments not requiring advice

The narrower-range investment includes the type of 'small savings' investment which does *not* necessitate the trustee's seeking advice before investing. The investments are set out in

Part I of the First Schedule to the 1961 Act and include, eg, Defence Bonds, National Savings Certificates, deposits in the National Bank and trustee savings banks, National Savings First Option Bonds (see SI 1992/1738).

Expert advice *must* be sought by trustees before investing in this class. Details are set out in Part II of the First Schedule to the Act, as amended. The following are included:

- Fixed interest securities issued by: the British Government (other than those in Part I); public authorities or nationalised industries in the United Kingdom; the government of any overseas territory within the Commonwealth; the International Bank for Reconstruction and Development.

- Securities, the payment on which is guaranteed by the government.

- Debentures issued: in the United Kingdom by a company incorporated there; by the Agricultural Mortgage Corporation.

- Deposits: by way of special investment in a trustee savings bank; in designated building societies.

- Mortgages of freehold property, and of leasehold property with an unexpired term of not less than 60 years.

16.4 Narrower-range investments requiring advice

Wider-range investments are enumerated in Part III of the First Schedule. Advice *must* be taken by the trustees. The investments include: shares in companies which meet the requirements noted above; shares in authorised building societies; units in authorised unit trusts.

16.5 Wider-range investments

Trustees may invest the entire fund in narrower-range securities. But where they wish to invest in wider-range investments the trust must be divided into two parts: the narrower-range part and the wide-range part.

- The narrower-range part of the fund may be invested only in Part I and Part II investments; the wider-range part may be invested in Part III investments only.

- The parts must be of equal value at the time the division is made: s 2(1).

- Once the division is made it is permanent: s 2(1).

- No property may be transferred from one part of the fund to the other unless a compensating transfer of property of equal value is made in the opposite direction: s 2(1).

16.6 Division of the fund and compensating transfers

16.7   Accruals to the trust fund after the division has been made, and withdrawals

The position regarding accruals is governed by s 2(3). If the property accrues to the trustee as owner or former owner of property comprised in either part of the fund, it is treated as belonging to that part of the fund; in any case, the trustee shall secure, by apportionment of the accruing property or the transfer of property from one part of the fund to the other, or both, that the value of each part of the fund is increased by the same amount: s 2(3)(a), (b).

Where a trustee acquires property in consideration of a money payment, 'the acquisition of the property shall be treated for the purposes for this section as investment and not as the accrual of property to the trust fund, notwithstanding that the amount of the consideration is less than the value of the property acquired': s 2(3).

Where in the exercise of any power or duty of a trustee property fails to be taken out of the trustee fund, nothing in [s 2] shall restrict his discretion as to the choice of property to be taken out: s 2(4).

The importance of preserving the fund outweighs success in its advancement. See *Nestlé v National Westminster Bank* (1992), in which the trustee bank was not liable for a decline in value of the trust fund as there was no default proved on the part of the bank.

16.8   Investment by trustees on mortgages of land

The statutory power is contained within the 1961 Act, First Schedule, Part II (narrower-range investments requiring advice). Mortgages of freehold property and leaseholds with an unexpired term of not less than 60 years are involved.

16.8.1   Restrictions

The following restrictions apply to an investment on mortgage by trustees:

- A first legal mortgage is permissible; second mortgages ought to be avoided. See *Lockhart v Reilly* (1857).
- A contributory mortgage (ie, one in which trustees join with other persons in making a joint loan) should be avoided: *Webb v Jonas* (1888).
- A mortgage of property of a wasting character ought not to be accepted: *Learoyd v Whiteley* (1887).

16.8.2   Other statutory provisions

The following should be noted:

- *Trustee Act 1925, ss 5, 6, 10.* These sections extend the general power to invest on mortgage. Section 5 enlarges powers of investment to include investments on a charge; s 6 authorises investment on mortgage in relation to land subject to drainage charges; s 10 allows trustees to agree not to call in a loan for a period not exceeding seven years, provided that interest is paid within at least 30 days after it becomes due, and provided there is no breach of any covenant by the mortgagor contained in the instrument of mortgage.

- *Trustee Act 1925, s 9*. Where a trustee improperly advances an excessive sum on mortgage it is deemed an authorised investment for the smaller sum, the trustee being liable only for the balance invested improperly, which he must make good, with interest.

The following statutory provisions affect the trustee's power to invest:

16.9 Miscellaneous statutory provisions concerning investment by trustees

- *Trustee Act 1925, s 2, as amended by Trustee Investments Act 1961, s 61*. A trustee may invest in securities even if they are redeemable and the price exceeds redemption value. He may retain such securities until redemption.
- *Trustee Act 1925, s 4*. A trustee is not liable for breach of trust merely because he continues to hold an investment which has ceased to be authorised by the trust instrument.
- *Trustee Act 1925, s 10, as amended by the Trustee Investments Act 1961, s 9*. This allows trustees who are lending money on the security of a company powers to concur in any scheme or arrangement for, eg, the reconstruction of the company, the sale of all or part of the company's property to another company, amalgamation, in like manner as if they were entitled to such securities beneficially.
- *Variation of Trusts Act 1958*. Should trustees view their existing powers of investment as inadequate or unsuitable, they may apply to the court, where the trust is private, for an order under the 1958 Act or under the Trustee Act 1925, s 57. In the case of a charitable trust, application may be made for a *cy-près* scheme (see Chapter 13), or for an order under the 1958 Act.

Among the recommendations of the 23rd Report of the Law Reform Committee (*The Powers and Duties of Trustees*, 1982) were the following:

16.10 Law reform and investment

- Investments should be divided into those which can be made without advice and those which can be made only with advice.
- Trustees should be allowed to invest in whatever proportions they thought fit.
- Trustees should be required to maintain a balance between income and capital so as to protect those interested in the trust fund.

- Investment in foreign securities should not be made unless authorised expressly by the trust instrument.

- Trustees' powers to invest in mortgages should be widened so as to permit investment in second mortgages.

- The statutory powers contained in the Trustee Investments Act 1961 are out of date and require revision.

16.11 Duty to act impartially

The trustee must act in the interests of *all* the beneficiaries, holding the scales evenly between them and favouring neither one nor another. The general duty is exemplified in the duty to convert and the duty to apportion, which are considered later.

The question of 'putting the beneficiaries' interests first' was discussed in *Cowan v Scargill* (1985), in which the duties of pension fund trustees were reviewed.

(i) Plaintiffs were trustees of a mineworkers' pension fund, appointed by the National Coal Board. Defendants were trustees appointed by the National Union of Mineworkers (NUM). An investment plan was submitted to the trustees for their approval. Defendants refused to concur in adopting the plan unless it was amended so that there would be no increase in the percentage of overseas investment. Deadlock resulted and plaintiffs applied to the court for directions, alleging that the defendants were acting in breach of their fiduciary duties as trustees of the fund.

(ii) The court held that defendants were in breach of their fiduciary duties. Trustees must exercise their powers in the beneficiaries' best interests without regard to their own personal views or interests; where a trust is required to provide financial benefits, maximising the beneficiaries' financial benefit is, subject to very rare exceptions, the trustees' paramount concern; in exercising investment powers, trustees must act prudently and reasonably; the restrictions which defendants were seeking were intended to carry out the policy of the NUM rather than being for the benefit of the beneficiaries. Indeed the restrictions which the NUM delegates were seeking to enforce would not result in any material benefit to the beneficiaries.

(iii) *Per* Megarry V-C:

'I can see no escape from the conclusion that the NUM trustees were attempting to impose the prohibitions in order to carry out union policy; and mere assertions that their sole consideration was the benefit of the beneficiaries do not alter that conclusion. If the NUM trustees were thinking only of the benefit of the beneficiaries, why all the references to union policy instead of proper explanation of how and why the prohibitions would bring benefits to the beneficiaires? No doubt some trustees with strong feelings find it irksome to be forced to submerge those feelings and genuinely put the interests of the beneficiaries first. Indeed, there are some who are temperamentally unsuited to being trustees, and are more fitted for campaigning for changes in the law. This, of course, they are free to do; but if they choose to become trustees they must accept it that the rules of equity will bind them in all they do as trustees.'

In *Harries v The Church Commissioners* (1992), the question of impartiality in relation to ethical considerations involved in a trust was considered. Persons who were concerned that the investment policy of the Church Commissioners in their administration of certain church funds failed to pay sufficient attention to the fund's fundamental purpose, sought a declaration that the Commissioners were under an obligation to have appropriate regard to the object of promoting the Christian faith through the church in their task of fund management.

The declaration was refused by the court. Normally, charitable trustees would be obliged to seek the maximum return on investments consistent with the demands of principles of commercial prudence. In this case the proper object of the funds held by the Commissioners was the provision of financial assistance to the clergy. The Commissioners' policy of excluding certain specified investments which might be of a morally offensive nature was proper because there remained available to the Commissioners adequate alternative investments. But they were correct in refusing to be more restrictive in their policy to an extent that might result in a risk of financial detriment to the proper object of the trusts. Weight could be given to ethical considerations provided that accepted investment principles were not jeopardised when investments were made.

The duty of a trustee to convert property may arise under the will or settlement, by statute (as in the Administration of Estates Act 1925); or under the rule in *Howe v Lord Dartmouth* (1802).

16.12   Duty to convert

The rule was explained in the following terms in *Hinves v Hinves* (1844):

16.12.1   Rule in *Howe v Dartmouth*

'Where personal estate is given in terms amounting to a general residuary bequest to be enjoyed by persons in succession, the interpretation the court puts on the bequest is that the persons indicated are to enjoy the same thing in

succession; and in order to effectuate that intention, the court as a general rule converts into permanent investments so much of the personalty as is of a wasting or perishable nature at the death of the testator, and also reversionary interests.'

A trustee who breaks the rule is liable for breach of trust: see *Bate v Hooper* (1855).

The object of the rule is to convert wasting property (such as copyrights), so that a remainderman, who might receive property which has depreciated in value, or who might receive nothing at all, is protected, and so that a tenant for life, who might obtain nothing from some parts of the trust property, eg, a reversionary interest, is also protected. The rule means, therefore, that: where in a will there is residuary bequest of personal estate which is to be enjoyed by persons in succession, and there is no intention on the part of the settlor that the property is to be enjoyed *in specie*, then the trustees are under a duty to convert all the property of a wasting, hazardous, reversionary, or unauthorised character into authorised investments.

16.12.2	Non-application of the rule

The rule does not apply to realty; only personalty is affected. It does not apply where any contrary intention is expressed (such as a direction in the will) or there is evidence of intention to exclude it: *Re Wareham* (1912). The rule applies only to a gift by will, not to property settled by deed. It has no application where there is no gift to persons in succession; specific legacies are excluded.

'As far as leaseholds held in trust for sale are concerned, the role of *Howe v Lord Dartmouth* is gone': *per* Tomlin J in *Re Trollope's WT* (1927).

The Law Reform Committee has suggested that the rule be replaced by a general duty under statute to hold a fair balance among the beneficiaries.

16.13 Duty to apportion

In general, the tenant for life is entitled to income, the remainderman to the capital. If there is such a duty, then the trustees have a further duty to apportion between capital and income until there is a conversion.

16.13.1	Rules regarding apportionment

The rules regarding apportionment are as follows:

- In the case of authorised securities, the tenant for life is entitled to the whole of the income as from the date of death: *Meyer v Simonsen* (1852).

- In the case of realty, no apportionment need be made: *Re Searle* (1900).

- In the case of leaseholds, the tenant for life is entitled to the whole of the income produced by a leasehold held on trust for sale.

- In the case of unauthorised pure personalty, there must be an apportionment which will give the tenant for life a fair yield from investments. Where there is no power to postpone sale, the securities must be valued as at one year from the testator's death; where there is a power to postpone sale, they must be valued as at the date of death. The tenant for life is entitled to a sum equivalent to four per cent of the value of the securities; the surplus will be considered as capital. See *Re Fawcett* (1940).

- In the case of reversionary interests, the rule in *Re Chesterfield's Trusts* (1833) applies. Under this rule, trustees must wait until the interest is sold or falls into possession, and on either of these events the sum is calculated which, if invested at the testator's death at four per cent compound interest, would have produced the sum actually received. The sum thus calculated is treated as capital; the rest as income.

16.13.2 Other apportionments

The rule in *Allhusen v Whittell* (1867) applies to other apportionments. The rule was explained by Lord Romer in *Corbett v IRC* (1938):

'For the purpose of adjusting rights as between the tenant for life and the remainderman of a residuary estate, debts, legacies, estate duties, probate duties and so forth are to be deemed to have been paid out of such capital of the testator's estate as will be sufficient for that purpose, when to that capital is added interest on that capital from the date of the testator's death to the date of the payment of the legacy or debt, or whatever it may have been, interest being calculated at the average rate of interest earned by the testator's estate during the relevant period.'

The rule will not apply if the residue is not settled on persons in succession.

The testator can exclude the operation of the rule by the use of appropriate words.

The Law Reform Committee has recommended the ending of the rule.

Duties of Trustees (2)

A trustee must confine himself to the class of investments permitted by the trust and avoid investments attended with hazard. He must have regard to suitability and the need for diversification.

Trustees may invest trust funds in investments authorised by the trust instrument and the provisions of the 1961 Act. Investments may be made in shares quoted on the Stock Exchange issued by companies with a total share capital of at least £1m.

The Act allows three categories of investment, which may be added to by Order in Council:

- *Part I investments.* This is the safer type of investment and does not necessitate the trustee's seeking advice before investing, eg, Defence Bonds. See First Schedule to 1961 Act, Part I.

- *Part II investments.* Expert advice must be sought by the trustees before investing. Examples: fixed interest securities issued by British Government (other than those in Part I); debentures; deposits in building societies.

- *Part III investments.* Advice must be taken by trustees. They include shares in authorised building societies, units in authorised unit trusts.

Where trustees wish to invest in wider-range investments (Part II), the trust must be divided into a narrower-range part and a wider-range part, the former to include Part I and II investments, the latter, Part III. Parts of the fund must be of equal value at the time of division. No transfer from one part to another may be made without a compensating transfer.

The importance of preserving the fund outweighs success in its advancement. See *Nestlé v National Westminster Bank* (1992).

Investment on mortgages is restricted to mortgages of freehold property and leaseholds with at least 60 years to run. Second mortgages ought to be avoided.

Where trustees view their existing powers as inadequate or unsuitable they may apply to the court for an order under the Variation of Trusts Act 1958, or under Trustee Act 1925, s 57.

Duty relating to investment: standard of care

Trustee Investments Act 1961: statutory powers

Investment on mortgages

Duty to act impartially

Trustees must act in the interests of all beneficiaries, favouring neither one nor the other. Beneficiaries' interests must be put first. See *Cowan v Scargill* (1985).

Duty to convert

The duty to convert may arise: under the will or settlement; by statute; under the rule in *Howe v Dartmouth* (1802).

The essence of the rule in *Howe v Dartmouth* is that where in a will there is residuary bequest of personal estate which is to be enjoyed by persons in succession and there is no intention on the settlor's part that the property is to be enjoyed *in specie*, the trustees are under a duty to convert all property of a wasting, hazardous nature into authorised investments.

The rule does not apply to realty, nor where a contrary intention is expressed, nor to property settled by deed.

Duty to apportion

A tenant for life is entitled to income, remainderman to the capital. Where there is such a requirement, the trustees must apportion between capital and income until there is a conversion. In the case of realty, no apportionment need be made. See: *Re Chesterfield's Trusts* (1833); *Allhusen v Whittwell* (1867); *Corbett v IRC* (1938).

Chapter 17

Duties of Trustees (3)

The trustee is under a duty to obey the directions contained within the instrument creating the trust. This duty must be obeyed save in circumstances in which a deviation from those directions is sanctioned by the court. In *Re New* (1901) the court gave its approval to the participation by trustees in a scheme of reconstruction involving a company in which the trust was a shareholder. Under the terms of the trust the trustees lacked the power to invest in the new types of security to be offered. The court empowered the trustees to accept the reorganisation scheme and to exchange its shares for newly-issued shares which promised to be more marketable.

Per Romer LJ:

'In the management of a trust ... it not infrequently happens that some peculiar state of circumstances arises for which provision is not expressly made by the trust instrument, and which renders it most desirable, and it may be even essential, for the benefit of the estate and in the interests of all the *cestuis que trust*, that certain acts should be done by the trustees which in ordinary circumstances they have no power to do. In a case of this kind, which may reasonably be supposed to be one not foreseen or anticipated by the author of the trust, where the trustees are embarrassed by the emergency that has arisen and the duty cast on them to do what is best for the estate, and the consent of all the beneficiaries cannot be obtained by reason of some of them not being *sui juris* or in existence, then it may be right for the court, and the court in a proper case would have jurisdiction, to sanction on behalf of all concerned such acts on behalf of the trustees as we have referred to ...

... The jurisdiction is one to be exercised with great caution, and the court will take care not to strain its powers ... it need scarcely be said that the court will not be justified in sanctioning every act desired by trustees and beneficiaries merely because it may appear beneficial to the estate; and certainly the court will not be disposed to sanction transactions of a speculative or risky character.'

There are now important exceptions to the wide general rule enunciated in *Re New* (1901). These include: exercise by the court of its inherent jurisdiction; exceptions under statute, including the important Variation of Trusts Act 1958.

17.1 Duty not to deviate from the trust

| 17.2 | **Inherent jurisdiction of the court** | Exceptions arising by virtue of the court's inherent jurisdiction are limited and are concerned largely with the sanctioning of departures from those terms of the trust which are involved with its administration and management. |

| 17.2.1 | Salvage, emergency and conversion | The following exceptions to the general rule against variation arise under this head: |

- In a case of absolute necessity, the court may sanction the mortgage or sale of part of an infant's beneficial interest for the benefit of the property retained - the so-called 'salvage case': *Re Jackson* (1882) (essential repairs to settled land).

- In the case of an emergency arising concerning the administration or management of property which had not been foreseen by the settlor and which could be dealt with only by giving extraordinary powers to the trustee. See *Re New* (1901) at para 17.1 above.

- The court may allow the conversion of an estate from realty to personalty in very rare cases where it has become necessary in the interests of an infant beneficiary: *Ashburton v Ashburton* (1801).

| 17.2.2 | Maintenance and compromise | These are further exceptions to the general rule: |

- The court has power to provide maintenance for the children of the testator where he has provided for them, but has postponed enjoyment of the property. *Per* Pearson J in *Re Collins* (1866):

  'Where a testator has made a provision for a family, using that word in the ordinary sense in which we take the word, ... but has postponed the enjoyment, either for a particular purpose or generally for the increase of the estate, it is assumed that he did not intend that these children should be left unprovided for or in a state of such moderate means that they should not be educated properly for the position and fortune which he designs them to have, and the court has accordingly found from the earliest times that where an heir-in-law is unprovided for, maintenance ought to be provided for him.'

- Where there are doubts or disputes concerning the rights of beneficiaries, the court may make a compromise 'so as to substitute certainty for doubt': *Brooke v Mostyn* (1864). See *Mason v Farbrother* (1983) - compromise effected concerning the precise meaning of an investment clause.

| 17.3 | **Statutory exceptions concerning variations** | Apart from the Variation of Trusts Act 1958 there are other statutory exceptions to the general rule against variation, arising from the Trustee Act 1925, the Settled Land Act 1925 and the Matrimonial Causes Act 1973. |

Trustee Act 1925, s 53:

'Where an infant is beneficially entitled to any property the court may, with a view to the application of the capital or income thereof for the maintenance, education or benefit of the infant, make an order for (a) appointing a person to convey such property; or (b) in the case of stock, or a thing in action, vesting in any person the right to transfer or call for the transfer of such stock, or to receive the dividends or income thereof, or to sue for and recover such thing in action, upon such terms as the court may think fit.'

See *Re Gower's Settlement* (1934) in which the court authorised the mortgage of an infant's entailed interest in remainder, for the purposes of maintenance.

See also *Re Meux* (1958), in which the court ordered, under s 53, the conveying of an infant's reversionary entailed interest in consideration of a sum to be paid to trustees on trust for the benefit of the infant.

Trustee Act 1925, s 57(1):

'Where in the management or administration of any property vested in trustees, any sale, lease, mortgage, surrender, release, or other disposition, or any purchase, investment, acquisition, expenditure, or other transaction, is in the opinion of the court expedient, but the same cannot be effected by reason of the absence of any power for that purpose vested in the trustees by the trust instrument, if any, or by law, the court may by order confer upon the trustees ... the necessary power for the purpose ...'

The court must be satisfied that the proposals are for the benefit of the trust in its entirety, and not merely for a beneficiary': *Re Craven's Estate (No 2)* (1937).

'The court may, from time to time, rescind or vary any order made under this section, or may make any new or further order': s 57(3).

Transactions sanctioned under s 57 have included: sale by trustees of a reversionary interest which, under the settlement, they were not empowered to sell until it fell into possession (*Re Cockerell's ST* (1956)); expenditure of capital to purchase the life tenant's interest (*Re Forster's Settlement* (1954)).

Note the comments of Lord Evershed in *Re Downshire* (1953):

'The object of s 57 was to secure that trust property should be managed as advantageously as possible in the interests of the beneficiaries, and, with that object in view, to authorise specific dealings with the property which the court might have felt itself unable to sanction under the inherent jurisdiction, either because there was no actual "emergency" or because of inability to show that the

17.3.1   Trustee Act 1925, s 53

17.3.2   Trustee Act 1925, s 57(1)

position which called for intervention was one which the creator of the trust could not reasonably have foreseen; but it was not part of the legislative aim to disturb the rule that the court will not rewrite a trust.'

17.3.3 Settled Land Act 1925, s 64(1)

Settled Land Act 1925, s 64(1):

'Any transaction affecting or concerning the settled land, or any part thereof, or any other land (not being a transaction otherwise authorised by this Act, or by the settlement) which in the opinion of the court would be for the benefit of the settled land, or any part thereof, or the persons interested under the settlement, may, under an order of the court, be effected by a tenant for life, if it is one which could have been validly effected by an absolute owner.'

See *Re Downshire* (1953); *Raikes v Lygon* (1988).

'Transaction' includes any sale, exchange or other disposition and 'any compromise or other dealing, or arrangement': s 64(2).

The section is not restricted merely to a variation of administrative matters related to a trust, but applies also to a variation of beneficial interests.

The section applies also to land held on trust for sale: *Re Simmons* (1956).

17.3.4 Matrimonial Causes Act 1973, s 24

On granting a decree of divorce, decree of nullity or judicial separation, or at any time thereafter (see *Jackson v Jackson* (1973)), the court may make an order 'varying for the benefit of the parties to the marriage and of the children of the family or either or any of them, any ante-nuptial or post-nuptial settlement (including such a settlement made by will or codicil) made on the parties to the marriage, and an order extinguishing or reducing the interests of either of the parties to the marriage under any such settlement': Matrimonial Causes Act 1973, s 24.

17.3.5 Mental Health Act 1983, s 96

Where a settlement has been made of any property of a patient and the Lord Chancellor or a nominated judge is satisfied at any time before the death of the patient, that a material fact was not disclosed when the settlement was made, he may by order vary the settlement in such manner as he thinks fit, and give any consequential directions: Mental Health Act 1983, s 96.

17.4 Variation of Trusts Act 1958

The Variation of Trusts Act 1958 was based upon the recommendations of the Law Reform Committee, following the decision of the House of Lords in *Chapman v Chapman* (1954).

Per Lord Simonds:

'This brings me to the question which alone presents difficulty in this case. It is whether the fourth category [the others were conversion, maintenance and salvage] which I call the "compromise category", should be extended so as to cover those cases in which there is no real dispute as to rights, and, therefore, no compromise, but it is sought by way of bargain between the beneficiaries in order to re-arrange the beneficial interests under the trust instrument so as to bind infants and unborn persons by order of the court. It is not the function of the courts to alter a trust instrument because alteration is thought to be advantageous to an infant beneficiary.'

Per Lord Morton:

'If the court had power to approve, and did approve schemes such as the present scheme, the way would be open for a most undignified game of chess between the Chancery Division and the legislature.'

The Act recognises four classes of person on whose behalf the court may act and approve variations in the trust:

- Persons who have, directly or indirectly, a vested or contingent interest under the trust, who are incapable of assenting by reason of infancy or other incapacity: s 1(l)(a).

- Persons (ascertained or not) who may become entitled, directly or indirectly, to an interest under the trust as being at a future date or on the happening of a future event a person of any specified description or a member of any specified class of persons. However this does not include any person who would be of that description, or a member of that class, as the case may be, if the said date had fallen or the said event had happened at the date of the application to the court: s 1(l)(b). See *Re Suffert's Settlement* (1961); *Re Moncrieff's ST* (1962); *Knocker v Youle* (1986).

- Unborn persons: s 1(l)(c).

- Persons in respect of any discretionary interest under a protective trust (see Chapter 7) where the interest of the principal beneficiary has not failed or determined: s 1(l)(d).

Section 1 of the 1958 Act applies to trusts of real *and* personal property arising before or after the passing of the Act.

17.5   Section 1

Applications to the court may be made by the life tenant, trustees, or any party entitled to the income of the trust fund. Trustees should apply only where they are satisfied 'that the proposals are beneficial to the persons interested and have a good prospect of being approved by the court, and, further, that if they do not make the application no one else will': *per* Russell J in *Re Druce's ST* (1962).

The court will not approve an arrangement on behalf of any person 'unless the carrying out thereof would be for the benefit of that person' but in the case of persons within s l(l)(d) their benefit is not essential for approval: see, eg, *Re Clitheroe's ST* (1959).

The term 'benefit' is 'plainly not confined to financial benefit, but may extend to moral or social benefit': *per* Megarry J in *Re Holt's Settlement* (1969). *Per* Lord Denning in *Re Weston's Settlement* (1969):

'The court should not consider merely the financial benefit to the infants or unborn children, but also their educational and social benefit. There are many things in life more worthwhile than money. One of these things is to be brought up in this our England, which is still "the envy of less happier lands". I do not believe it is for the benefit of children to be uprooted from England and transported to another country simply to avoid tax ... The avoidance of tax may be lawful, but it is not yet a virtue. The Court of Chancery should not encourage or support it - it should not give its approval to it - if by so doing it would imperil the true welfare of the children, already born or yet to be born ... The long and short of it is, as the judge said, that the exodus of this family to Jersey is done to avoid British taxation ... If it really be for the benefit of the children, let it be done. Let them go, taking their money with them. But if it be not truly for their benefit, the court should not countenance it. It should not give the scheme its blessing ...'

Per Ungoed Thomas in *Re Van Gruisen's WT* (1964):

'The court is not merely concerned with the actuarial calculation ... the court is also concerned whether the arrangement as a whole, in all the circumstances, is such that it is proper to approve it. The court's concern involves, *inter alia*, a practical and business-like consideration of the arrangement, including the total amount of the advantages which the various parties obtain and their bargaining strength.'

The word 'arrangement' as used in the context of s l may be 'deliberately used in the widest possible sense so as to cover any proposal which any person may put forward for varying or revoking the trust': *per* Evershed MR in *Re Steed's WT* (1960). See also *Re Ball's Settlement* (1968). Variations of a fraudulent nature, or contrary to public policy, will not be sanctioned by the court: *Re Wallace's Settlement* (1968).

Per Megarry, J:

'If to a fair, cautious and enquiring mind the circumstances of the appointment, so far as known, raise a real and not merely a tenuous suspicion of fraud on the power, the approval of the court ought to be withheld until that suspicion is dispelled.'

In *Re Pettifor's WT* (1966), it was stated that the Act was not concerned with the variation of trusts to cover impossible contingencies; it was held inappropriate, therefore, for an application to be made to cover the contingency of the birth of further children to a woman aged seventy.

It has been suggested that variation is effected by the arrangement approved by the court and not by the court order itself: *Re Holt's Settlement* (1968).

The following comments on the Act are of particular interest.

- *Per* Lord Evershed in *Re Steed's WT* (1960):

  'The court must regard the proposal as a whole, and so regarding it, then ask itself whether in the exercise of its jurisdiction it should approve that proposal on behalf of a person who cannot give a consent, because he is not in a position to do so. If that is a right premise, then it follows that the court is bound to look at the scheme as a whole, and when it does so, to consider, as surely it must, what was the intention of the benefactor ... The court must, albeit that it is performing its duty on behalf of some person who cannot consent on his or her own part ,regard the proposal in the light of the purpose of the trust as shown by the evidence of the will or settlement itself, and of any other relevant evidence available ... It is the agreement which has to be approved, not just the limited interest of the person on whose behalf the court's duty is to consider it.'

- *Per* Buckley, J in *Re Moncrieff's ST* (1962):

  (The court's approval of arrangements had been requested on behalf of the statutory next of kin of Mrs Parkin. At the date of application her next of kin was the first respondent, an infant adopted son. In the event of Mrs Parkin's surviving him, her next of kin would be the four infant grandchildren of her maternal aunt. They and the trustees were made respondents.)

  'Section 1 of the 1985 Act enables me to approve the arrangement on behalf of "any person (whether ascertained or not) who may become entitled, directly or indirectly, to an interest under the trusts as being at a future date or on the happening of a future event a person of any specified description or a member of any specified class of persons ...". The first respondent would fall within that description, but the section goes on: "so however that this paragraph shall not include any person who would be of that description, or a member of that class, as the case may be, if the said date had fallen or the said event had happened at the date of application to the court ....." The first respondent is excluded, therefore, from the persons on whose behalf I can sanction the arrangement under s 1(1)(b), but none of the other persons who might become entitled to participate in the estate of the settlor were she to survive the first respondent and then die intestate is excluded because none of them would be within the class of next of kin if she died today. Therefore I am in a position to approve the arrangement on behalf of all persons whether ascertained or not who might become interested in the settlor's estate at a future date with the exception of the first respondent.'

- *Per* Lord Reid in *IRC v Holmden* (1968):

  'Each beneficiary is bound because he has consented to the variation. If he was not of full age when the arrangement was made he is bound because the court was authorised by the Act to approve it on his behalf and did so by making an order ... The arrangement must be regarded as an arrangement made by the beneficiaries themselves. The court merely acted on behalf of or as representing those beneficiaries who were not in a position to give their own consent and approval.'

17.6	**Duty to hand over trust funds to the right persons**	Trust property must be distributed only to the person(s) entitled. There are cases, however, where the court may excuse a mistake made honestly and reasonably and in which the trustee is protected by statute.
17.6.1	Aspects of trustees' liability	Trustees are liable when they act on an incorrect construction of the trust instrument: *Re Hulkes* (1886). They are liable, further, where they rely on a forged document: *Eaves v Hickson* (1861), in which trust money was paid to a person not entitled, on the basis of a forged marriage certificate.

Trustees have a right to demand that a person who claims to be a beneficiary should prove his title: *Hurst v Hurst* (1874).

Trustees who have doubts as to a claimant's title should apply to the court for directions: *Merlin v Blagrave* (1858).

Where trustees cannot trace a beneficiary they should pay his money into court: see *Re Benjamin* (1902).

Trustees are not obliged to hand over trust funds to the mortgagee of a beneficiary where accounts are pending between mortgagor and mortgagee: *Hockey v Weston* (1898).

The Trustee Act 1925, s 27, as amended, has application even though there is a provision to the contrary in the trust instrument. This gives a measure of protection to trustees who have to distribute trust property.

Trustees may give notice to persons entitled to real or personal property by advertising in the London Gazette (and, in the case of land, in a newspaper circulating in the district in which the land is situated) and 'by other like notices ... as would ... have been directed by a court ... in an action for administration', of their intention to effect a distribution.

The notice must require any interested person to forward particulars of his claim to the trustees within a stated time (usually not less than two months).

At the expiration of the advertised time the trustees may distribute on the basis of those claims of which they have notice. They are then fully protected. (See also Charities Act 1993, s 14.)

Nothing in the section prejudices the right of a person to follow the property into the hands of any other person, other than a purchaser, who may have received it: s 27(2)(a).

Per Page-Wood VC in *Gosling v Gosling* (1859):

> 'The principle of this court has always been to recognise the right of all persons who attain the age of [18] to enter upon the absolute use and enjoyment of the property given to them by a will, notwithstanding any direction by the testator to the effect that they are not to enjoy it until a later age - unless during the interval the property is given for the benefit of another.'

In *Saunders v Vautier* (1841), the testator bequeathed stock on trust so that dividends might be accumulated until X should attain the age of 25, then to transfer the principal plus accumulated dividends to X. When X reached the age of 21 he claimed to have the fund transferred to him.

Per Lord Langdale:

> 'Where a legacy is directed to accumulate for a certain period, or where the payment is postponed, the legatee, if he has an absolute indefeasible interest in the legacy, is not bound to wait until the expiration of that period, but may require payment the moment he is competent to give a valid discharge.'

A beneficiary who is *sui juris* and absolutely entitled has the right to terminate a trust irrespective of the wishes of the settlor or trustees. This will apply also if there are several beneficiaries each of whom is *sui juris* and absolutely entitled: *Barton v Briscoe* (1822). The rule appears to have application even where the trust instrument contains a contrary provision.

The circumstances outlined above necessitate the trustees' conveying the trust property, thus bringing the trust to an end. See *IRC v Hamilton-Russell Executors* (1943).

Per Walton J in *Stephenson v Barclays Bank Trust Co Ltd* (1975):

'It appears to me that once the beneficial interest holders have determined to end the trust they are not entitled, unless by agreement, to the further services of the trustees. Those trustees can of course be compelled to hand over the entire trust assets to any person or persons selected by the beneficiaries against a proper discharge, but they cannot be compelled, unless they are in fact willing to comply with the directions, to do anything with the trust fund which they are not in fact willing to do.'

Duties of Trustees (3)

The trustee is under a duty to obey the directions in the trust instrument. In some few cases there are exceptions to this rule.

Duty not to deviate from the trust

The court may sanction departures from terms of the trust relating to administration and management in cases of *salvage* (eg, essential repairs), *emergency* (where unforeseen, extraordinary action is required), and *conversion* of an estate from realty to personalty where necessary. The court also has the power to provide maintenance of children where the settlor has provided for them, but has postponed enjoyment of the property.

Inherent jurisdiction of the court

The following should be noted:

- Trustee Act 1925, s 53. The court may make an order concerning the application of capital or income for the maintenance, benefit or education of an infant beneficially entitled.

- Trustee Act 1925, s 57(1). The court may empower trustees to carry out transactions in the interests of the trust and in the absence of powers within the trust instrument.

- Matrimonial Causes Act 1973, s 24. The court is empowered to vary settlements for the benefit of the parties to the marriage and children.

Statutory exceptions concerning variation of trusts

The court may act and approve variations in a trust on behalf of those who cannot assent because of infancy or other incapacity; unborn persons; persons who have a discretionary interest under a protective trust where the interest of the principal beneficiary remains; persons who may become entitled directly or indirectly to an interest under the trusts as being at a future date or on the happening of a future event a person of any specified description or member of any specified class of persons: s 1.

Variation of Trusts Act 1958

The section applies to trusts of real and personal property.

The proposed variation must be for the benefit of the persons concerned. 'Benefit' is not confined to financial benefit, but may extend to moral or social benefit.

Variations of a fraudulent nature will not be sanctioned.

Duty to hand over trust funds to the right persons

Trust property must be distributed only to the persons entitled. Trustees may be liable when they act on an incorrect construction of the trust instrument. They have the right to demand that those who claim to be beneficiaries should prove their title. Trustee Act 1925, s 27, protects trustees who advertise their intention to effect distribution. At the expiration of the advertised time the trustees may distribute on the basis of the claims of which they have notice; they are then fully protected.

Duty where beneficiaries are entitled to end the trust

A beneficiary who is *sui juris* and absolutely entitled has the right to terminate a trust irrespective of the wishes of the settlor or trustees. The rule seems to have application even where the trust instrument contains a contrary provision. See *Saunders v Vautier* (1841). In these circumstances the trustees must convey the trust property so as to bring the trust to an end. See *IRC v Hamilton-Russell Executors* (1943).

Chapter 18

Powers of Trustees (1)

The *duties* of the trustee, which were considered in previous chapters, are linked to the *powers* given to him under the instrument creating the trust or under statute. In general, a trustee may, subject to restrictions contained in the settlement or imposed by statute, perform all the acts necessary to carry out the terms of the trust. In this chapter we outline the power of sale, the power to give receipts, to insure, to compound liabilities and to act in relation to reversionary interests.

18.1 The general powers of the trustee

A trustee has the power to sell, exchange and mortgage the trust property; but this power derives only from statute, order of the court, or an authority, express or implied, in the trust instrument. In the case of a trust to sell land, trustees have all the powers of a tenant for life arising under the Settled Land Act 1925 (and these include powers of sale, exchange and mortgage): Law of Property Act 1925, s 28(1).

18.2 The trustee's power of sale

Under Law of Property Act, s 32(1), which has application to all settlements coming into operation after 1911, where a settlement of personal property or of land held on trust for sale contains a power to invest money in the purchase of land, such land shall, unless the settlement provides otherwise, be held by the trustee on trusts for sale; 'and the net rents and profits until sale, after keeping down costs of repairs and insurance and other outgoings, shall be paid or applied in like manner as the income of investments representing the purchase money would be payable or applicable if a sale had been made and the proceeds had been duly invested in personal estate'.

18.2.1 Law of Property Act 1925, s 32(1)

A 'trust for sale', in relation to land, means an immediate binding trust for sale, whether or not exercisable at the request or with the consent of any person, and with or without a power at discretion to postpone the sale: Law of Property Act 1925, s 205(1)(xxix). It may arise: expressly from the wording of the settlement; or by statute, as where, eg, persons are jointly entitled to land; or where trustees lend money on mortgage and, as a result of a foreclosure, the property is vested in them. See also the Administration of Estates Act 1925, s 33, which is outlined in para 18.2.5.

A direction which imposes a 'trust either to retain or sell the land' is construed as a trust to sell combined with a power to postpone the sale: Law of Property Act 1925, s 25(4). (Prior to the Act, the direction was construed as depending on intention.)

Operation of the section may be excluded expressly or by necessary implication. See *Re Hanson* (1928).

18.2.2   Trustee Act 1925, s 12

Where a trust for sale or power of sale of property is vested in a trustee, he may sell, or concur with others, in selling all the property or any part of it, subject to prior charges (or not) and in lots, by public auction or private contract, subject to any conditions relating to title as he thinks fit: Trustee Act 1925, s 12. Division of the land may be horizontal, vertical or made in any other way. Thus the trustee is given a wide freedom as to the manner and mode of his conduct of a sale of land.

18.2.3   Trustee Act 1925, s 16

Where trustees are authorised by the trust instrument or by law to pay or apply capital money, subject to the trust, for any purpose or in any manner, they have power to raise the money required by sale, conversion, calling in, or mortgage of all the trust property or any part of it for the time being in possession: Trustee Act 1925, s 16. For a proposed borrowing to come within s 16, it must be shown that the very manner in which the capital money is to be applied is authorised by the settlement or under law: *Re Suenson-Taylor's ST* (1974). In this case trustees were empowered 'within their absolute discretion' to acquire investments as a substitute for existing investments or to invest any capital moneys which they already held as part of the trust fund. The trustees wished to mortgage land which they held for purposes of investment with the object of purchasing further land for purposes of investment. The court held that the powers of the trustees did not include a specific power to acquire additional assets or investments and that the proposed borrowing was not for a purpose which was authorised by the settlement or by law.

18.2.4   Trustee Act 1925, ss 13(1), (2)

No sale made by a trustee may be impeached by a beneficiary on the ground that any of the conditions subject to which the sale was made may have been 'unnecessarily depreciatory', unless it can be shown that the consideration for sale was thereby rendered inadequate. No sale may be impeached, after execution of the conveyance, unless it appears that purchaser and trustee were acting in collusion at the time when the contract for sale was made. *Buttle v Saunders* (1950)) allowed the court to formulate the general principle that trustees have a duty of an overriding nature to obtain for their beneficiaries the best price they can. The facts were that trustees for sale of land had made an oral agreement to sell that land to Mrs Simpson [S] for £6,142. Before the contract was signed, and after preparation of the appropriate documents, a beneficiary, Canon Buttle [B], made an offer of

£6,500 for the land, which he wanted to purchase for a charity. The trustees considered that the negotiations with S were so advanced that they could not honourably terminate them by withdrawing from the agreement. B brought an action intended to restrain the trustees from selling below the price in his offer. The trustees counterclaimed, seeking the court's directions. *Per* Wynn-Parry, J:

'It has been argued on behalf of the trustees that they were justified in the circumstances in not pursuing B's offer and in deciding to go forward with the transaction with S. It is true that persons who are not in the position of trustees are entitled, if they so desire, to accept a lesser price than that which they might obtain on the sale of property, and not infrequently a vendor, who has gone to some length in negotiating with a prospective purchaser, decides to close the deal with that purchaser, notwithstanding that he is presented with a higher offer. It rebounds to the credit of a man who acts like that in such circumstances. Trustees, however, are not vested with such complete freedom. They have an overriding duty to obtain the best price which they can for their beneficiaries. It would, however, be an unfortunate simplification of the problem if one were to take the view that the mere production of an increased offer at any stage, however late in the negotiations, should throw on the trustees a duty to accept the higher offer and resile from the existing offer. For myself, I think that trustees have such a discretion in the matter as will allow them to act with proper prudence. I can see no reason why trustees should not pray in aid the common-sense rule underlying the old proverb: "A bird in the hand is worth two in the bush." I can imagine cases where trustees could properly refuse a higher offer and proceed with a lower offer. Each case, of necessity, must depend on its own facts ...

... In regard to the case now before me, my view is that the trustees and their solicitors acted on an incorrect principle. The only consideration which was present to their minds was that they had gone so far in negotiations with S that they could not properly, from the point of view of commercial morality, resile form those negotiations. That being so, they did not to any extent, probe B's offer as, in my view, they should have done. It seems to me that the least the trustees should have done would have been to have said to him: "You have come on the scene at a late stage ... You must submit in the circumstances to somewhat stringent terms ..." I have not the slightest doubt that B would have agreed to them and the matter would have been carried out ...'

It was held that the trustees must accept B's offer.

18.2.5	Administration of Estates Act 1925, s 33	Under the Administration of Estates Act 1925, s 33, the death of a person intestate as to any real or personal estate, such estate shall be held by his personal representatives as to the real estate upon trust to sell the same, and as to the personal estate upon trust to call in, sell and convert any part not consisting of money, with power to postpone the sale and conversion.
18.2.6	Settled Land Act 1925, s 38	A tenant for life may sell the settled land or any part, or any easement, right or privilege over or in relation to the land, and may make an exchange of the settled land, or any part, or of any easement, right or privilege: Settled Land Act 1925, s 38.
18.2.7	Settled Land Act 1925, s 67	Where personal chattels are settled so as to devolve with settled land, or are settled together with land, or upon trusts declared by reference to the trusts affecting land, a tenant for life may sell those chattels and the money arising from the sale will be considered as capital money: Settled Land Act 1925, s 67. But a sale under this section may not be undertaken without a court order.
18.2.8	Law of Property Act 1925, s 130(5)	Where personal chattels are settled without reference to settled land on trusts creating entailed interests, the trustees, with the consent of the usufructuary (the person having a limited interest in the property) for the time being, if of full age, may sell the chattels, and proceeds of the sale will be held in trust for 'and shall go to the same persons successively, in the same manner and for the same interests', as the chattels sold would have been held and gone, had they not been sold: Law of Property Act 1925, s 130(5). The income of investments representing the proceeds of sale will be applied accordingly.

18.3 The trustee's power to give receipts

The trustee's power to give receipts is governed by the Trustee Act 1925, s 14. The section has application notwithstanding anything to the contrary which might have been stated in the instrument creating the trust.

18.3.1	Trustee Act 1925, s 14(1)	Trustee Act 1925, s 14(1): 'The receipt in writing of a trustee for any money, securities, or other personal property or effects payable, transferable, or deliverable to him under any trust or power shall be a sufficient discharge to the person paying, transferring, or delivering the same and shall effectively exonerate him from seeing to the application or being answerable for any loss or misapplication thereof.'
18.3.2	Trustee Act 1925, s 14(2)	Trustees Act 1925, s 14(2), amended by the Law of Property (Amendment) Act 1926, does *not*, except where the trustee is a trust corporation (see Chapter 14), enable a *sole trustee* to give a valid receipt for proceeds of sale or other capital money arising under trust for sale of land, or capital money arising under the Settled Land Act 1925.

The rule which demands that where there are two or more trustees, a valid receipt may be given only as the result of their joint action, remains unaltered by s 14.

The trustee's power to delegate was discussed in Chapter 15.

18.4   The trustee's power to delegate

In the absence of an express provision in the trust instrument, a trustee is not bound to insure the trust property: *Bailey v Gould* (1840). He has a statutory power arising out of the Trustee Act 1925.

18.5   The trustee's power to insure property

Under the Trustee Act 1925, s 19, a trustee may insure against loss or damage by fire any building or other insurable property to any amount, including the amount of any insurance already on foot, not exceeding three fourth parts of the full value of the building or property, and pay the premiums out of income, without obtaining the consent of any person who may be wholly or partly entitled to that income.

This section has no application to any building or property which a trustee is bound to convey absolutely to any beneficiary upon being requested to do so: s 19(2).

The power may be excluded or varied by the instrument creating the trust: see s 69(2).

Under s 20(1), money receivable by trustees or any beneficiary under a policy of insurance is capital money for the purpose of the trust or settlement. If such money is receivable by any person other than the trustees, that person must pay the residue, after costs of recovering and receiving it, to the trustees: s 20(2).

18.5.1   Application of insurance money

Such money, if receivable in respect of property held upon trust for sale, shall be held upon the trusts and subject to the powers and provisions applicable to money arising by sale under such trust: s 20(3).

Such money may be applied by the trustees in rebuilding, reinstating, replacing or repairing the property lost or damaged, subject to obtaining the required consents: s 20(4).

Nothing in the section prejudices or affects the rights of persons to require the money, or any part of it, to be applied in rebuilding, reinstating or repairing the property, or the rights of any mortgagor, lessor or lessee, whether under any statute or otherwise: s 20(5).

The following recommendations referring to insurance were included in the Report, *The Powers and Duties of Trustees, 1982*:

18.5.2   Recommendations of the Law Reform Committee, 23rd Report

• Trustees should be placed under a duty to insure against any risk in all the circumstances in which an ordinary prudent man of business would so insure.

• All trustees should be empowered to insure the trust property up to its full replacement value in all cases in which it would be sensible to do that, and, in other cases, up to its market value.

• Trustees should be empowered to pay insurance premiums out of capital as well as income, but should make the payments in such a way as to maintain the balance between the interests of the life tenant and remainderman.

18.6   The trustee's power to compound liabilities

The Trustee Act 1925, s 15, is concerned with the settling of claims made against, or on behalf of, the trust:

'A personal representative, or two or more trustees acting together, or, subject to the restrictions imposed in regard to receipts by a sole trustee not being a trust corporation, a sole trustee ... may, if and as he or they think fit,

(a) accept any property, real or personal, before the time at which it is made transferable or payable; or

(b) sever and apportion any blended trust funds or property; or

(c) pay or allow any debt or claim on any evidence that he or they think sufficient; or

(d) accept any composition or any security, real or personal, claimed; or

(e) allow any time of payment of any debt; or

(f) compromise, compound, abandon, submit to arbitration, or otherwise settle any debt, account, claim, or thing whatever relating to the testator's or intestate's estate or to the trust; and for any of these purposes may enter into, give, execute ... instruments of composition or arrangement, releases, and other things as to him or them seems expedient, without being responsible for any loss occasioned by any act or thing so done by him or them in good faith.'

In *Re Ridsdel* (1947) it was held that a judicial trustee has the power to effect a compromise with a debtor.

In *Re Earl of Strafford* (1979), the testator, by his will had settled land and bequeathed his chattels on trust by which life interests were given to a number of beneficiaries. The trustee and beneficiaries became involved in a dispute concerning the nature of an allocation of various chattels. The Court of Appeal held that the surrender of a limited interest under a settlement merely eliminated a pre-existing interest but left the trust intact. A trustee had power, therefore, to compromise a claim to trust property in consideration of a surrender by adverse claimants of their life interests under the trust. The essence of s 15 was its conferring on the trustee of 'wide and flexible' powers of compromising disputes.

The Trustee Act 1925, s 22, affords a measure of protection to trustees in relation to trust property which includes any share or interests in property not vested in trustees.

Section 22(1):

> 'Where trust property includes any share or interests in property not vested in the trustees, or proceeds of the sale of such property, or any other thing in action, the trustees may, on the same falling into possession, or becoming transferable or payable:
>
> (a) agree or ascertain the amount or value thereof or any part thereof in the manner they consider fit;
>
> (b) accept in, or towards satisfaction thereof, at market or current value, or upon any valuation, authorised investments;
>
> (c) allow deductions for charges and expenses which they consider reasonable;
>
> (d) execute a release in respect of the premises so as to discharge parties from liability concerning matters within the scope of the release.'

In these circumstances, the trustees are not responsible for any loss occasioned by any act done by them in good faith.

Under the Trustee Act 1925, s 22(2), the trustees are under no obligation and are not chargeable with any breach of trust by reason of any omission to apply for a stop or other order upon property out of or on which a share or interest or other thing in action is derived, payable or charged. Nor are they responsible for any omission to take any proceedings on account of any act, default or neglect on the part of those in whom such securities or other property are for the time being, or had at any time been, vested, 'unless and until required in writing so to do by some person, or the guardian of some person, beneficially interested under the trust, and unless also due provision is made to their satisfaction for payment of the costs of any proceedings required to be taken.'

Under a *proviso* to the section nothing in sub-section (2) is to relieve the trustees of the obligation to get in and obtain payment or transfer of such share or interest or other thing in action on the same falling into possession.

The trustees 'may, for the purpose of giving effect to the trust, or any of the provisions of the instrument, if any,

18.7   Trustee's powers in relation to reversionary interests

18.7.1   Trustee Act 1925, s 22(1)

18.7.2   Trustee Act 1925, s 22(2)

creating the trust or of any statute, from time to time (by duly qualified agents) ascertain and fix the value of any trust property in such manner as they think proper, and any valuation so made in good faith shall be binding upon all persons interested under the trust.'

18.8   Trustee's power to claim reimbursement

Trustee's power to claim reimbursement was discussed in Chapter 15 .

Summary of Chapter 18

Powers of Trustees (1)

The trustee may, subject to restrictions imposed by the trust instrument or statute, perform all those acts necessary to carry out the terms of the trust.

The trustee's general powers

The trustee may sell, exchange or mortgage trust property.

The power of sale

- Law of Property Act 1925, s 32(1)

  A trust for sale (immediate and binding) is implied where land has been purchased by the trustees of a personalty settlement.

- Trustee Act 1926, s 12

  This gives the trustee a wide freedom as to the manner of sale, allowing him to sell, eg, all or any part of the property.

- Trustee Act 1925, s 16

  Trustees who have to pay or apply capital money are empowered to raise it by sale of the trust property in possession.

- Trustee Act 1925, s 13

  No sale by a trustee may be impeached by the beneficiaries unless it can be shown that because of the conditions of the sale the consideration for sale had been rendered inadequate. See *Buttle v Saunders* (1950).

- Administration of Estates Act 1925, s 33; Settled Land Act 1925, s 38

  The former section empowers personal representatives of an intestate to hold his real estate on trust to sell the same. The latter section allows a tenant for life to sell the settled land or any part of it, or easements, rights, attached.

The trustee's power to give receipts is governed by Trustee Act 1925, s 14. Generally there needs to be only a single trustee of land; but two or more are needed so as to give a valid receipt for capital money when land is sold.

The power to give receipts

The power to delegate was considered in Chapter 15.

The power to delegate

A trustee's statutory power to insure arises under Trustee Act 1925, s 19. He may insure buildings or other insurable

The power to insure property

property and pay premiums out of income without obtaining consent from those entitled to that income.

The section does not apply to property which a trustee is bound to convey absolutely upon request from a beneficiary: s 19(2).

Under s 20, money received under an insurance policy is capital money for the purposes of the trust. It may be applied by the trustees so as to rebuild or replace the property lost or damaged.

The Law Reform Committee has recommended that all trustees should be under a duty to insure in circumstances in which an ordinary prudent business man would insure.

The power to compound liabilities

Under s 15 of Trustee Act 1925, two or more trustees acting together may accept property before the time at which it is made transferable or payable, may accept any composition or any security, real or personal, for any debt or property claimed, may allow any time of payment of any debt, and may compromise, compound or otherwise settle any debt or account relating to the trust. See *Re Ridsdel* (1947); *Re Earl of Strafford* (1979).

The power of dealing with reversionary interests

Under Trustee Act 1925, s 22, where the trust property includes property not vested in the trustees, they are permitted to agree a valuation for such property or accept authorised investments in, or towards, satisfaction of the property, or execute a release. In these circumstances the trustees will not be responsible for any loss occasioned by any act they have performed in good faith.

The power to claim reimbursement

See Chapter 15.

Chapter 19

Powers of Trustees (2)

Beneficiaries who are not yet entitled to income or who are minors can be assisted by the exercise of the power possessed by trustees to allow *maintenance*. A further power allows payment or application of capital money, and is known as the power of *advancement*. Both are discussed in this chapter.

Trustees may, during a period when the beneficiary is under the age of 18, allow some part of the income of the trust property, to be used for his *maintenance, education or benefit*. If, on attaining the age of 18, the beneficiary has not a vested interest in the income, the trustees must, in general, pay the income of the property to him.

'A trust to apply the whole or part as the trustees may think fit of the income for the maintenance of children is an obligatory trust': *per* Jessel MR in *Wilson v Turner* (1883).

Where there is a discretionary power of maintenance, the trustees, in exercising that power, should consider the minor's benefit and should take into account the principles the court would be likely to apply in granting maintenance to a minor: *Re Lofthouse* (1885).

Where the trustees have exercised their discretion with honesty, the court will not generally interfere: *Re Bryant* (1894).

Should the trustees fail to exercise their discretion, the court may intervene and make an appropriate order: *Stopford v Lord Canterbury* (1840).

There are circumstances in which the court is empowered to allow maintenance. In *Wellesley v Wellesley* (1828), Lord Redesdale referred to the court's power as stemming from jurisdiction 'with respect to the income of the property, to take care of it for the benefit of the children, to apply it for the benefit of the children, as far as it may be beneficial for them that it should be so applied, and to accumulate any surplus, if any surplus there should be'.

In exceptional circumstances *capital* may be used for purposes of maintenance: *Ex p Green* (1820).

'However large a child's fortune may be, whilst the father is of ability to maintain the child, he must perform his duty, and no part of the child's fortune is to be applied for that purpose': *per* Langdale MR in *Douglas v Andrews* (1849).

19.2.3	The statutory power

Under the Trustee Act 1925, s 31(1), power is given to apply income for maintenance and to accumulate surplus income during a minority.

Where property is held in trust for a person for a vested or contingent interest, then during his infancy, the trustees may, at their sole discretion, pay to his parent or guardian, or otherwise apply for or towards his *maintenance, education or benefit*, the whole or part of the income of the property as may be reasonable. This applies whether or not there is any other fund applicable to the same purpose, or any person bound by law to provide for his maintenance or education.

If the person, on attaining the age of 18, has no vested interest in the income, the trustees must pay the income of the property, and of any accretion thereto, until he attains a vested interest therein, or dies, or until his interest fails.

The Trustee Act 1925, s 31(2) provides for the accumulation of the balance of income not applied in maintenance. If the person for whom property is held in trust attains the age of 18 or marries under that age, and his interest in the income during his infancy or until his marriage is a vested interest, or, on attaining the age of 18, or on marriage under that age, he becomes entitled to the property from which the income arose (in fee simple, or for an entailed interest), the trustees must hold the accumulations in trust for him absolutely.

In any other case the trustees must hold the accumulations as an accretion to the capital of the property from which such accumulations arose, and as one fund.

A *proviso* to s 31(1) states that in deciding whether the whole or any part of the income of the property is to be paid during a minority, the trustees must have regard to the age of the minor, his *requirements* and *generally to the circumstances of the case*. In particular they must consider what other income, if any, is applicable for the same purposes. Where the trustees have notice that the income of more than one fund is applicable for those purposes, then, so far as is practicable, unless the entire income of the fund is paid or the court otherwise directs, a proportionate part only of the income of each fund shall be applied or paid.

An express trust for accumulation will exclude s 31: *Re Stapleton* (1946).

19.2.4	The problem of contingent interests

Section 31 will apply 'in the case of a contingent interest only if the limitation or trust carries the intermediate income of the property': s 31(3).

A contingent gift by will of residuary personalty *does* carry with it all the income produced by it after the testator's death: *Re Adams* (1893).

A residuary bequest, vested or contingent, which is expressly deferred to some future date, does *not* carry intermediate income: *Re Oliver* (1947). Law of Property Act 1925, s 175(1):

'A contingent future specific devise or bequest of property, whether real or personal, and a contingent residuary devise of freehold land, and a specific or residuary devise of freehold land to trustees upon trust for persons whose interests are contingent or executory shall, subject to the statutory provisions relating to accumulations [see Law of Property Act 1925, ss 164-166], carry the intermediate income of that property from the death of the testator, except so far as such income, or any part thereof, may be otherwise expressly disposed of.'

A pecuniary legacy does *not* generally carry intermediate income (*Re Raine* (1929)), unless the testator has directed in specific terms that the legacy should be set aside from his estate for the legatee's benefit, or the testator has demonstrated an intention that the income is to be devoted to maintenance or education, or the testator was the legatee's father or stood *in loco parentis* to him: *Re Pollock* (1943).

In *Re Sharp's ST* (1972), it was held that a beneficiary not yet of age is entitled to the accumulated intermediate income *only* if his interest is not defeasible. *Per* Pennycuick, V-C: Under the 1925 Act, s 31(2)(3), a beneficiary who has a vested interest (or a contingent interest which has been declared to be carrying intermediate income) is entitled to the income which is accumulated during his minority if on attaining his majority he "becomes entitled to the property from which such income arose in fee simple, absolute or determinable, or absolutely, or for an entailed interest". It being agreed that "in fee simple absolute or determinable" has application to realty only, and "absolutely" to personalty only, then on the question as to whether the later expression includes a vested interest which was liable to defeasance, it is held that it does not. (*Re Buckley's Trusts* (1883) was applied.)

19.3 The trustee's power of advancement

The trustee may be empowered by statute, by the provisions of the settlement, or the court may exercise its powers, to advance *up to one half of capital* held on trust for the advancement or benefit of any person entitled to the capital of the trust property or any share in it. The courts now tend to give a wide construction to 'advancement or benefit'.

Per Lord Radcliffe in *Pilkington v IRC* (1964):

'The general purpose of the power of advancement is to allow the trustees in a proper case to anticipate the vesting in possession of an intended beneficiary's contingent or reversionary interest and paying or applying it immediately for his benefit. By so doing they released it from the trusts of the settlement and accelerated the enjoyment of his interest (though normally only with the consent of a prior tenant for life); and where the contingency upon which the vesting of the beneficiary's title depended failed to mature or there was a later defeasance or, in some cases, a great shrinkage in the value of the remaining trust funds, the trusts as declared by the settlement were materially varied through the operation of the power of advancement.'

The word 'advancement' means, in this context, according to Lord Radcliffe:

'The establishment in life of the beneficiary who was the object of the power, or, at any rate, some step that would contribute to the furtherance of his establishment. Thus it was found in such phrases as "preferment or advancement" (*Lowther v Bentinck* (1874)), "business, profession or employment or ... advancement or preferment in the world" (*Roper-Curzon v Roper-Curzon* (1871)) and "placing out or advancement in life" (*Re Breed's Will* (1875)).'

The trustees must satisfy themselves that the exercise of the power will be of benefit to the beneficiary: see *Re Pauling's Settlement* (1963).

The exercise of the power must be *bona fide*: *Molyneux v Fletcher* (1898), in which an advance to a beneficiary in order that it would be used to repay a debt owed to the trustee by the beneficiary's husband, was held to constitute a breach of trust.

Where the power is given for exercise during the period of the beneficiary's minority only, and it is exercised improperly after the beneficiary has reached the age of majority, the trustee is liable to make refund: *Re Ward's Trusts* (1872).

19.3.1 Power of the court in exceptional circumstances

In exceptional circumstances the court may apply capital for the purposes of advancement: *Clay v Pennington* (1837). See also *Worthington v McCraer* (1856): a trustee without the express power may be allowed by the court to make payment.

19.3.2 Statutory power

Trustee Act 1925, s 32(1):

'Trustees may at any time or times pay or apply any capital money subject to a trust, for the advancement or benefit, in such manner as they may, in their absolute discretion, think fit, of any person entitled to the capital of the trust property or of any share thereof, whether absolutely or contingently on his attaining any specified age or on the occurrence of any other event, and whether in possession or remainder or reversion, and such payment or application may be made notwithstanding that the interest of such person is liable to be defeated by the exercise of a power of appointment or revocation, or to be diminished by the increase of the class to which he belongs.'

The section has no application to trusts created before the commencement of the Act: s 32(3).

The section has application only where the trust property consists of 'money or securities or of property held upon trust for sale calling in and conversion, and such money or securities, or the proceeds of such sale calling in and conversion are not by statute or in equity considered as land, or applicable as capital money for the purposes of the Settled Land Act 1925': s 32(2).

The section can be excluded by the settlor.

A *proviso* to s 32(1) states that money paid or applied for a person's advancement or benefit must not exceed altogether in amount 'one-half of the presumptive or vested share of that person in the trust property'. Further, if that person is or becomes absolutely and indefeasibly entitled to a share in the trust property, 'the money so paid or applied shall be brought into account as part of such share'. No such payment or application is to be made so as to prejudice any person liable to any prior life or other interest, whether vested or contingent, in the money paid or applied 'unless such person is in existence and of full age and consents in writing to such payment or application'. See *Henley v Wardell* (1988), in which it was held that the advancement of capital without the consent of a prior income beneficiary given pursuant to statute is invalid, and this is so even where the power of advancement is expressed as being subject to an uncontrolled discretion, unless s 32(1)(c) has been excluded *in express terms*.

In *Re Abergavenny' Trusts* (1981), trustees had been given wide powers to pay out to the plaintiff (as life tenant) 'one half of the value of the settled fund'. The precise computation of the settled fund was at the discretion of the trustees. In 1965 the trustees had exercised their power in full; later, however, the value of the retained assets had risen considerably. The question arose as to whether the trustees could make further payments to the plaintiff. It was held that no further payment was permissible since the payment in 1965 of the half share did represent the full extent of the power of the trustees.

The following have been held to be valid occasions for the application of the power of advancement: emigration (*Re England* (1830)); furnishing a house (*Perry v Perry* (1870)); establishing a husband in business (*Re Kershaw's Trust* (1868)); payment of a sum to charity at the request of a beneficiary who felt that he had a moral obligation (*Re Clore's ST* (1966)).

19.3.3   Examples of application of the power

19.3.4	Application of the money advanced

Per Willmer LJ in *Re Pauling's ST* (1963):

'If the trustees make the advance for a particular purpose which they state, they can quite properly pay it over to the advancee if they reasonably think they can trust him or her to carry out the prescribed purpose. What they cannot do is to prescribe a particular purpose, and then raise and pay the money over to the advancee leaving him or her entirely free, legally and morally, to apply it for that purpose or to spend it in any way he or she chooses, without any responsibility on the trustees even to inquire as to its application.'

19.4 The trustee's power to apply to the court

Trustees may apply to the court for directions and for the determination of questions arising from their management and administration of the trust. A usual method of application is by originating summons.

A trustee will be personally liable for costs if the court decides that the matter in question might have been dealt with more appropriately in some other way: *Re Wilson* (1885).

Trustees may apply to the court for directions when they are considering the exercise of their discretionary powers: *Talbot v Talbot* (1967). But the court will not allow itself to be used by trustees so as to relieve themselves of the duty to apply their minds and discretion to particular problems arising from the administration of the trust.

19.4.1 Direction of the court

Rules of the Supreme Court Order 85 allows an action to be brought by a trustee in relation to the execution of a trust under the direction of the court.

An action may be brought for the *determination* of the following questions: any questions arising in the execution of a trust; any questions as to the composition of a class of persons having a 'claim against the estate of a deceased person or a beneficial interest in the estate of such a person or in any property subject to a trust'; any question as to the rights or interests of a person claiming to be a creditor of the estate of a deceased person or to be entitled under a will or on the intestacy of a deceased person or to be beneficially entitled under a trust.

An action may be brought for any of the following *reliefs*: an order requiring a trustee to furnish and verify accounts; an order requiring payment into court of money held by a person in his capacity as trustee; an order directing a person to do or abstain from doing a particular act in his capacity as trustee; an order approving any sale, purchase, compromise or other transaction by a person in his capacity as trustee; an order directing an act to be done in the execution of a trust which the court could order to be done if the trust were being administered or executed under the direction of the court.

There may be circumstances in which a trustee will be allowed to exercise his powers only with the sanction of the court. Such circumstances may arise, eg, where judgment has been given for the execution of the trust by the court; where an injunction has been granted; where a receiver has been appointed. See *Mitchelson v Piper* (1836). A decree for administration will not result in the trustee's being absolved from further performance of his duties; but the sanction of the court will be needed for each future transaction: *Re Viscount Furness* (1946). Where trustees have paid the trust fund into court under the Trustee Act 1925, s 63, they must not exercise further any of their powers: *Re Nettlefold's Trusts* (1888).

19.4.2   Sanction of the court

When the trustee has completed his trusteeship he is entitled to have his accounts examined and settled, and to be given a formal discharge.

The trustee has a right to be given a receipt for any funds paid over by him.

He may demand a release by deed if there is no writing to indicate what the trusts were, or the precise size of a trust fund, or where he has been asked to do 'that which is not in accordance with the tenor of the trusts': *King v Mullins* (1852).

In the absence of special circumstances, a trustee cannot insist on a release under seal. See *Re Cater's Trust (No 2)* (1858), in which trust funds had been resettled, so that trustees of the original settlement were allowed to claim from the beneficiaries appropriate releases under seal.

19.5   The trustee's power to demand a discharge

Summary of Chapter 19

Powers of Trustees (2)

Trustees are empowered, during a beneficiary's minority, to allow some part of trust income to be used for his maintenance, benefit and education.

Power to allow maintenance

Where the trustee exercises his express discretionary power of maintenance with honesty, the court will not generally interfere: *Re Bryant* (1904). Where trustees fail to exercise their discretion, the court may intervene.

Express power

The court's inherent power stems from the court's general right to take care of the income of trust property for the benefit of the children. In exceptional circumstances (see *Ex p Green* (1820)), the court may sanction the use of capital for maintenance.

Court's inherent jurisdiction

Under Trustee Act 1925, s 31, the trustees are empowered to apply funds for maintenance, education or benefit of beneficiaries, and to accumulate the balance of income not applied in maintenance. Trustees must have regard to the age, of the beneficiary, his requirements and the circumstances of the case. They must consider what other income, if any, is applicable for the same purpose.

Statutory power

Section 31 has application in the case of a *contingent interest* only if the limitation or trust carries the intermediate income of the property: s 31(3). See Law of Property Act 1925, s 175(1). Note *Re Sharp's ST* (1971): a beneficiary not yet of age is entitled to accumulated income only if his interest is not defeasible.

Trustees may be empowered, or the court may exercise its powers, to advance up to one half of the capital held on trust for the advancement or benefit of a person entitled to the capital of the trust property or any share in it. 'Advancement' is construed widely; it involves steps that contribute to the 'furtherance of the beneficiary's establishment in life'. See *Pilkington v IRC* (1964).

Power of advancement

Trustees must satisfy themselves that the exercise of the power will be of benefit to the beneficiary.

The court may, in exceptional circumstances, apply capital for the purposes of advancement.

Trustees may at any time pay or apply capital money subject to a trust for the advancement of a beneficiary. The money paid or applied must not exceed altogether one-half of the presumptive or vested share of the beneficiary in the trust property. See *Henley v Wardell* (1988). Trustees may not leave the beneficiary entirely free to apply the money as he thinks fit: see *Re Pauling's ST* (1964).

Power to apply to the court

Trustees may apply to the court for directions and for the determination of questions relating to their management of the trust. But the court will not allow trustees to evade the responsibility of exercising their discretion.

Rules of the Supreme Court Order 85 allows a trustee to bring an action for the determination of questions arising, eg, from the rights of those who claim to be creditors of the estate.

In some cases a trustee will be allowed to exercise his powers only with the sanction of the court, eg, where a receiver has been appointed. See *Mitchelson v Piper* (1836).

Power to demand a discharge

When a trustee has completed his trusteeship he is entitled to an examination of accounts and to be given a formal discharge (by deed, if, eg, there is no writing to indicate the precise size of the trust fund).

Chapter 20

Breach of Trust (1)

A breach of trust results generally from some improper act or omission concerning the administration of a trust or the interests of the beneficiaries arising under it. It concerns some failure on the part of the trustee to carry out his duties or some abuse of his powers. See, eg, *Bartlett v Barclays Bank Trust Co* (1980) - breach of trust arising from trustees ignoring the hazardous nature of an investment in certain land development projects. Other examples of situations involving a breach of trust by trustees would include paying trust property to the wrong person, purchasing trust property without authorisation, failure to act impartially as between beneficiaries.

20.1 The essence of breach of trust

A trustee is *personally liable* for a breach of trust which arises through his default. Whether or not that breach results from conduct which is fraudulent or innocent (as where he acts in a manner intended to benefit the trust property and in ignorance of the real nature of his activities) may not always be of relevance.

The general rule is that a trustee's liability for any breach of his duties is *strict*; he is 'bound to conduct the business of the trust in such a way as an ordinary prudent man would conduct a business of his own': *per* Cross J in *Re Lucking's WT* (1968). See also *Re Speight* (1883) and Chapter 15.

20.2 Liability of trustees to the beneficiaries

The general measure of damages resulting from a breach of trust is the loss caused to the trust estate, directly or indirectly: *Knott v Cottee* (1852), in which trustees who made unauthorised investments were liable for all the losses arising when those investments were eventually realised.

'The obligation of a defaulting trustee is essentially that of effecting restitution to the trust estate': *per* Brightman LJ in *Bartlett v Barclays Bank Trust Co* (1980). See also *Re Dawson* (1966): the obligation is a personal one, and its extent ought not to be limited by the principles of the common law as they relate to remoteness of damage.

A trustee who fails to sell unauthorised investments when under a duty to do so will be liable to make good the difference between the price eventually obtained and the higher price which could have been obtained: *Fry v Fry* (1859). In this case, a testator, who died in 1834, had stated in his will that the Langford Inn was to be sold as soon as was convenient by

20.2.1 Measure of damage

auction or private sale 'and for the most money that could reasonably be obtained for the same'. Sale was not easy and the trustees advertised it at a price of £1,000. An offer of £900 was rejected. The opening of a railway in 1843 took from the establishment almost all its coach traffic. A further advertisement produced no offer. The court held the trustees liable because of their negligent conduct in not selling the Inn. The court ordered that the estates of the trustees were to be considered liable for a sum amounting to the difference between the sum which might be obtained eventually and £900.

Should a trustee improperly realise a security, he is obliged to replace it or make good any difference between that which he obtained and the value of the security at the date proceedings commenced: *Re Massingberd's Settlement* (1890). In that case, trustees were empowered to invest in Government or real securities. In 1875 they sold Consols and invested the proceeds in unauthorised mortgages which were called in; the money invested was recovered in its entirety. In 1887 proceedings commenced; Consols were higher than in 1875. The trustees said that their obligation extended only to production of the capital sum. The Court of Appeal held that they were obliged to produce the stock sold or its equivalent in terms of present monetary values.

Where a trustee is directed to purchase a specified security and, in the event, makes no investment, and the security increases in price, he may be ordered to purchase the amount of securities he might have obtained had he purchased them at the correct time: *Cann v Cann* (1884).

Where a trustee lends trust funds, in breach of trust, to some person who has notice of the trust, and those funds are subsequently employed for purposes of trade, the trustee must replace them with interest.

Where a breach is 'innocent', in that the trustee has made no use of trust funds for his own purposes, his measure of responsibility remains, nevertheless, the actual loss which is shown to have occurred.

Where a loss on the realisation of the trust property is inevitable, the trustee's responsibility for a breach of trust which has directly increased that loss will be confined to the actual loss: *Re Godwin's Settlement* (1918).

The liability of the trustee is usually for the actual loss in each transaction; hence the loss resulting from one transaction may not be compensated by a gain in the other.

In *Dimes v Scott* (1828), trustees had retained money which ought to have been invested in Consols and which, as a result,

20.2.2   The problem of setting-off

had depreciated. Later it was so invested, but at a lower rate than that which would have been obtained had the trustees obeyed the directions set out in the will. The trustees wished to set off, against their liability, the extra Consols which their delay had allowed them to purchase. It was held that they could not do so because they were not entitled to an advantage which had accrued accidentally from their delay.

In *Wiles v Gresham* (1854), trustees of a marriage settlement had acted negligently in failing to get in a debt of £2,000 from the husband, and, as a result, the amount was lost. Other parts of the trust fund were invested in unauthorised purchases of land. Later, the husband, out of his own funds, increased the value of the land. A claim was made against the trustees for the £2,000, and they attempted to set off against it the gain which had resulted from the increased value of the land. It was held that the two transactions were quite distinct, and set-off was not allowed.

In general, the trustee who is ordered to make good any loss suffered by the trust must pay interest. Thus, a trustee who fails to invest the trust funds as required for an unreasonable period of time will be charged interest.

20.2.3   The problem of interest

The rate was fixed for some time at four per cent. In *Bartlett v Barclays Bank Trust Co (No 2)* (1980), Brightman LJ argued for a more realistic approach to the problem:

'In my judgment, a proper rate of interest to be awarded, in the absence of special circumstances, to compensate beneficiaries and trust funds for non-receipt from a trustee of money that ought to have been received is that allowed from time to time on the court's short-term investment account, established under the Administration of Justice Act 1965, s 6(1).'

To some extent, the high interest rates reflect erosion in the value of money as the result of inflation, said Brightman LJ.

If a high rate of interest is payable, a proportion of the interest should be added to capital so as to help to maintain the value of the corpus of the trust estate.

Compound interest may be charged where the trustee was under a duty to accumulate: *Re Barclay* (1899). Where he has used the money in trade, compound interest may be charged: see *A-G v Alford* (1855). In *O'Sullivan v Management Agency* (1985) (see para 15.4.1), Waller, LJ considered the award of compound interest:

'With one reservation I would not award compound interest. The reservation is with regard to the foreign royalties under the publishing agreement. In that case there were secret deductions which were not used in the joint interests of the plaintiff and the companies ... A substantial proportion of those royalties were diverted to foreign subsidiaries of the defendants without the plaintiff's knowledge. Accordingly it is to be inferred that the defendants had the use of money for commercial purposes and [it has been conceded] that compound interest should be charged. In so far as it has been shown clearly that it was not used for commercial purposes then only simple interest should be charged ... It is clear from this that the basis for ordering compound interest is that the defendant has actually used the money in trade. The principle therefore is that he must disgorge the profits which he has made.'

20.2.4   Joint and
           several liability

In general, where a breach of trust has resulted from the actions of two or more trustees, their liability is considered to be joint and several, so that each is liable for the entire loss, even though all are not equally blameworthy: *A-G v Wilson* (1840).

Where judgment is obtained against all the trustees, a beneficiary may execute judgment against any one of them. 'All parties to a trust are equally liable; there is between them no primary liability': *per* Leach MR in *Wilson v Moore* (1833).

Constructive trustees are included in the rule: *Cowper v Stoneham* (1893).

In the case of a breach of trust by a former trustee, a new trustee will not be held liable. But should the new trustee have discovered the breach, he is obliged to compel the former trustee who was responsible to remedy the loss.

A retiring trustee will be liable for breaches of trust for which he is responsible. He is liable also if his retirement is in contemplation of, and was intended to make possible, a breach which actually occurs: *Head v Gould* (1898).

Per Kekewich, J:

'In order to make a retiring trustee liable for breach of trust committed by his successor you must show, and show clearly, that the very breach of trust which was in fact committed was not merely the outcome of the retirement and new appointment, but was contemplated by the former trustee when such retirement and appointment took place ... It will not suffice to prove that the former trustees rendered easy or even intended, a breach of trust, if it was not in fact committed. They must be proved to have been guilty as accessories before the fact of the impropriety actually perpetrated.'

Liability will continue against the estate of a deceased trustee.

A trustee-beneficiary who has committed a breach of trust may not claim any interest in the estate until the breach has been made good: *Re Rhodesia Goldfields* (1910). His interest may be applied so as to make good the default. Where he has assigned his beneficial interest, the assignee will stand in the same position as the assignor, even though the breach occurred *after* the assignment: *Doering v Doering* (1889).

20.2.5 Trustee-beneficiaries

An injunction may be granted so as to restrain a breach of trust, as where trustees intend to distribute the trust estate on terms other than those specified in the trust instrument: *Fox v Fox* (1870); or where trustees intend to mortgage the trust property where such a measure was unnecessary: *Rigall v Foster* (1853). See Chapter 3.

20.2.6 Injunctions

In general, property subject to a trust may be considered as belonging to the trustees *and* the beneficiaries; as a consequence, it may be stolen from any one of them. Under the Theft Act 1968, a trustee is liable for theft if he 'dishonestly appropriates property belonging to another with the intention of permanently depriving the other of it': s 1(1).

20.3 **The problem of criminal liability**

Theft Act 1968, s 5(2):

'Where property is subject to a trust, the persons to whom it belongs shall be regarded as including any person having a right to enforce the trust, and an intention to defeat the trust shall be regarded accordingly as an intention to deprive of the property any person having that right.'

The general rule, under s 4(2), is that a person cannot steal land. But there is an exception in the case of 'a trustee or personal representative ... [who] appropriates the land or anything forming part of it, by dealing with it in breach of the confidence reposed in him': s 4(2)(a). A trustee who makes an unauthorised disposition of land, intending permanently to deprive a beneficiary of it, may be guilty of theft under the 1968 Act.

In *A-G's Reference (No 1 of 1985)*, it was held that an employee who makes a secret profit by selling his own goods on the employer's premises, is not guilty of the theft of that money; that person, who was in a fiduciary position, was not a trustee within the meaning of the Theft Act 1968, s 5.

The general rule states that a trustee is not liable for the defaults of his co-trustee(s): see, eg, *Re Lucking's WT* (1967).

20.4 **Liability of trustees *inter se***

Exceptions to the rule include: where the trustee hands trust property to a co-trustee without taking steps to ensure its correct application (*Bone v Cooke* (1824)); where a trustee allows

20.4.1 Exceptions to the rule

his co-trustee to receive the trust property without any enquiry as to his dealings with it (*Marriott v Kinnersley* (1830)); where the trustee is aware of a contemplated or actual breach of trust and fails to take appropriate steps so as to prevent this occurring (*Millar's Trustees v Polson* (1897)).

20.4.2   Civil Liability (Contribution) Act 1978

Under the Civil Liability (Contribution) Act 1978, any person liable in respect of any damage suffered by another person may recover contribution from any other person liable in respect of the same damage (whether jointly with him or otherwise): s 1(1).

In any proceedings for contribution under s 1, the amount of the contribution recoverable from any person shall be such as may be found by the court to be just and equitable having regard to the extent of that person's responsibility for the damage in question: s 2(1).

A person is liable in respect of any damage for the purposes of this Act if the person who suffered it (or anyone representing his estate or dependants) is entitled to recover compensation from him in respect of that damage (whatever the legal basis of his liability, whether tort, breach of contract, breach of trust or otherwise): s 6(1).

20.4.3   Trustee Act 1925, s 30(1)

Trustee Act 1925, s 30(1):

'A trustee shall be chargeable only for money and securities actually received by him notwithstanding his signing any receipt for the sake of conformity, and shall be answerable and accountable only for his own acts, receipts, neglects, or default, and not for those of any other trustee, nor for any banker, broker, or other person with whom any trust money or securities may be deposited, nor for the insufficiency or deficiency of any securities, nor for any loss, unless the same happens through his own wilful default.'

'Wilful default' was considered in *Re City Equitable Fire Insurance Co* (1925) as 'either a consciousness of negligence or breach of duty, or a recklessness in the performance of a duty': *per* Maugham J.

In *Re Vickery* (1931) it was held that a loss occasioned by the behaviour of a solicitor who had absconded after refusing to hand over money, did not amount to wilful default on the part of the executor (who had been aware of the background of the solicitor, which included his having been suspended from practice at one time). *Per* Maugham, J:

'It is essential in this case to guard oneself against judging the conduct of the defendant in the light of subsequent events. To have employed a new solicitor as soon as the defendant became aware that X [the absconding solicitor] was a person with a tarnished reputation for honesty would certainly have meant further costs. It might have proved quite unnecessary even on the supposition that X was a rogue. Even a man of the world might have thought that the sum involved ... was far too small to make it probable that the solicitor would be likely - unless, indeed, in the case of stern necessity - for such a sum to expose himself to the orders of the court and to the action of the Law Society. Nor must it be forgotten that upon the facts as I find them it was not until September 1927 [one year after X's employment commenced] that defendant had any real reason for suspecting that X was unworthy of confidence and it seems that after that date he kept on pressing for an immediate settlement and kept on being assured that a settlement would immediately take place ... I have come to the conclusion that defendant was on any view of the facts guilty only of an error of judgment, and this, in the case of a loss occasioned by a solicitor's defalcations, does not amount to wilful default on the part of the executor. The action fails and must be dismissed.'

In some cases a trustee was able to claim a complete indemnity from his co-trustees. (But see now the Civil Liability (Contribution) Act 1978 which has introduced flexibility in the place of rigid rules. The cases below are useful in the interpretation of the situation which existed before the Act.)

20.4.4   Indemnity

- Where one trustee alone has benefited from the breach of trust.

  Per Cotton LJ in *Bahin v Hughes* (1886):

  'I think it wrong to lay down any limitation of the circumstances under which one trustee would be held liable to the others for indemnity, both having been held liable to the *cestui que trust*; but so far as cases have gone at present, relief has only been granted against a trustee who has himself got the benefit of the breach of trust, or between whom and his co-trustees there has existed a relation which will justify the court in treating him as solely liable for the breach of trust.'

- Where the trustee is also a beneficiary and has exclusively obtained a benefit from the breach of trust, he is liable to the value of his beneficial interest: *Chillingworth v Chambers* (1896).

  Per Kay LJ:

  'On the whole I think that the weight of authority is in favour of holding that a trustee who, being also *cestui que trust*, has received, as between himself and his co-trustee an exclusive benefit by the breach of trust, must indemnify his co-trustee to the extent of his interest in the trust fund, and not merely to the extent of the benefit which he has received. I think that the plaintiff must be treated as having received such an exclusive benefit.'

In this case both plaintiff and defendant were trustees. The plaintiff's wife was a beneficiary, and on her death, he became a beneficiary. The trustees had made an unauthorised investment and a resulting deficiency had been made good out of the plaintiff's interest.

The plaintiff claimed contribution from defendant, but failed.

- Where one of the trustees is a solicitor and the breach has been committed solely as the result of acting on his advice, the solicitor-trustee must indemnify his co-trustees.

In *Re Partington* (1887), the trustees of a fund were A (a solicitor) and B, the testator's widow. Following a breach of trust, A took responsibility for the administration of the trust, but it was held that he had not given B sufficient advice concerning an unauthorised investment which he made. B was entitled to an indemnity in the circumstances.

In *Head v Gould* (1898), it was held that the mere fact that one trustee was a solicitor was not, in itself, sufficient to entitle a co-trustee to an indemnity where the non-solicitor trustee had been an active participator in the breach of trust complained of, and was not proved to have participated merely in consequence of the advice and control of the solicitor-trustee.

Breach of Trust (1)

A breach of trust results generally from an improper act or omission concerning the administration of a trust or the interests of the beneficiaries. See *Bartlett v Barclays Bank Trust Co* (1980).

The essence of breach of trust

A trustee is personally liable for a breach of trust resulting from his default.

Liability of trustees to beneficiaries

See Chapter 15 on the standard of care. In general, the trustee's liability is strict; the appropriate expected standard is that of an ordinary prudent business man. See *Re Lucking's WT* (1968).

The measure of damage is the loss caused directly or indirectly to the trust estate: *Knott v Cottee* (1852). The defaulting trustee is expected to effect restitution to the trust estate. Where a breach is 'innocent', the trustee remains responsible for the actual loss which is shown to have occurred.

Loss resulting from one transaction may not be set-off or compensated by a gain in another. See *Dimes v Scott* (1828); *Wiles v Gresham* (1854).

In general, the trustee who is ordered to make good any loss suffered by the trust must pay interest, eg, as where he fails to invest trust funds for an unreasonable period of time. Compound interest may be charged where, eg, the trustee has used money for the purposes of trade.

Where a breach of trust results from the actions of two or more trustees, their liability is considered as joint and several; each is liable for the entire loss even though all are not equally blameworthy. A retiring trustee will be liable for breaches of trust for which he was responsible.

A trustee-beneficiary who has committed a breach of trust may not claim any interest in the estate until the breach has been made good.

Injunctions may be granted (see Chapter 3) so as to restrain a breach of trust. See *Fox v Fox* (1870).

Under the Theft Act 1968, a trustee is liable for theft if he 'dishonestly appropriates property belonging to another with the intention of permanently depriving the other of it': s 1(1). An intention to defeat a trust is regarded as an intention to

The problem of criminal liability

deprive of the property any person having the right to enforce the trust: s 5(2). See *A-G's Reference (No 1 of 1985)*.

Liability of trustees
inter se

A trustee is not generally liable for the defaults of his co-trustees. See *Re Lucking's WT* (1967).

Exceptions to the rule include: where, eg, the trustee hands trust property to co-trustees without taking steps to ensure its correct application; where the trustee fails to take steps to prevent a breach, having become aware of its contemplated commission.

Under the Civil Liability (Contribution) Act 1978, any person liable in respect of any damage suffered by another person may recover contribution from any other person liable in respect of the same damage (whether jointly with him or otherwise): s 1(l).

A trustee is chargeable for money and securities received by him, notwithstanding his signing any receipt for the sake of conformity and is answerable only for his own acts and defaults, and not for those of any other trustee, unless this happens through his own wilful default: Trustee Act 1925, s 30(1). See *Re Vickery* (1931).

Where one trustee alone has benefited from the breach, relief may be granted against him. Where the trustee is also a beneficiary and has exclusively obtained a benefit from the breach, he is liable to the value of his beneficial interest: *Chillingworth v Chambers* (1896). Where one of the trustees is a solicitor and the breach has been committed solely as the result of action taken on his advice, he must indemnify his co-trustees. See *Head v Gould* (1898).

Chapter 21

Breach of Trust (2)

A trustee who is personally liable for a breach of trust may be relieved wholly or partly from that liability in certain circumstances where he has acted *honestly and reasonably*. This general principle finds expression in the Trustee Act 1925, s 61, which was based upon the Judicial Trustees Act 1896, s 3. A number of the cases cited here were decided within the context of the 1896 Act; they remain of relevance in the interpretation of the 1925 Act.

Trustee Act 1925, s 61:

> 'If it appears to the court that a trustee, whether appointed by the court or otherwise, is or may be personally liable for any breach of trust, whether the transaction alleged to be a breach of trust occurred before or after the commencement of this Act, but has acted honestly and reasonably, and ought fairly to be excused for the breach of trust and for omitting to obtain the directions of the court in the matter in which he committed such breach, then the court may relieve him either wholly or partly from personal liability for the same.'

'The grit [of the section] is in the words "reasonably and ought fairly to be excused for the breach of trust".': *per* Kekewich J in *Perrins v Bellamy* (1898). In this case, the trustees of a settlement had erred in thinking that they possessed a power of sale; they had sold some leaseholds with the result that there was a considerable reduction in income. Had the power of sale existed, the sale would have been considered proper. In the event, the trustees were excused. *Per* Kekewich, J:

> 'These trustees have commmitted a breach of trust and they are responsible for it. But then the statute comes in [NB: reference is being made to the predecessor of the Trustee Act 1925, s 61, namely, the Judicial Trustees Act 1896, s 3] and the very foundation is that the trustee whose conduct is in question "is or may be personally liable for any breach of trust". I am bound to look at the rest of the section by the light of those words, and with the view that, in cases falling within the section, the breach of trust is not of itself to render the trustee personally liable ... He is not to be held personally liable if he "has acted honestly and reasonably, and ought fairly to be excused for the breach of trust". In this case ... the word "honestly" may be left

21.1   The protection of trustees

21.1.1   Trustee Act 1925, s 61

out of consideration ... In the present case there is no imputation of any dishonesty whatever. The Legislature has made the absence of all dishonesty a condition precedent to the relief of the trustee from liability ...

... I venture, however, to think that, in general, and in the absence of special circumstances, a trustee who has acted "reasonably" ought to be relieved, and that it is not incumbent on the court to consider whether he ought "fairly" to be excused, unless there is evidence of a special character showing that the provisions of the section ought not to be applied in his favour ... The only question is whether the trustee acted reasonably. In saying that, I am not unmindful of the words of the section which follow, and which require that it should be shown that the trustee ought "fairly" to be excused, not only for "the breach of trust", but also "for omitting to obtain the directions of the court in the matter in which he committed such breach of trust". I find it difficult to follow that. I do not see how the trustee can be excused for the breach of trust without being also excused for the omission referred to, or how he can be excused for the omission without also being excused for the breach of trust ...

... But if the court comes to the conclusion that a trustee has acted reasonably, I cannot see how it can usefully proceed to consider, as an independent matter, the question whether he has or has not omitted to obtain the directions of the court.'

The court does not lay down any general rules concerning the exercise of its discretion under this section: *Re Kay* (1897).

'Fairly' refers to fairness to the trustee and to others who may be affected: *Marsden v Regan* (1954).

The burden of establishing that he has acted reasonably and honestly is on the trustee: *Re Stuart* (1897). *Per* Stirling J:

'This matter has been considered by Byrne J in *Re Turner* (1897), where he says this ... "I think that if Mr Turner [the trustee] was - and he may well have been - a businesslike man, he would not, before lending his money, have been satisfied without some further inquiry as to the means of the mortgagor and as to the nature and value of the property upon which he was about to advance his money." Certainly, it is fair in dealing with such a question to consider whether [the trustee] would have acted with reference to these investments as he did if he had been lending money of his own'.

In this case, a trustee had proceeded on the basis of a valuation which had stated only the amount for which the property might be considered to be good security. The value of the property was not stated. The trustee advanced more than two-thirds of the amount given in the valuation. The valuer had been employed by the solicitor who was acting on behalf of the mortgagor. Relief was not allowed by the court.

In the context of s 61, 'reasonableness' has to be determined by reference to the specific circumstances of each particular case. See *Perrins v Bellamy* (1898):

21.1.2   Reasonableness

A trustee must have obtained skilled advice if he is to be considered as having acted 'reasonably'. See *National Trustees Co of Australasia v General Finance Co of Australasia* (1905).

In *Re Kay* (1897), a testator left over £20,000 with liabilities of, apparently, only £100. Before advertising for claims the executor paid the widow a legacy of £300. It was learned later that the estate was insolvent because of a large claim for the fraudulent misappropriation of rents. The executor was granted relief.

Wilful default in failing to sue a debtor to the estate was excused where the trustee had reasonable grounds for believing that proceedings would have been to no effect: *Re Roberts* (1897).

Trustees who acted *bona fide* in accordance with what was generally held to be the law, supported by judicial authority, but which was later overruled by the House of Lords, were held entitled to be excused: *Re Wightwick's WT* (1950).

No relief was given where a solicitor-trustee failed to interpret correctly the provisions of a statute. *Per* Buckley J in *Ward-Smith v Jebb* (1965):

'A prudent man whose affairs were affected by a statute would either satisfy himself that he fully understood its effect or would seek legal advice. A solicitor-trustee could not be heard to say that it was reasonable to apply a lower standard to him.'

In this case the solicitor-trustee had made a mistake in his interpretation of a statute as a result of which payments had been made, incorrectly, from the trust fund.

Relief may be granted to a paid trustee in appropriate circumstances. *Per* Wilberforce J in *Re Pauling* (1963):

'Where a bank undertakes to act as a paid trustee of a settlement created by a customer, and so deliberately places itself in a position where its duty as trustee conflicts with its interest as a banker, we think that the court should be very slow to relieve such a trustee under the provisions of the section.'

'If honesty and reasonableness are both made out, there is a case for the court to consider whether the trustee ought fairly to be excused for the breach, looking at all the circumstances': *National Trustees Co of Australasia v General Finance Co of Australasia* (1905).

In *Re Rosenthal* (1972), it was held that a trustee was not entitled to relief where, although he had acted honestly, he had not, as a professional trustee, acted reasonably (having paid estate duty levied on a specific devise out of general residue). In this case, X made a specific devise of a house to Y; residuary estate was given on trust for sale to Z, subject to a direction to trustees to pay the debts, testamentary and funeral expenses. The house was transferred to Y by trustees, but without any provision having been made for Y to pay the appropriate estate duty on it. Y sold the house and went to live abroad. Trustees paid £270 from the residue towards the liability. Z issued an originating summons asking for a declaration that the trustees were not entitled to do so. One of the trustees, T, had acted as solicitor to the estate and claimed that the trustees were able to treat the estate duty as a testamentary expense so that it could be paid from residue. The court held that it was not a testamentary expense and that transfer of the house to Y could not be considered a breach of trust if the trustees were pepared to take the risk of having personally to pay the estate duty on it. Hence, there was no question of relief under s 61. But payment of the £270 from residue was a breach of trust. T was not entitled to relief under s 61 and a declaration was granted.

21.1.3   Agreement or concurrence of the beneficiary

The general rule is that a beneficiary who acquiesces in a breach of trust, or consents to, or concurs in, or grants a release to the trustee, will have no claim against the trustee.

Where one of several beneficiaries consents to a breach, the rights of the others are not affected: *Ghost v Waller* (1846).

A consent or release by a beneficiary who is not *sui juris* is to no effect: *Lord Montford v Lord Cadogan* (1816).

'A consent which is not free is no consent at all': *per* Stuart VC in *Stevens v Robertson* (1868).

It might be possible to infer the beneficiary's acquiescence from a considerable lapse of time, or from conduct: *Egg v Devey* (1847). But note the comment of Cross J in *Holder v Holder* (1968): 'One cannot lay down a hard and fast rule to the effect that knowledge of the legal consequences of known facts is or is not essential to the success of the plea [of acquiescence]'.

Where a beneficiary who is *sui juris* authorises a trustee's acts in sure knowledge of their nature and consequence, he cannot afterwards complain of those acts: *Fletcher v Collis* (1905).

Per Wilberforce J in *Re Pauling's Settlement* (1963):

'The result of [the authorities] appears to me to be that the court has to consider all the circumstances in which the concurrence of the *cestui que trust* was given with a view to seeing whether it is fair and equitable that, having given his concurrence, he should afterwards turn round and sue the trustees: that, subject to this, it is not necessary that he should know that what he is concurring in is a breach of trust, provided that he fully understands what he is concurring in, and that it is not necessary that he should himself have directly benefited by the breach of trust.'

See also *Re Freeston's Charity* (1978) (presumed acquiescence of beneficiary in relation to Universities and Colleges (Trusts) Act 1943, s 2(1)).

The Trustee Act 1925, s 62 (as subsequently amended) deals with the power to make a *beneficiary* indemnify for a breach of trust. Section 62(1):

21.1.4   Impounding a beneficiary's interest

> 'Where a trustee commits a breach of trust at the instigation or request or with the consent in writing of a beneficiary, the court may, if it thinks fit, make such order as to the court seems just, for impounding all or any part of the interest of the beneficiary in the trust estate by way of indemnity to the trustee or persons claiming through him.'

This section applies to breaches of trust committed as well before as after the commencement of the Act: s 62(2).

The power to impound a beneficiary's interest in this context will not be lost by an assignment of that interest: *Bolton v Curre* (1895).

A trustee who wishes to rely on s 62 must show that the beneficiaries knew the facts which amounted to a breach of trust: *Re Somerset* (1894).

In *Re Somerset* (1894) trustees of a marriage settlement expended an excessive sum by way of mortgage; the loan was made at the instigation, and with the consent in writing, of X, the tenant for life. The security proved to be inadequate and X and his infant children sued the trustees for breach of trust. The trustees claimed that they were entitled to impound X's life interest so as to assist in meeting the claim upon them. The Court of Appeal refused, on the ground that X had never intended to be a party to a breach of trust; he had left the question of the mortgage to the trustees. *Per* Lindley MR:

> 'In order to bring a case within the section the *cestui que trust* must instigate, or request, or consent in writing to some act or omission which is itself a breach of trust, and not to some act or omission which only becomes a breach of trust by reason of want of care on the part of the trustees ... But if all that a *cestui que trust* does is to instigate, request or consent in writing to an investment which is authorised by the terms of the power, the case is, I think, very different. He has a right to expect that the trustees will act with proper care in making the investment and if they do not

they cannot throw the consequences on him unless they can show that he instigated, requested, or consented in writing to their non-performance of their duty in this respect.'

21.1.5   Discharge from bankruptcy

A trustee who becomes bankrupt and is subsequently discharged is discharged from all 'bankruptcy debts' (as defined in the Insolvency Act 1986, s 382(1)), and these will include claims arising from a breach of trust. But, under, s 281(3): 'Discharge does not release the bankrupt from any bankruptcy debt which he incurred in respect of, or forebearance in respect of which was secured by means of, any *fraud or fraudulent breach of trust* to which he was a party.'

21.1.6   Limitation of actions

Under the Limitation Act 1980, s 21(3), an action by a beneficiary to recover trust property or in respect of any breach of trust cannot be brought after the expiration of *six years* from the date on which the right of action accrued. For the purposes of this sub-section, the right of action shall not be treated as having accrued to any beneficiary entitled to a future interest in the trust property until the interest fell into possession.

The date on which the right of action accrues is, in the case of a breach of trust, the date on which the breach occurred, eg, the date on which an unauthorised investment was made: *Re Swain* (1891).

Where a beneficiary is under a disability, time runs only from the ending of the disability: s 28. A person is under a 'disability', for purposes of s 28, while, eg, under the age of 18, or of unsound mind.

A disability occurring after the right of action has accrued and time has begun to run, does not prevent the limitation period running.

In the case of fraud, Limitation Act 1980, s 21(1), provides:

'No period of limitation prescribed by this Act shall apply to an action by a beneficiary under a trust, being an action: (a) in respect of any fraud or fraudulent breach of trust to which the trustee was a party or privy; or (b) to recover from the trustee trust property or the proceeds of trust property in the possession of the trustee,or previously received by the trustee and converted to his use.'

'Fraud' is used 'in the equitable sense to denote conduct by the defendant ... such that it would be against all conscience for him to avail himself of the lapse of time': *per* Lord Denning in *King v Parsons & Co* (1973).

The 'fraud' must have been perpetrated on the individual wishing to take advantage of s 21(1)(a). See *Thorne v Heard* (1895).

The phrase 'trust property or the proceeds of trust property' extends to the rents and profits which the trustee may be assumed to have derived from the possession of the trust property: *Re Howlett* (1949). Mere receipt of the property will not suffice; it is necessary to show that the trustee has possession of the trust property, or that he has converted for personal use the property or proceeds of sale.

'Staleness of demand as distinguished from the Statute of Limitations and analogy to it may furnish a defence in equity to an equitable claim': *per* Lord Lindley in *Re Sharpe* (1892).

'Nothing in this Act [Limitation Act 1980] shall affect any equitable jurisdiction to refuse relief on the ground of acquiescence or otherwise': s 36(2).

The phrase 'or otherwise' seems to refer to the equitable doctrine of laches: 'Equity aids the vigilant, not the indolent'.

See *Lindsay Petroleum Oil Co v Hurd* (1874)(lapse of time is of much signifcance); *Brooks v Muckleston* (1909).

Tracing is a proprietary remedy allowing a claimant to protect his title to trust assets which have come into the hands of another. The general principle of tracing rests on the rule that 'an abuse of trust can confer no rights on the party abusing it, nor on those who claim in privity with him': *per* Lord Ellenborough in *Taylor v Plumer* (1815).

In *Agip Ltd v Jackson* (1989) Millet J stated that tracing at common law serves an evidential purpose:

'Tracing at common law enables the defendant to be identified as the recipient of the plaintiff's money and the measure of his liability to be determined by the amount of the plaintiff's money he is shown to have received. The common law has always been able to follow a physical asset from one recipient to another. Its ability to follow an asset in the same hands into a changed form was established in *Taylor v Plumer*. In following the palintiff's money into an asset purchased exclusively with it, no distinction is drawn between a chose in action such as the debt of a bank to its customer and any other asset (*Re Diplock* (1948)). But it can only follow a physical asset, such as a cheque or its proceeds, from one person to another. It can follow money but not a chose in action ...'

At common law the legal owner may follow an asset so long as he retains the property in it and so long as it can be identified in its original or converted form.

There were *limitations* to tracing at *common law*.

The remedy was not available in the case of equitable interests in property. *Re Diplock* (1948):

'The common law did not recognise equitable claims to property, whether money or any other form of property. Sovereigns in A's pocket either belonged to A or they belonged in law to B. The idea that they could belong in law to A and they could nevertheless be treated as belonging to B was entirely foreign to the common law.'

Similarly, funds which had become mixed with other funds could not be traced at common law. *Per* Millett J in *Agip Ltd v Jackson* (1989):

'Money can be followed at common law into and out of a bank account and into the hands of a subsequent transferee, provided that it does not cease to be identifiable by being mixed with other money in the bank account derived from some other source: *Banque Belge v Hambrouck* (1921).'

Re Diplock (1948):

'It was the materialistic approach of the common law coupled with and encouraged by the limited range of remedies available to it that prevented the common law from identifying money in a mixed fund. Once the money of B had become mixed with the money of A, its identification in a physical sense became impossible. Owing to the fact of mixture there could be no question of ratification of an unauthorised act, and the only remedy of B, if any, lay in an action for damages.'

Because of the very large number of transfers of money effected through the medium of payment into bank accounts, and the money transferred becoming mixed in the accounts of payees with other funds, the common law ceased to provide an effective proprietary remedy. Tracing in equity, with its much wider scope, was used in increasing measure.

21.3 Tracing trust property in equity

Tracing in equity may be applied where, eg, the property in question is in the hands of trustees (or others with whom there is a fiduciary relationship) or where the trustee has been adjudged bankrupt.

21.3.1 Claims *in rem*

Per Millett J in *Agip Ltd v Jackson* (1989):

'The tracing claim in equity gives rise to a proprietary remedy which depends on the continued existence of the trust property in the hands of defendant. Unless he is a *bona fide purchaser for value without notice*, he must restore the trust property to its rightful owner if he still has it. [But even a volunteer who has received trust property cannot be made subject to a personal liability to account for it as a constructive trustee if he has parted with it without having previously acquired some knowledge of the existence of the trust].'

The remedy *in rem* is available only if there is a fiduciary relationship, which is not restricted to trustee and beneficiary. If there is no such relationship, there is no right to trace in equity. See *Chase Manhattan Bank v Israel-British Bank* (1981).

The right to trace in equity is dependent, therefore upon the tracer being a beneficial owner of an equitable interest in the property.

The title of a *bona fide* purchaser for value without notice will be voidable.

In the case of the innocent volunteer (as distinct from a purchaser for value without notice), note *Re Diplock* (1948):

'Where the innocent volunteer mixes money of his with money which in equity belongs to another person, or is found in possession of such a mixture, although that other person cannot claim a charge on the mass superior to the claim of the volunteer, he is entitled to a charge ranking *pari passu* with the claim of the volunteer.'

The claimant's money must continue to be identifiable. *Re Diplock* (1948):

'The equitable remedies presuppose the continued existence of the money either as a separate fund or as part of a mixed fund or as latent in property acquired by means of such a fund. If, on the facts of any individual case, such a continued existence is not established, equity is as helpless as the common law itself.'

Tracing will not be allowed if the result proves inequitable. (See *Lipkin Gorman v Karpnale* (1991).)

In general, a claimant who succeeds in a tracing claim is entitled to receive interest.

With regard to the mixing of trust funds, the following rules apply:

21.3.2 The mixing of trust funds

- Where a trustee purchases property with both his own and trust money, the beneficiaries will have a first charge on the property he has purchased: *Re Oatway* (1903).

- Where a trustee mixes funds with his own in a single banking account, the beneficiaries have a first charge on the resulting mixed fund. Where he draws upon that account for his own purposes, there is a presumption that he has drawn first on his own money. He is deemed not to have drawn on the trust fund until his own money has been exhausted, irrespective of the order in which funds have been paid in: *Re Hallett's Estate* (1880). See also *Borden v Scottish Timber Products* (1981); *Re Registered Securities* (1991).

In *Re Hallett's Estate* (1880), X [Hallett], a solicitor and the trustee of his marriage settlement had paid money arising from that trust into his personal banking account. His work as a solicitor involved his acting for Y; she had entrusted him with money intended to be used for purposes of investment and a proportion of this money had been paid by X into his account. X made a number of payments from and into his own banking account. He had incurred further debts at the date of his death, at which time the account contained sufficient funds to satisfy the claims of the trustees of the marriage settlement and of Y. There were insufficient funds to satisfy X's personal debts.

An action for the administration of X's estate was commenced. The principal problem was: could the trust and Y claim in priority to X's creditors? The Court of Appeal held, first, that the trust and Y were entitled to a charge upon funds in the banking acount in priority to X's general creditors; and, secondly, the various drawings by X from the account were to be considered as payments of his own money, not that of Y or the trust.

- Where a trustee of two trusts mixes the funds in a single account and draws for his own private purposes on that account, the rule, known as the rule in *Clayton's Case* (1816), applies to his drawings, namely, 'first in, first out'. The first item on the debit side of the account is reduced by the first item on the credit side.

The rule applies only to banking accounts and only where there is a single, unbroken account. The rule has no application where a trustee has earmarked a specific withdrawal as a withdrawal of trust funds.

21.3.3   Claims *in personam*

The House of Lords confirmed in *Re Diplock* (1948) the right of, eg, an unpaid creditor or legatee to bring an action in equity against those persons to whom an estate had been distributed wrongfully. It matters not that the distribution was made wrongfully as the result of a mistake in law or in fact. Nor does it matter that the recipients had no title, or were strangers to the trust. *Re Diplock* (1948):

'As regards the conscience of the defendant on which in this, as in other jurisdictions, equity is said to act, it is *prima facie*, at least, a sufficient circumstance that the defendant ... has received some share of the estate to which he was not entitled.'

See *Re Leslie Engineer's Co* (1976).

Breach of Trust (2)

In certain circumstances in which a trustee has acted honestly and reasonably, he may be relieved from liability arising from a breach of trust.

Protection of trustees

- Trustee Act 1925, ss 61, 62

    Under Trustee Act 1925, s 61, if the trustee has acted honestly and reasonably and ought fairly to be excused for the breach, 'then the court may relieve him wholly or partly from personal liability for the same'.

    The burden of showing that he has acted reasonably and honestly is on the trustee. 'Reasonableness' is to be determined by reference to each specific case: Thus, a trustee should have obtained skilled advice in appropriate circumstances. Relief may be granted to a paid trustee in appropriate circumstances: see *Re Pauling* (1963). A beneficiary who acquiesces in a breach of trust or consents to or concurs in it, will have no claim against the trustee.

    Trustee Act 1925, s 62, allows for the impounding of a beneficiary's interest in the case of some breaches of trust, eg, as where the trustee commits a breach of trust at the instigation, or with the consent, of the beneficiary. The power to impound will not be lost by an assignment of the interest. It must be shown that the beneficiaries were aware of the facts which constituted the breach: see *Re Somerset* (1984).

- Bankruptcy

    A trustee who becomes bankrupt and is subsequently discharged, is discharged from all bankruptcy debts, and these will include claims arising from a breach of trust.

- Limitation Act 1980, s 21

    Under the Limitation Act 1980, s 21(3), an action by a beneficiary to recover trust property or in respect of any breach of trust must be brought within six years from the date on which the right of action accrued.

    Time runs, in the case of a breach of trust from the date on which the breach occurred. A person is under a disability during his minority, or while of unsound mind. No period of limitation applies to an action brought by a beneficiary for breach of trust in respect of fraud: s 21(1).

Nothing in the 1980 Act affects any refusal of relief on the ground of acquiescence or otherwise: s 36(2). Reference to the equitable doctrine of laches seems implied here.

Tracing trust property at common law

Tracing is a proprietary remedy allowing a claimant to protect his title to any trust assets which are in the hands of another. The legal owner may, at common law, follow an asset so long as he retains property in it and as long as it can be identified in its original or converted form.

Limitations to the remedy at common law were: its lack of availability in the case of equitable interests in property; its inapplicability to funds which had become mixed with other funds. See *Banque Belge v Hambrouck* (1921); *Agip v Jackson* (1989).

Tracing trust property in equity

The doctrine of tracing trust property in equity has application, eg, where the property is in the hands of trustees (or others with whom there is a fiduciary relationship) or where a trustee has been adjudicated bankrupt. The claim in equity means that, unless defendant is a bona fide purchaser for value without notice, he may be obliged to restore the trust property to its rightful owner if he still has it.

Essentially, the right to trace in equity depends upon the tracer being the beneficial owner of an equitable interest in the property.

Tracing will not be allowed if the result proves inequitable. See *Lipkin Gorman v Karpnale* (1991).

Where trust funds are mixed, the following principles apply:

- Trustee purchases property with both his own and trust money: beneficiaries have first charge on property purchased. (See *Re Registered Securities* (1991).

- Trustee mixes funds with his own in a single banking account: beneficiaries have first charge on mixed fund.

- Trustee of two trust funds mixes them in single account upon which he draws: 'first in, first out', is presumed to apply to his drawings. See *Clayton's Case* (1816); *Re Hallett's Estate* (1880).

- The House of Lords confirmed in *Re Diplock* (1948) right of an unpaid creditor or legatee to bring action in equity against persons to whom an estate had been distributed wrongly.

Recommended Reading List

Edwards & Stockwell, *Trusts and Equity* (Pitman)

Hanbury & Maudsley, *Modern Equity* (Stevens)

Hayton, *Law Relating to Trusts and Trustees* (Butterworths)

Keeton & Sheridan, *Digest of the English Law of Trusts* (Butterworths)

Maitland, *Lectures on Equity* (Cambridge University Press)

McLoughlin & Rendell, *Law of Trusts* (MacMillan)

Parker & Mellows, *Modern Law of Trusts* (Sweet & Maxwell)

Pettit, *Equity and the Law of Trusts* (Butterworths)

Riddall, *The Law of Trusts* (Butterworths)

Snell, *Principles of Equity* (Sweet & Maxwell)

General texts

Burn, *Trusts and Trustees – Cases and Materials* (Butterworths)

Harris, *Variation of Trusts* (Sweet & Maxwell)

Middleton & Phillips, *Charities* (Jordans)

Oakley, *Constructive Trusts* (Sweet & Maxwell)

Case books & specialist texts

Index